# KARDIO

# KARDIO: A Study in Deep and Qualitative Knowledge for Expert Systems

Ivan Bratko, Igor Mozetič, and Nada Lavrač

Foreword by Donald Michie

The MIT Press
Cambridge, Massachusetts
London, England

This book was set in T<sub>E</sub>X
by Darko Levstek
and printed and bound in the United States of America

Library of Congress Cataloging-in-Publication Data

Bratko, Ivan.
  KARDIO: a study in deep and qualitative knowledge for expert
  systems / Ivan Bratko, Igor Mozetič, Nada Lavrač.

  Bibliography: p.
  Includes index.
  ISBN 0-262-02273-7
  1. KARDIO (Computer program) 2. Arrhythmia--Diagnosis--Data
processing. 3. Expert systems (Computer science) I. Mozetič,
Igor. II. Lavrač, Nada. III. Title.
RC685.A65B69 1988      616.1'2807547'02--dc19      88-22504
                                                      CIP

DEC, DECsystem-10, VAX and VMS are trademarks
 of Digital Equipment Corporation
UNIX is a registered trademark of AT&T Bell Laboratories
Sun-2/xxx is a trademark of Sun Microsystems. Inc.

# Contents

1 **Introduction**                                                                    **1**

  1.1  Deep and qualitative knowledge ........................... 1

  1.2  Transformations between knowledge representations ....... 11

  1.3  Overview of KARDIO ................................... 21

      1.3.1 The ECG diagnosis problem ........................ 21

      1.3.2 Qualitative model of the heart ..................... 25

      1.3.3 Qualitative simulation algorithm ................... 32

      1.3.4 Implementation of the simulation algorithm ........ 35

      1.3.5 Compilation of deep model into surface
           representation ..................................... 37

      1.3.6 Compression of the arrhythmia-ECG base
           using inductive learning tools ...................... 39

      1.3.7 Summary of representations and
           AI techniques in KARDIO ........................ 42

      1.3.8 Introducing abstraction hierarchy into and
           learning of qualitative models ..................... 44

      1.3.9 Completeness assessment and clinical applicability ... 45

  1.4  Comparison with other approaches to qualitative modeling 47

2 **Qualitative Model of the Heart**                                                  **53**

  2.1  Describing arrhythmias .................................. 53

      2.1.1 Electrophysiology of the heart ..................... 53

      2.1.2 Qualitative description of ECG ..................... 55

      2.1.3 Simple cardiac arrhythmias ........................ 60

      2.1.4 Examples ......................................... 61

  2.2  The model .............................................. 68

      2.2.1 Overview of the model ............................ 68

      2.2.2 Qualitative state of the heart ..................... 71

      2.2.3 Constraints over states ........................... 76

      2.2.4 Rules in the model ............................... 79

3  Model Interpretation and Derivation
   of Surface Knowledge                                            95
   3.1  Formalization and implementation of the model ........... 95
        3.1.1 Formalization in predicate calculus ................. 96
        3.1.2 Depth-first forward simulation ...................... 98
        3.1.3 Breadth-first forward simulation ................... 100
        3.1.4 Backward simulation ............................... 109
        3.1.5 Soundness proof of the simulation algorithm ....... 112
   3.2  Derivation of arrhythmia-ECG knowledge base .......... 118

4  Knowledge Base Compression by Means
   of Machine Learning                                            127
   4.1  Learning from examples ................................. 127
        4.1.1 Definition of the learning task .................... 127
        4.1.2 The AQ algorithm ................................. 131
   4.2  Compression of the arrhythmia-ECG base ............... 135
        4.2.1 Motivation and overview .......................... 135
        4.2.2 Transformations of the reduced arrhythmia-ECG
              base into the form appropriate for learning ........ 139
        4.2.3 Conditions for preserving the equivalence
              of rule sets ..................................... 144
        4.2.4 Results of knowledge base compression ............ 150
   4.3  Comparison of compressed prediction rules
        with medical literature ................................ 155

5  Further Developments: Hierarchies and
   Learning of Models                                             161
   5.1  Overview of the model learning system ................. 161
   5.2  Knowledge representation .............................. 164
        5.2.1 Deductive nonrecursive database
              formalism (DNDB) .............................. 164
        5.2.2 Representing qualitative models ................... 166
        5.2.3 Hierarchy of models ............................. 167
   5.3  Learning functions of components ...................... 171
   5.4  Debugging a hypothesized model ....................... 174
   5.5  Interpreting a model .................................. 179
        5.5.1 Hierarchical diagnosis ........................... 180
        5.5.2 Backward diagnosis ............................. 183
   5.6  Experiments and results ............................... 186

**References**                                                     **191**

**Appendix**
   A     Part of Surface Arrhythmia-ECG Base....................199
   B     Compressed Diagnostic Rules...........................219
   C     Compressed Prediction Rules ..........................237

**Index**                                                          **257**

# Foreword

The pages which follow can be likened to the logs, charts and maps of a voyage to a new world. In these territories of the future we see humanly assimilable knowledge custom-manufactured from nothing more substantial than logical specifications.

In the early 1980's the dawning recognition of this possibility led a number of laboratories to launch a collectively planned set of trials. The first experiment offered for the scrutiny of the International School for the Synthesis of Expert Knowledge (ISSEK) was Alen Shapiro's semi-automatic synthesis of a self-articulate knowledge-base concerning a selected chess end-game, subsequently documented in his book "Structured Induction in Expert Systems." This important work fell marginally short of ISSEK's stipulation that newly minted knowledge should be truly substantial in amount. A year or so later the KARDIO work described in this volume had passed the required level, and after satisfactory completion of clinical evaluation we certificated it as a fully acceptable proof of concept. To us, KARDIO had demonstrated beyond reasonable doubt that large-scale automatic synthesis of human-type knowledge was technically feasible.

I have selected "human-type" with care. Why not just write "human"? The point is crucial to the reader's chances of grasping the nature of the enterprise. That part of existing cardiological knowledge which was explicitly represented in KARDIO was *not* the diagnostic part to be found in texts of clinical practice or in the heads of the authors of such texts. The role of the consultant physicians who collaborated in the project was to help the KARDIO team to design the logical model of the heart which was then used as a *de novo* generator of diagnostic rules. Professor Bratko and his colleagues judged that existing clinical knowledge was not of an explicitness or completeness to support a useful exercise of extraction from specialists and enhancement in the machine. From the start, therefore, **they had no other option but to construct the required corpus of knowledge from scratch** — by machine derivation, that is to say, from a compact logical specification. By doing so, Bratko, Lavrač and Mozetič reaped the reward of guaranteed completeness and correctness in the finally synthesized expert system.

The technological and social potential of the Yugoslav discovery has been discussed elsewhere. Turning to its intellectual aspect, we note that it unites the two most active growing-points in the study of knowledge-based systems, namely logic programming and machine learning. Professor Bratko is an authority on the application to artificial intelligence of programming in logic. His tutorial "Prolog Programming for Artificial Intelligence" published by Addison-Wesley has enjoyed widespread success in communicating this theme in depth. As to machine learning, the present book should dispel any remaining doubts concerning the wisdom contained in John McCarthy's celebrated dictum that a representational form adequate for telling a machine something is a virtual pre-requisite for enabling the machine to learn that something for itself. In the case of KARDIO, the adequate representational form for the underlying physiology was that of *qualitative descriptions*, expressed in a logic language and not the traditional quantitative representation. "KARDIO: a Study in Deep and Qualitative Knowledge for Expert Systems" supplies a long-unfulfilled need for solid foundations from which to teach and illustrate this key principle. The book's style, both concrete and theoretically illuminating, will be found well suited to advanced-level undergraduate courses, and also to postgraduate and post-doctoral study in universities, institutes and industrial laboratories.

Four hundred years ago in his "Advancement of Learning" Francis Bacon developed his revolutionary concept of a voyage along the Intellectual Coast of unfolding knowledge, and called for a *New Engine* to serve as "helps for the mind." I congratulate New Engineers Bratko, Lavrač and Mozetič on their remarkable accomplishment.

Donald Michie
The Turing Institute, Glasgow
July 1988

# Preface

First generation expert systems rely on the use of surface, or shallow knowledge, described as associational or heuristic. Second generation expert systems technology is characterized by two additional features: deep knowledge and machine learning. Deep knowledge enables an expert system to reason from "first principles," which improves the system's robustness, explanation capability and verifiability. In relation to deep knowledge, *qualitative* modeling (as opposed to traditional quantitative modeling) is being recognized as increasingly important.

This book presents an in-depth case study in building expert systems featuring deep knowledge, qualitative modeling and machine learning. The relevant techniques are demonstrated in full detail in the development of a medical expert system for ECG diagnosis. The system comprizes a qualitative model of the electrical system of the heart and the heart arrhythmias—possible failures of the system. The model was compiled by means of qualitative simulation and machine learning techniques into various representations that are suited for particular expert tasks, such as diagnosis and prediction.

Further, a hierarchical organization of a qualitative model is investigated, and an experiment completed whereby the construction of a deep model was automated by means of machine learning techniques.

This study shows how the qualitative modeling approach, using logic-based representations, and machine learning technology can be used to construct knowledge bases whose complexity is far beyond the capability of traditional, dialogue based techniques for knowledge acquisition. We expect that the KARDIO "knowledge acquisition cycle" will become a standard technique in the development of practical expert systems. It has already been used in the development of other expert systems, for example at the Turing Institute by Danny Pearce in a system for diagnosing a satellite power supply system.

The book is intended for readers with general interest in expert systems, and more particularly, in the technology of the second generation expert systems and its practical application to difficult problems.

From the specific application point of view, this book will be of interest to those working in the medical informatics and medical expert systems. The text and the appendices contain all the necessary information for complete reconstruction of KARDIO. In particular, the qualitative model of the electrical system of the heart can be used in further developments in this application area. It has already been used in such a study by Jim Hunter of the University of Aberdeen and his colleagues as a standard for the behavior of the heart.

The book assumes that the reader is familiar with the basics of expert systems and artificial intelligence (such as chaining mechanisms and search strategies), some basics of predicate logic, and introductory knowledge of Prolog.

Chapter 1 surveys the main techniques and results, to give the reader a general and complete overview. The distinctions between deep and shallow knowledge, qualitative and quantitative knowledge in expert systems are introduced. The KARDIO project is reviewed and compared with other approaches to qualitative modeling. The remaining chapters are refinements on particular aspects.

Chapter 2 gives complete details of the qualitative model of the heart developed in this study.

In Chapter 3, algorithms for qualitative simulation are developed and applied to the heart model. This resulted in automatic generation of ECG descriptions for all possible combinations of cardiac arrhythmias. This representation occupies 5 MB of store and can be viewed as an automatically generated surface knowledge base for ECG diagnosis.

Chapter 4 describes a procedure, based on machine learning techniques, by which the whole 5 MB surface representation was compressed into a compact form which is also conceptually more meaningful to the human expert.

Chapter 5 presents further developments: introducing hierarchy into a qualitative model, exploiting hierarchy in diagnosis, and machine-aided development of qualitative models based on interactive use of machine learning techniques.

# Acknowledgements

Many people contributed to the KARDIO project at various stages of development. Medical doctors of the University Medical Center at Ljubljana, who acted as domain specialists are: Matija Horvat, Bojan Čerček, Anton Grad, and Primož Rode. Other medical doctors who helped with testing and in other respects, include Aleš Blinc, Matija Cevc, Ciril Grošelj, Matjaž Klemenc, and Samo Ribarič. Peter Macfarlane of The Western Royal Infirmary, Glasgow, G. van Herpen of University Hospital, Leiden, The Netherlands, and Matija Horvat participated as medical specialists in the evaluation of the KARDIO knowledge base.

On the AI side, we want to thank Donald Michie for his continuous interest in the project from its beginning, for numerous discussions, methodological suggestions, and encouragement. Ryszard Michalski helped with discussions on the use of the AQ learning method for knowledge compression and machine-aided construction of qualitative models. Nicolas Mars and Judith Richards helped with the international evaluation of KARDIO. Many of our colleagues were involved in the project in various technical aspects; among them are: Damjan Bojadžiev, Alojz Černe, Neža Mramor – Kosta, Jurij Škrlj, Marjan Vlašič, and Tatjana Zrimec.

This work was first presented in detail at an ISSEK workshop (International School for the Synthesis of Expert Knowledge). We are grateful to ISSEK members for their valuable suggestions and encouragement to publish this work in book form.

The following institutions provided environment in which this work was done: Jožef Stefan Institute, Ljubljana; Edvard Kardelj University, Faculty of Electrical Engineering and Computer Science, Ljubljana; Department of Computer Science, University of Illinois at Urbana-Champaign; University Medical Center, Ljubljana; the Turing Institute, Glasgow; and AI Center, Department of Computer Science, George Mason University, Fairfax.

The KARDIO project was continuously supported by the Research Community of Slovenia. Additional support came from: the European Economic Community within the COST-13 project in Artificial Intelligence and Pattern Recognition (subprojects Machine Learning and Knowledge Acquisition, and AI in the Medical Science); Fulbright Foundation; National Science Foundation; Office of Naval Research; Defense Advanced Research Project Agency; U.S. Army Research Institute for the Behavioral and Social Sciences through its European Science Coordination Office. The opinions expressed in this book are those of the authors and do not necessarily represent those of the supporting institutions.

The following figures in the book were reproduced, with permission, from M.J. Goldman, Principles of Clinical Electrocardiography, 9th edition, copyright Lange Medical Publications, 1976: 2.1–2.8, 3.1–3.4.

Ivan Bratko, Igor Mozetič, Nada Lavrač
Ljubljana, Yugoslavia
August 1988

# KARDIO

# Chapter 1

# Introduction

This book presents a study in building expert systems featuring deep knowledge, qualitative modeling and machine learning. The techniques employed are demonstrated in detail in the development of a medical expert system, called KARDIO, for the ECG diagnosis of disorders in the heart, known as cardiac arrhythmias.

In this chapter we introduce the distinctions between deep and surface knowledge, qualitative and quantitative knowledge in expert systems; illustrate these representations by examples and discuss their advantages and drawbacks in general; outline techniques for transformations between various representations and illustrate these transformations by examples; review the KARDIO project in which these techniques were applied on a large scale problem; and compare KARDIO with other approaches to qualitative modeling.

## 1.1 Deep and qualitative knowledge

In general, the type of knowledge in an expert system can be characterized along several dimensions, such as:

- surface vs. deep
- quantitative vs. qualitative

Knowledge is said to be *surface*, or *shallow*, if it directly states the relation between problem specification and problem solution without referring to the underlying principles. Typically, surface-level knowledge is used in solving problems *efficiently*, although without any reference to, or understanding of, the underlying *causal relations* on which the solution is based. Therefore surface-level knowledge is also called "operational" knowledge. We will be using the terms shallow and surface interchangeably in this context.

The distinction between operational knowledge and deep knowledge also applies to human problem solving. Human experts, when confronted with a problem from their domain, normally do not have to think hard about the solution; they already *know* the answer. They simply retrieve the answer from their "operational knowledge base." Only occasionally, when faced with an unusual problem, the answer cannot simply be retrieved but has to be *derived* by reasoning from "first principles," which is, according to Steels (1985), a distinguishing feature of second generation expert systems. For that, a deeper model of the same domain is necessary. Such a model states the first principles or basic rules of the game from which operational decisions can be derived.

A large majority of the so-called first generation expert systems comprise knowledge bases which can be characterized as shallow or surface. Also, a large majority of traditional computer applications are based on *quantitative* models as opposed to *qualitative* ones. The KARDIO project, described in this book, is interesting because the prevailing type of knowledge in the system is deep, capturing the underlying causal structure of the problem domain. This enables the system to reason from first principles. Also, knowledge in KARDIO can be characterized as qualitative as opposed to quantitative.

In this section we clarify the differences between these types of knowledge (shallow vs. deep, qualitative vs. quantitative) and indicate their advantages and drawbacks. This is done best by means of an example. Figure 1.1 shows a simple electric circuit consisting of a battery, a bulb, and a switch. Imagine that the problem is to diagnose the bulb on the basis of some available observations. The possible diagnostic outcomes correspond to the functional states of the bulb: *bulb_ok* or *bulb_blown*. The observations that are available to the diagnostician are the external manifestations of the circuit: the lightness of the bulb and the position of the switch. For simplicity we will assume that the battery is intact and so is the switch.

Here are some rules that could be useful in such a diagnostic micro

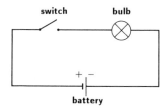

**Figure 1.1**  A simple electric circuit.

expert system:

> IF   *bulb_light*   THEN   *bulb_ok*
>
> IF   *switch_on*   AND   *bulb_dark*   THEN   *bulb_blown*

These rules represent *surface knowledge* since they define "surface relations" between the observables and the diagnoses without mentioning any underlying principles, involving electrical voltage, current, power, etc. So the diagnostic problem is solved without making reference to any of these deeper principles about how the circuit works, or about what causes what.

Figure 1.2 shows a more sophisticated model of the circuit, which can also be used for our diagnostic task. This model mentions some concepts from physics: voltages, currents, Ohm's law, Kirchhoff's law, etc. Here, the domains for voltages and currents are real numbers. This model is deep with respect to the simple diagnostic rules considered above. The model is also *quantitative* because the variables in the model take numerical values and the relations between them are stated numerically. There are also some definitions that establish the link between these underlying principles, described quantitatively, and the surface parameters of the system that are observable by the user. Such a parameter is the position of the switch, and its relation to the underlying physics is: whenever the switch is on, the electrical resistance of the switch is zero. This is stated in the model formally as:

$$switch\_on \quad \Longleftrightarrow \quad R_s = 0$$

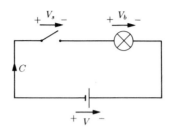

$$V - Vs - Vb = 0$$
$$V_s = C * R_s$$
$$V_b = C * R_b$$
$$P_b = C * V_b$$

$$P_b = 0 \quad \Longleftrightarrow \quad dark$$
$$P_b > 0 \quad \Longleftrightarrow \quad light$$
$$switch\_on \quad \Longleftrightarrow \quad R_s = 0$$
$$switch\_off \quad \Longleftrightarrow \quad R_s = \infty$$
$$bulb\_ok \quad \Longleftrightarrow \quad 0 < R_b < \infty$$
$$bulb\_blown \quad \Longleftrightarrow \quad R_b = \infty$$

**Figure 1.2**   A quantitative deep model of a simple electric circuit. $P_b$ is power on the bulb, $R_b$ and $R_s$ are the resistances of the bulb and the switch, respectively. The voltages, currents and resistances are represented by real numbers. Resistances are assumed constant.

This quantitative model is of course more sophisticated than our initial simple diagnostic model. The new model comprises knowledge that is deep from the point of view of the initial model. Diagnostic rules of the surface model can be derived from the deep model. In addition, the deep model can answer many other types of questions, which the surface model cannot. For example, what position should the switch be in if bulb light is desired? Or, what is the current in a blown bulb?

In spite of this, for a practical application a simple surface model may be more appropriate. There are some disadvantages of our deep quantitative model with respect to the particular task of diagnosing the bulb:

- To execute the quantitative model in the usual way numerically, we have to know numerical values of the parameters of the circuit, e.g., the resistance of the bulb.
- The quantitative model requires more computation than the simple surface model.
- Some of the computation is quite unnecessary; in particular, it is unnecessary to know exact numerical values of the currents and voltages in the circuit.

In addition to these, the quantitative model is not quite correct. In the model the relation between the voltage and the current on the bulb is namely stated as linear, but that is not really true because the resistance of the bulb depends on its temperature which, in turn, depends on the power on the bulb.

Thus for the diagnostic task at hand, yet another type of model is more appropriate. This is shown in Figure 1.3. This model is, again, deeper than our simple initial diagnostic rules. On the other hand, it is *qualitative*: the parameters of the circuit are represented by qualitative values. In general, in such a qualitative model we have to choose a suitable *space* for the values of each of the parameters. In our case, a suitable space for voltages and currents consists of three values:

$$+ \qquad 0 \qquad -$$

These qualitative values correspond to the numerical value of a parameter being positive, zero, or negative, respectively. So for a numerical parameter $x$, the corresponding qualitative value is defined by the following:

if  $x > 0$  then  $+$

if  $x = 0$  then  $0$

if  $x < 0$  then  $-$

Our set of qualitative values is naturally ordered thus:

$$- \; < \; 0 \; < \; +$$

---

% Quantity space for voltages and currents: +, 0, −

% Circuit definition, battery voltage is assumed positive

```
circuit( SwitchPos, BulbState, Lightness)   :-
   sum( SwVolt, BulbVolt, +),           % Battery volt. is +
   switch( SwitchPos, SwVolt, Curr),
   bulb( BulbState, Lightness, BulbVolt, Curr).
```

% Switch definition: switch( SwitchPos, Voltage, Current)

```
switch( on, 0, AnyCurrent).              % Voltage zero
switch( off, AnyVoltage, 0).             % Current zero
```

% Bulb definition: bulb( BulbState, Lightness, Voltage, Current)

```
bulb( blown, dark, AnyVoltage, 0).    % Current zero
bulb( ok, light, +, +).
bulb( ok, light, −, −).
bulb( ok, dark, 0,  0).
```

% Laws of qualitative summation

```
sum( +, +, +).      % Positive plus positive gives positive
sum( +, 0, +).
sum( +, −, Any).   % Positive plus negative gives anything
sum( 0, +, +).
sum( 0, 0, 0).
sum( 0, −, −).
sum( −, +, Any).
sum( −, 0, −).
sum( −, −, −).
```

---

**Figure 1.3** A qualitative model of a simple electric circuit consisting of a battery, a switch and a bulb. The model is represented in logic as a Prolog program.

Such an ordered (possibly partially ordered) value space for a parameter is often called *quantity space* (e.g., Forbus 1984).

The model in Figure 1.3 is represented by logic clauses in which all the variables are assumed to be universally quantified. The form of these clauses is such that they can be directly accepted and executed as a Prolog program. The notational conventions chosen here are those of the Edinburgh Prolog (Pereira, Pereira, and Warren 1978; also used in Clocksin and Mellish 1981 or Bratko 1986). According to these conventions, the names of variables start with capital letters, and constant symbols start with lower case letters.

The circuit, as a system, is specified by a set of its components (bulb, switch) and the way they are interconnected. The behavior of the system can thus be derived from the behavior of its components. On the other hand, the behavior of the components is defined as a law. The lawful behavior of the bulb is defined by the predicate:

**bulb( BulbState, Lightness, Voltage, Current)**

where the four arguments are:

- **BulbState** is the functional state of the bulb: **ok** or **blown**.
- **Lightness** is the lightness of the bulb: **light** or **dark**.
- **Voltage** is the voltage on the bulb.
- **Current** is the current in the bulb.

For example, the assertion

**bulb( blown, dark, AnyVoltage, 0)**

says that a blown bulb is dark, the voltage is anything, and the current is zero.

In the model we also have the predicate

**sum( X, Y, Z)**

which defines the laws for qualitative summation in our simple 3-valued quantity space, so that **X** plus **Y** gives **Z**. For example, the assertion

**sum( +, +, +)**

says that the sum of two positive values is a positive value. On the other hand,

**sum( +, −, Anything)**

says that the sum of a positive and a negative value can be anything (notice that **Anything** above is the name of a variable whose value is completely unconstrained): it can be either **+**, **0** or **−**. Since the result of summation in this case is not unique, our qualitative model can be said to be *nondeterministic*. Nondeterminism of this kind is rather typical of qualitative models. In our example nondeterminism is due to information loss in abstracting real numbers to qualitative values.

Notice the specification of qualitative behavior of the intact bulb, illustrated in Figure 1.4. This qualitative behavior corresponds to *any* numerical function $y = f(x)$ that passes through the origin and has the property:

$$\text{if} \quad x > 0 \quad \text{then} \quad y > 0$$
$$\text{if} \quad x < 0 \quad \text{then} \quad y < 0$$

Our qualitative model of the relation betweeen the current and the voltage on the bulb is thus *correct* although less *precise* than the quantitative model. We can state a qualitative model correctly without knowing the exact relation between the voltage and the current.

The model in Figure 1.3 can be run as a Prolog program directly. It can be asked any of the three important types of question, explained below: prediction type, diagnostic type and control type.

*Diagnostic-type question*: Given the inputs to the system and the observable manifestations, what is the system's functional state (normal or malfunctioning; what is the failure?); for example, if the switch position is "on" and the lightness is "dark," what is the status of the bulb? This question is posed to Prolog as:

**?−    circuit( on, BulbState, dark).**

It is inferred from the model that

**BulbState = blown**

*Prediction-type question*: Here we are interested in what will be the observable result of some "input" to the system and some given functional state of the system. For example, what will be the lightness of the bulb if the switch is on ("input") and the bulb is intact (functional state):

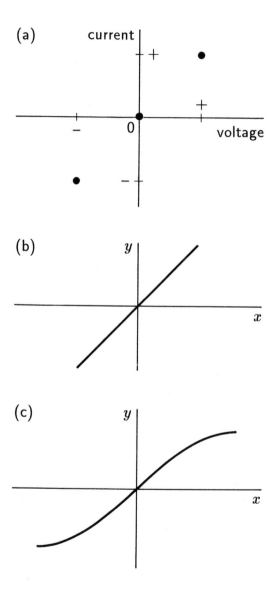

**Figure 1.4** (a) A qualitative model of the intact bulb. Notice that this qualitative relation corresponds to any function $y = y(x)$ such that: $y(0) = 0$, if $x > 0$ then $y > 0$, if $x < 0$ then $y < 0$. (b) and (c) are examples of such functions.

```
?—  circuit( on, ok, Lightness).

Lightness  =  light
```

*Control-type question*: Here we are interested in knowing what should be the "input" control into the system to achieve a desired "output"; for example, what position should the switch be in if light is desired:

```
?—  circuit( SwitchPos, ok, light).

SwitchPos  =  on
```

Other terms that are sometimes associated with qualitative knowledge, although they are not equivalent, are: "causal knowledge," or "commonsense knowledge," or "naive physics." In the case of KARDIO, of course, the word naive physics would correspond to "naive physiology." The KARDIO model of the physiological processes in the heart is qualitative in the sense that it does not deal with electrical signals represented numerically as voltages in time. Instead, electrical signals are represented by *symbolic descriptions* that specify qualitative features of signals. Such a qualitative approach has several advantages over conventional numerical modeling. Among the advantages are:

- The qualitative view is closer to actual medical descriptions of and reasoning about the physiological processes and failures in the heart.

- To execute the model we do not have to know exact numerical values of the parameters in the model.

- The qualitative simulation is computationally less complex than numerical simulation. (This advantage of course disappears in cases when qualitative model produces overly underdetermined situations that entail many ambigous behaviors, leading to combinatorial explosion.)

- The qualitative simulation can be used for constructing explanations of the mechanisms of failures of the system that is being modeled more naturaly than in numerical modeling.

## 1.2 Transformations between knowledge representations

Obviously not all forms of knowledge are equally suitable for all tasks. Some representations are better suited for answering prediction-type questions that involve reasoning from causes to consequences. Other representations better suit diagnostic questions that involve reasoning backwards, from consequences (known manifestations) to causes (diagnoses).

Here the important difference between both tasks was in the direction of inference. Another dimension of difference may come from the necessity of using deep knowledge. So the task of *explaining* a device may require reference to the underlying mechanisms (deep knowledge). On the other hand, for simple-minded and efficient diagnosis, surface knowledge may be sufficient or even preferable to deep since typically the use of surface knowledge is operationally more efficient.

Therefore it is sensible to use different representations of the knowledge for different types of task. Once we have *some* representation, it is most convenient to automatically transform this representation into the one that is best suited for the particular task at hand.

This leads to the question of transformations between various representations. The particular kinds of transformations carried out in the KARDIO study are:

(1) deep model $\longrightarrow$ surface knowledge

(2) surface knowledge $\longrightarrow$ compressed diagnostic rules

(3) surface knowledge $\longrightarrow$ compressed prediction rules

(4) surface knowledge $\longrightarrow$ deep model

The first three transformations were completely automatic whereas the fourth one was semi-automatic and required human interaction. This interaction is necessary because normally surface knowledge does not sufficiently constrain the deep model. Various deep models can explain the given surface behavior, so additional constraints on the deep model are needed.

The first transformation, from deep model to surface knowledge, was done by means of exhaustive simulation based on deep model

(Mozetič, Bratko and Lavrač 1984). The computational process employed in simulation was deduction. The difference between deep model and the corresponding surface knowledge can be characterized as *intensional vs. extensional* representation of the same information. The deep model is a set of logical axioms and the surface knowledge is the set of all theorems that follow from these axioms and are of interest from the "surface point of view" (that is disregarding "intermediate events").

The surface representation is thus a set of simple rules that look like a long table. Such a table is, of course, typically much bulkier than the deep model. However, the information required by the diagnostic or prediction-type questions is stated explicitly in the table and simply has to be retrieved. Therefore the surface representation is suitable for efficient machine use for diagnosis and prediction, but it has an important disadvantage that is due to its size: it may be too complex for *humans* to study and to understand as a whole. Hence the need for a more compact and yet shallow representation, which led to transformations 2 and 3: from surface knowledge to compressed prediction and diagnostic rules.

The compression transformations 2 and 3 were in the case of KARDIO carried out by means of inductive learning programs (Mozetič 1985a, 1986). The idea is to use individual facts from the surface-knowledge as examples for a learning program. The learning program then formulates compact rules defining a particular concept, e.g., a diagnostic class, as required. Normally in learning, an inductive program will generalize, obtaining rules that are more general than the examples. Thus in machine learning the transformation between the example set and the learned rules need not be truth preserving. However, if we use *all* the statements in the surface knowledge as learning examples, thus covering the total problem space, and if our learning program has the property of perfect reproduction of the learning set, then the learned rules are a compressed representation of and equivalent to the original surface knowledge.

It is important that the compressed rules be easy to understand by humans. The importance of generating *comprehensible* rules by machine learning programs was argued by Michie (e.g., 1986a, b) and is now generally recognized. In the case of KARDIO special effort was

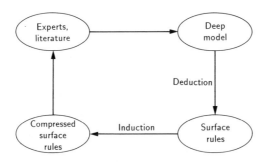

**Figure 1.5**  A knowledge acquisition cycle.

made in this respect. The compressed representations thus obtained (after steps 2 or 3) are compact and largely comprehensible. These representations are therefore most suitable for human experts to study and compare with the existing human codifications of the same knowledge. This comparison completes what we here refer to as a *knowledge acquisition cycle* (Figure 1.5). The comparison between the original human codifications and the generated compressed representation offers a powerful possibility for knowledge validation. Differences between the original human codification and a compressed representation can result from either:

(1)  an error in compressed representation, or

(2)  a slip in the human codification.

In the former case, the error is clearly a consequence of an error in the deep model since both the deductive and inductive derivation steps in Figure 1.5 are truth preserving. Thus in this case the knowledge acquisition cycle provides a feedback loop for verifying and correcting the deep model. In the latter case, a slip in the human codification, the knowledge acquisition cycle will expose blemishes in the existing, original expert formulations and may thus help to improve those. In the KARDIO study both effects were noticed.

The KARDIO study shows that this knowledge acquisition cycle, involving qualitative modeling and machine learning technology, can be used to construct knowledge bases whose complexity is far beyond the capability of traditional, dialogue based techniques for knowledge acquisition. We believe the KARDIO knowledge acquisition paradigm will become a standard method in the development of practical expert systems. For example, it has also been adapted in the development of a satellite power supply fault diagnosis system by Pearce (1988).

We shall here illustrate the knowledge acquisition cycle in detail by examples from the domain of electric circuits, such as the one in Figure 1.1. To make the problem slightly more interesting, we will this time consider the circuit in Figure 1.6. We will assume that the battery in this circuit provides sufficient power input to the bulbs for any combination of the positions of the switches. So all three of the bulbs will normally be bright whenever there is some current input.

Simply executing the logic model of the circuit on Figure 1.6 as a Prolog program for all possible positions of the three switches (on or off) and states of the bulbs (ok or blown), we get a surface, extensional representation of this circuit. Part of this representation is shown in Figure 1.7 as a set of ground facts about **circuit2** relation.

These surface-type facts can be used as rules for diagnosing the circuit. For example, one of the lines in the table can be read as a diagnostic rule: if the switches 1 and 2 are on, switch 3 is off, and all the bulbs are dark, then bulbs 2 and 3 could be ok. Consider a situation where: bulb 1 is dark, switch 1 is on and switch 3 is on. Using lines 5 to 7 in the table of Figure 1.7, we can find that bulb 1 is blown. On the other hand, we cannot say anything definite about bulbs 2 and 3: each of them can be either intact or blown.

For a more complex system, a corresponding table of ground facts such as the one in Figure 1.7 would be impractically long as a representation that is intended to be understood by humans. A more compact and structured representation would be desirable. Such a compressed representation can often be obtained by machine learning methods. We will here illustrate the principle with our circuit example.

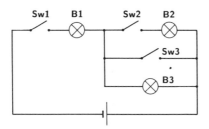

```
circuit2( Sw1, Sw2, Sw3, B1, B2, B3, L1, L2, L3)  :-
    VSw3 = VB3,
    sum( VSw1, VB1, V1),
    sum( V1, VB3, +),
    sum( VSw2, VB2, VB3),
    switch( Sw1, VSw1, C1),
    bulb( B1, L1, VB1, C1),
    switch( Sw2, VSw2, C2),
    bulb( B2, L2, VB2, C2),
    switch( Sw3, VSw3, CSw3),
    bulb( B3, L3, VB3, CB3),
    sum( CSw3, CB3, C3),
    sum( C2, C3, C1).
```

**Figure 1.6** A more interesting circuit and its corresponding deep qualitative model (intensional representation). The laws for switch, bulb and summation are as in Figure 1.3. The variables beginning with L denote the lightness of bulbs, and the variables beginning with C the currents in bulbs and switches.

We can compress the extensional representation of Figure 1.7 by means of an inductive learning program as follows. Suppose that we just need a compact rule for diagnosing bulb 1. An appropriate formulation of the compression task for a learning program would then be as follows: each situation is described in terms of six observable *attributes* of the circuit. These six attributes and their possible values are:

| *Attribute* | *Possible values* |
|---|---|
| Switch1 | on, off |
| Switch2 | on, off |
| Switch3 | on, off |
| Light1 | light, dark |
| Light2 | light, dark |
| Light3 | light, dark |

The possible diagnoses with respect to bulb 1 are: ok and blown. Each possible situation is then taken by a learning program as a training example, described in terms of the six attributes and the diagnostic *class* to which it belongs (ok or blown).

---

**circuit2( on, on, on, ok, ok, ok, light, dark, dark)**
**circuit2( on, on, on, ok, ok, blown, light, dark, dark)**
**circuit2( on, on, on, ok, blown, ok, light, dark, dark)**
**circuit2( on, on, on, ok, blown, blown, light, dark, dark)**
**circuit2( on, on, on, blown, ok, ok, dark, dark, dark)**
**circuit2( on, on, on, blown, ok, blown, dark, dark, dark)**
**circuit2( on, on, on, blown, blown, ok, dark, dark, dark)**
**circuit2( on, on, on, blown, blown, blown, dark, dark, dark)**
**circuit2( on, on, off, ok, ok, ok, light, light, light)**
**circuit2( on, on, off, ok, ok, blown, light, light, dark)**
**circuit2( on, on, off, ok, blown, ok, light, dark, light)**
**circuit2( on, on, off, ok, blown, blown, dark, dark, dark)**
**circuit2( on, on, off, blown, ok, ok, dark, dark, dark)**
**circuit2( on, on, off, blown, ok, blown, dark, dark, dark)**
**circuit2( on, on, off, blown, blown, ok, dark, dark, dark)**
**circuit2( on, on, off, blown, blown, blown, dark, dark, dark)**
. . .

---

**Figure 1.7** Part of a shallow, extensional representation of the circuit in Figure 1.6. The complete table of all ground facts about this circuit would comprise 64 lines. The arguments of **circuit2** relation are: the positions of the three switches, the states of the three bulbs, and the lightness of each of the bulbs.

(a)

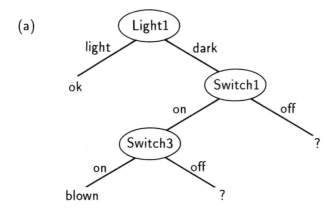

(b)

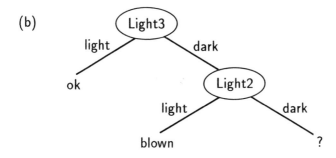

**Figure 1.8** Compressed diagnostic rules, in the form of decision trees, generated by the Assistant learning program from the table of Figure 1.7. (a) tree for bulb 1; (b) tree for bulb 3. The question mark denotes "ok or blown."

We can use for compression any inductive learning program that accepts learning examples in the above form, such as programs of the TDIDT family (Top-Down Induction of Decision Trees, e.g., Quinlan 1986) or the AQ family (e.g., Michalski 1983). Here we present the compression results obtained with a general inductive learning shell Assistant Professional (e.g., Cestnik, Kononenko, and Bratko 1987) that belongs to the TDIDT family. Compact decision trees for bulbs 1 and 3 generated by Assistant are shown in Figure 1.8. Here it is assumed that the diagnostic procedure only involves observing the lightness of bulbs and the positions of switches, but it does not involve manipulating switches.

Similarly we could construct a decision tree for diagnosing Bulb2. These trees are now sufficient for diagnosing each of the three bulbs individually, irrespective of the other two. The three trees are, however, not quite sufficient for diagnosing the whole circuit. The following example explains why not. Consider a situation where: switch 1 is on, switch 3 is off, and all the three bulbs are dark. According to the diagnostic tree 1 (Figure 1.8), bulb 1 can be in any state, either ok or blown. Similarly, according to Figure 1.8, bulb 3 can be either intact or blown. This could now be (incorrectly) understood that all the four theoretically possible combinations of the states of bulb 1 and bulb 3 are in fact possible in the present situation. In particular, in one such combination both bulbs are intact. However, looking back at the circuit itself (Figure 1.6) it becomes clear that with this setting of the switches (Switch1 = on, Switch3 = off), bulb 1 and bulb 3 cannot be both intact and dark! Obviously at least one of them must be blown. Superficially it might seem there is something wrong with the diagnostic trees of Figure 1.8. However the trees themselves are correct since they are only intended to produce *partial* diagnoses (tree 1 only diagnoses bulb 1), but the possible *combinations* of these partial diagnostic results are not necessarily all correct. Thus for diagnosing the complete circuit, we have also to consider the combined diagnoses, that is the states of *all* three bulbs. One simple way to do this is to consider these combinations as diagnostic classes. Combinations in our case are triples, for example (blown, ok, ok). So for the complete system we have eight classes altogether $(2 * 2 * 2 = 8)$. A diagnostic decision tree thus constructed for the whole circuit is shown in Figure 1.9. According to this tree, for the combination of observable attributes where switch 1 is on, switch 3 is off, and all the bulbs are dark, it is not possible that *both* bulb 1 and bulb 3 be intact at the same time (the path in the tree: Light1 = dark, Switch1 = on, Switch3 = off).

It is interesting to note that, although our diagnostic problem with three bulbs looks very simple, the tree in Figure 1.9 contains some decisions that may not be immediately obvious. An example is the path Light1 = light, Light3 = dark, and Switch3 = off. This

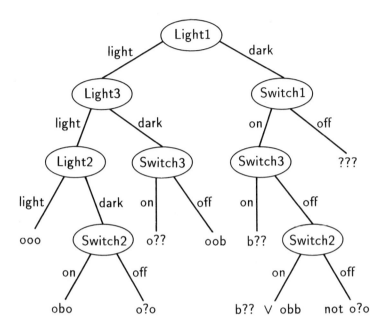

**Figure 1.9** A compressed diagnostic rule for the complete circuit of Figure 1.6, generated from the table of Figure 1.7.

path ends with a leaf labeled oob. This may appear surprizing because the information along the path is directly concerned only with bulbs 1 and 3. Thus it would seem that we cannot tell anything about bulb 2, and that correct diagnosis would be o?b. However, the information along the path is in fact sufficient for the conclusion Bulb2 = ok, which is explained by the following argument. Because bulb 1 is light, there must be electric current in bulb 1. Therefore there must also be current in the right part of the circuit (bulbs 2 and 3). Now, because bulb 3 is dark and switch 3 is off, this current can only be in bulb 2. Therefore bulb 2 must be ok.

Other types of descriptions (other than decision trees) of diagnoses are obtained by other inductive learning programs. The NEWGEM program (Mozetič 1985b), for example, generates descriptions in Figure 1.10. NEWGEM was eventually used in the large scale compres-

| | | |
|---|---|---|
| [Bulb1=blown] | ⇐ | [Switch1=on] & [Switch3=on] & [Light1=dark] |
| [Bulb1=ok] | ⇐ | [Light1=light] |
| [Bulb1=?] | ⇐ | [Switch1=off] |
| | ∨ | [Switch3=off] & [Light1=dark] |
| | | |
| [Bulb2=blown] | ⇐ | [Switch2=on] & [Light2=dark] & [Light3=light] |
| [Bulb2=ok] | ⇐ | [Light2=light] |
| [Bulb2=?] | ⇐ | [Light2=dark] & [Light3=dark] |
| | ∨ | [Switch2=off] |
| | | |
| [Bulb3=blown] | ⇐ | [Light2=light] & [Light3=dark] |
| [Bulb3=ok] | ⇐ | [Light3=light] |
| [Bulb3=?] | ⇐ | [Light2=dark] & [Light3=dark] |
| | | |
| [Bulbs=???] | ⇐ | [Switch1=off] |
| [Bulbs=not o?o] | ⇐ | [Switch1=on] & [Switch2=off] & [Switch3=off] & [Light1=dark] |
| [Bulbs=b?? ∨ obb] | ⇐ | [Switch1=on] & [Switch2=on] & [Switch3=off] & [Light1=dark] |
| [Bulbs=b??] | ⇐ | [Switch1=on] & [Switch3=on] & [Light1=dark] |
| [Bulbs=oob] | ⇐ | [Light2=light] & [Light3=dark] |
| [Bulbs=o??] | ⇐ | [Switch3=on] & [Light1=light] |
| [Bulbs=o?o] | ⇐ | [Switch2=off] & [Light3=light] |
| [Bulbs=obo] | ⇐ | [Switch2=on] & [Light2=dark] & [Light3=light] |
| [Bulbs=ooo] | ⇐ | [Light2=light] & [Light3=light] |

Figure 1.10 Compressed descriptions of diagnoses for the circuit of Figure 1.6, derived by the NEWGEM learning program. The upper three sets of rules apply to individual bulbs, the lower set of rules applies to the whole circuit. The expression **[Bulb=?]** denotes cases where the state of the bulb is unknown, i.e., either ok or blown.

sion exercise in KARDIO, described in Chapter 4. NEWGEM belongs to the AQ family of learning programs, also described in Chapter 4.

In the case of KARDIO, the combinations of simple defects were far too numerous to allow the generation of a decision rule for the complete system (the heart) for all the combined defects (in the style of Figure 1.9). Therefore diagnostic rules were constructed for individual simple diagnoses. It was proved that no extra rules need to be added to retain logical equivalence in this particular case (details are in Chapter 4).

## 1.3 Overview of KARDIO

The KARDIO project started in 1982. The results reported in this book were obtained in the period 1982–1987. The following are important publications that correspond to the milestones of the project: Bratko et al. (1982) is an attempt to develop an ECG diagnosis expert system without a deep model; the first results on introducing a deep qualitative model of the heart were presented in (Mozetič, Bratko, and Lavrač 1983); the version of the model essentially the same as the present version was developed in Mozetič (1984); the model and model-based derivation of surface knowledge were presented at the ISSEK 84 Workshop (International School for the Synthesis of Expert Knowledge) in a substantial technical report (Mozetič, Bratko, and Lavrač 1984); KARDIO-E, an expert system that uses the derived surface knowledge is described in Lavrač et al. (1985); Mozetič (1985a, 1986) describes the compression of surface knowledge using machine learning; Mozetič (1987a,b, 1988) introduces abstraction hierarchy into the heart model and an approach to learning of qualitative models; some of the presentation in this section is based on an earlier paper (Bratko, Mozetič, and Lavrač 1986).

### 1.3.1 The ECG diagnosis problem

The heart can be viewed as a mechanical device with an electrical control system. This electrical system works completely autonomously within the heart and is responsible for generating the rhythmical stimulation impulses that cause the contraction of the heart muscle. For proper functioning of the heart, the stimuli have to reach the atria (upper part of the heart) somewhat earlier than the ventricles (lower part of the heart). This is coordinated by the electrical control system schematically shown in Figure 1.11.

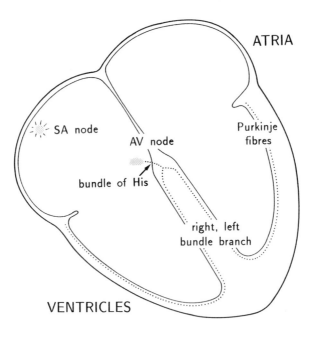

**Figure 1.11** A scheme of the electrical control system of the heart. The nodes generate electrical impulses. The dotted lines represent conduction paths for impulses.

The contractions of the heart muscle cause changes in the electrical potentials in the body. The changes of these potentials in time can be recorded as an electrocardiogram (ECG). Disturbances in the functioning of the heart are reflected in the ECG curves. The interpretation of ECG signals is concerned with the question: If a given ECG curve is not normal, what disorders in the heart could have caused this abnormality?

Our study was limited to the electrical activity of the heart and was not concerned with the mechanical failures of the heart muscle. Various disorders can occur in the electrical control system of the heart. For example, an impulse generator may become silent, or an extra generator may appear, or some electrical conductance may become blocked or partially blocked, or the rate of a generator may increase, rhythm become irregular, etc. These disorders are called *cardiac arrhythmias.* There are about 30 basic disorders that are of general interest in medical practice. Each of these disorders causes some characteristic changes in the ECG.

There can be several disorders simultaneously present in the heart. Combined disorders are called *multiple arrhythmias* as opposed to *simple arrhythmias* that correspond to single, basic disorders. The combinatorial nature of arrhythmias complicates the ECG interpretation problem because of the large number of potentially possible combinations. In principle, by way of combining simple disorders, the number of combined arrhythmias grows exponentially with the number of constituent simple arrhythmias. In the medical literature on the cardiac arrhythmias (e.g., Goldman 1976) there is no systematic description of ECG features that correspond to pairs of simple arrhythmias, let alone triple and even more complicated arrhythmias which, on the other hand, are not very rare in the medical practice.

In addition to this, multiple arrhythmias are hard to diagnose because there is no simple rule for combining ECGs that correspond to constituent disorders. In other words, if we know which ECGs correspond to any constituent simple disorder, in general it is not clear how to "sum" these ECGs into a "combined" ECG that corresponds to combinations of simple disorders. More formally, we do not know any function (of acceptable complexity) for computing an ECG description of a combined arrhythmia $Arr_1 \& Arr_2$, say, from the ECG descriptions $ECG_1$ and $ECG_2$ that correspond to $Arr_1$ and $Arr_2$ on their own:

$$Arr_1 \implies ECG_1$$
$$Arr_2 \implies ECG_2$$
$$Arr_1 \& Arr_2 \implies f(ECG_1, ECG_2)$$
$$f = ?$$

In the rules above it is assumed that those disorders not explicitly mentioned in the left hand side of a rule are not present. So the first rule above, for example, means: if there is simple disorder $Arr_1$ present and the rest of the heart is normal then the corresponding ECG is $ECG_1$.

The fact that we do not know the combination function $f$ for ECGs suggests that we need a special rule for each combined arrhythmia. If such rules are to be specified manually, extracted from human experts by traditional methods of knowledge acquisition, the combinatorial number of arrhythmias is prohibitive. It is true that not all combinations of simple arrhythmias are physiologically possible, but as shown by this study the number of physiologically possible arrhythmias and their corresponding ECGs is still high. Also, to guarantee the completeness of manual construction of such a knowledge base, mathematically possible combinations would still have to be considered even if they turn out to be physiologically unfeasible. It is interesting that no estimate of the number of physiologically possible combined arrhythmias can be found in the medical literature on cardiac arrhythmias and ECG interpretation.

These were the initial reasons that we approached the problem of multiple arrhythmias by constructing a deep qualitative model of the heart. Any combination of disorders can be inserted into the model that enables the system to reason about multiple arrhythmias from first principles.

Starting with this deep model, we carried out the transformations in the knowledge-acquisition cycle discussed earlier (Figure 1.5). These transformations are for the case of KARDIO shown in Figure 1.12. In this figure the representations are arranged so as to emphasize the distinction between the deep and surface levels.

We used the deep model for the automatic synthesis (through simulation) of the surface, operational representation of the ECG interpretation knowledge. This representation facilitates fast ECG diagnosis, but is rather complex in terms of memory space (about 5 MB). Therefore, as Figure 1.12 shows, we compressed this knowledge base by means of an inductive learning program. The thus obtained representation is compact and diagnostically efficient.

In the remainder of this section we give an overview of the model of

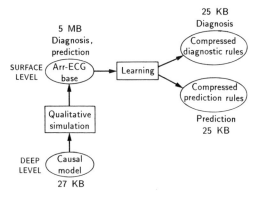

**Figure 1.12** Deep and surface levels of cardiological knowledge and transformations between these representations.

the heart, the qualitative simulation algorithm and its efficient implementation, the synthesized surface knowledge base and its subsequent compression. We also indicate how abstraction hierarchy was introduced into the qualitative model, and used in diagnosis and learning. Finally we assess the completeness and clinical applicability of KARDIO knowledge bases.

## 1.3.2 Qualitative model of the heart

Our qualitative model of the electrical activity of the heart specifies causal relationships between objects and events in the heart. These include electrical impulses, ECG signals, impulse generation, impulse conduction and summation. The model can be thought of as an electric network, as shown in Figure 1.13. However, signals that propagate in this network are represented qualitatively by symbolic descriptions rather than by voltage vs. time relations.

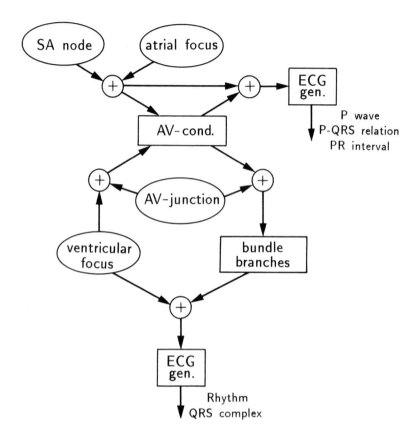

**Figure 1.13** Model of the heart as a network composed of impulse generators, conduction paths, impulse summators and ECG generators.

Ingredients of the model are:

(a) nodes of the network

(b) a dictionary of simple arrhythmias related to heart disorders

(c) "legality" constraints over the states of the heart

(d) "local" rule sets

(e) "global" rules

These ingredients are reviewed in more detail below.

(a) *nodes of the network*

- impulse generators
- conduction pathways
- impulse summators
- ECG generators

These elements are illustrated in Figure 1.14. Recall that the word "impulse" in this figure refers to a symbolic description, so these elements are in fact operators on descriptions. Impulse generators and conduction pathways can be in normal or abnormal functional states. For example, a generator can generate impulses or be silent; a conduction pathway can conduct normally or be blocked or partially blocked in various ways—it may just cause a delay of an impulse, or it can suppress every second or third impulse, etc. These abnormal states of individual elements correspond to simple disorders of the heart.

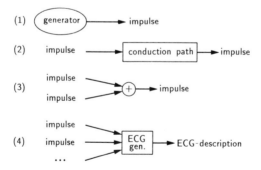

**Figure 1.14** Building blocks for the heart model.

(b) *dictionary of simple arrhythmias related to heart disorders*

Each simple arrhythmia is defined in terms of the functional states of the components of the heart. Roughly speaking, each simple arrhythmia corresponds to a disorder in one of the heart's components.

(c)  *"legality" constraints over the states of the heart*

These are defined by a predicate on the functional state of the heart that recognizes certain categories of states that are rejected by the model as "illegal." These categories include:

- logically impossible states
- physiologically impossible states
- "medically uninteresting" states

A state is logically impossible if one of the heart's components is in two different states at the same time. An example of a physiologically impossible state is a situation in which two generators in the atria discharge impulses permanently. An example of a medically uninteresting state is one in which there is no atrial activity and the AV-conduction is blocked. In such a case the block has no effect on the function of the heart and also cannot be detected in the ECG.

(d)  *"local" rule sets*

These specify the behavior of individual components of the heart (generators, summators and conduction pathways) in the presence of various abnormal states.

(e)  *"global" rules*

These rules define causal relations between impulse generators and conduction pathways in the heart, electrical impulses and ECG features; these rules also reflect the structure of the network in Figure 1.13.

All the rules in the model essentially have the syntax of first order predicate calculus, more precisely, the syntax that is accepted by Prolog under the Edinburgh notational conventions (Pereira, Pereira and Warren 1978).

Rules are composed of subexpressions in specialized languages for describing the state of the heart, impulses that are conducted through the heart, and ECG patterns. For example, the term

**heart( atr_focus: permanent( regular, between_100_250))**

is a partial specification of the state of the heart. It says that the atrial focus is discharging permanent impulses (as opposed to occasional) with a regular rhythm at the tachycardic rate (i.e., somewhere between 100 and 250). Each statement about the state of the heart specifies the functional state of a component of the heart (the atrial focus in the example above).

The following is an example of an ECG description:

**[rhythm_QRS = irregular] &**
**[dominant_P = abnormal] &**
**[rate_of_P = between_100_250] &**
**[relation_P_QRS = after_P_some_QRS_miss] &**
**[dominant_PR = prolonged] &**
**[dominant_QRS = normal] &**
**[rate_of_QRS = between_60_100 ∨ between_100_250]**

This specification consists of values assigned to qualitative ECG attributes that are normally used in the cardiological literature, such as the rhythm and the shape and the rate of P waves (illustrated in Figure 1.15). Notice that the description above gives two values for the rate of QRS waves: it can be either normal (**between_60_100**) or tachycardic (**between_100_250**).

Impulses are described by terms of the form illustrated by the following example:

**permanent( atr_focus: form( unifocal, regular, between_100_250))**

This says that there are unifocal permanent impulses with the tachycardic rate and regular rhythm at the atrial focus.

Figure 1.16 shows two examples of global rules and some local rules that specify the behavior of the individual components of the heart. The first global rule in Figure 1.16 says:

IF

the atrial focus discharges permanent impulses
at some rhythm **Rhythm** and rate **Rate**

THEN

there will be impulses at the atrial focus
characterized by **Origin**, **Rhythm** and **Rate**

WHERE

**Origin**, **Rhythm** and **Rate** must satisfy the
**atr_focus** relation

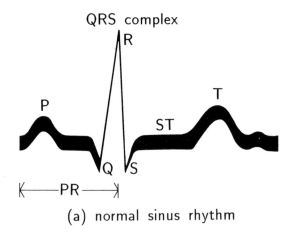

QRS complex

(a) normal sinus rhythm

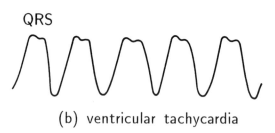

QRS

(b) ventricular tachycardia

**Figure 1.15** (a) ECG curve corresponding to one beat of one beat of the normal heart. Marked are features that are normally looked at by an ECG diagnostician. (b) ECG curve corresponding five beats in the case of arrhythmia ventricular tachycardia. This abnormal ECG is characterized by its higher rate ("tachycardia," between 100 and 250 beats per minute), and the "wide" shape of the QRS complexes.

The **atr_focus** relation describes the behavior of the atrial focus. This relation is partially specified in Figure 1.16 by local rules. It says that the atrial focus can be quiet, behave "unifocally" discharging impulses at a normal or tachycardic rate with the regular rhythm, or be "wandering," discharging impulses with irregular rhythm at normal or tachycardic rate, etc.

% Two global rules

[heart( atr_focus: permanent( Rhythm, Rate))]  ⟹
[permanent( atr_focus: form( Origin, Rhythm, Rate))]  &
atr_focus( Origin, Rhythm, Rate).

[permanent( atria: form( _, Rhythm0, Rate0)),
 heart( av_conduct: State)]  ⟹
[permanent( av_conduct: form( State, Rhythm1, Rate1))]  &
av_conduct( State, Rhythm0, Rhythm1, Rate0, Rate1).

% Some local relations

```
atr_focus( atr_focus, quiet,    zero           ).
atr_focus( atr_focus, regular,  between_60_100  ).
atr_focus( atr_focus, regular,  between_100_250 ).
atr_focus( wandering, irregular, between_60_100  ).
```
. . .

```
av_conduct( normal, Rhythm, Rhythm, Rate, Rate ) :-
    Rate -< between_250_350.
av_conduct( delayed, Rhythm, Rhythm, Rate, Rate ) :-
    Rate in [under_60, between_60_100, between_100_250].
av_conduct( progress_delayed, regular, irregular,
            Rate0, Rate ) :-
    poss_reduced( Rate0, Rate ).
```
. . .

```
poss_reduced( Rate,            Rate ) :-
    Rate >- zero, Rate -< between_250_350.
poss_reduced( between_60_100,   under_60        ).
poss_reduced( between_100_250, between_60_100 ).
```
. . .

**Figure 1.16**  Two global rules and some local rules of the heart model. Global rules are, from the point of view of Prolog, unit clauses of the form: $A \Longrightarrow B\&C$, which can in the model be read: if $A$ then $B$ where $C$. A special rule-interpreter in Prolog uses rules of this type. Local rules specify the behavior of individual components of the heart and are directly executed by the Prolog system as rules of a Prolog program.

The second global rule in Figure 1.16 can be read:

IF

> in the atria there are permanent impulses of some rhythm **Rhythm0** and rate **Rate0**, and the state of the AV conductance is **State**

THEN

> there are impulses of type **State**, rhythm **Rhythm1** and rate **Rate1** at the exit from the AV conductance

WHERE

> **State**, **Rhythm0**, **Rhythm1**, **Rate0** and **Rate1** have to satisfy the relation **av_conduct**

The **av_conduct** relation is specified by a set of local rules, as a directly executable Prolog procedure. This procedure qualitatively defines the physiology of the AV conductance pathway. As can be seen from the definition of the relation **av_conduct** in Figure 1.16, the components of the heart can behave nondeterministically in the sense that they can react to the same input with different responses at the output. For example, the **av_conduct** relation says that the output impulse rate is *possibly* reduced with respect to the input rate. That is, the two rates can be qualitatively equal or different.

Complete details of the model are in Chapter 2.

## 1.3.3    Qualitative simulation algorithm

Formally, the qualitative simulation consists of theorem proving and theorem generation. Although the global rules have the syntax of Prolog they are not directly executed by Prolog's own interpreting mechanism. The main reason is the need for additional control to improve the executional efficiency. Thus the qualitative simulation is done by a special rule-interpreter implemented in Prolog.

Each simulation run consists of the following steps:

(1) Instantiate the model by a given arrhythmia, using the definitions of arrhythmias in terms of the heart disorders.

(2) Check the resulting functional state of the heart against the legality constraints (logical, physiological, medically interesting).

(3) Execute the model by triggering the rules until a state is reached in which no rule fires (this process is combinatorial due to the nondeterministic nature of the heart's components).

(4) Collect the proved assertions about ECG and then construct an ECG description that corresponds to the given arrhythmia.

The complex part above is step 3. It is based on the forward chaining of global rules in the model. The simulator starts with some initial database of facts (initially these just specify the state of the heart) and then keeps firing the global rules until no more rules can fire. The constraint here is that no rule is repeatedly executed on the same piece of information. Execution of rules generates new assertions that are added into the database. These new assertions are regarded as hypotheses that can later be proved false, which causes backtracking. Backtracking to a previous point occurs when the current content of the database is found inconsistent, i.e., some assertion has been generated which leads to contradiction. More precisely, the rule triggering process is as follows.

Assume that there is a hypothesis $A$ in the database. Then apply a global rule of the form

$$A \implies B \ \& \ C$$

In general, in such rules, $A$ and $B$ are Prolog terms and $C$ is a Prolog goal that can directly be executed by Prolog. The precondition matching is simply the logic unification. Normally, $C$ is a call to evaluate a local relation. Thus, to apply a rule of the above form, do the following:

Evaluate $C$;
if $C$ is false then $A$ must be false—discard it;
otherwise, if $C$ is true, assert a new hypothesis $B$ and
continue firing rules.

In the case that $C$ is false, a contradiction has been detected and backtracking is to be done. This process terminates when there is no further rule to fire. At that stage, all the remaining hypotheses in the database are accepted as true since there is now no way of showing them to contradict. Among these facts there are also statements about ECG. The simulator collects those statements and forms an ECG description

(1) By the definition of **[atrial_tachycardia, wenckebach]** instantiate the state of the heart to:

**heart( sa_node: permanent( quiet, zero)) &**
**heart( atrial_focus: permanent( regular, between_100_250)) &**
**heart( av_conduct: progress_delayed) &**

. . .

(2) The assertion

**heart( atrial_focus: permanent( regular, between_100_250))**

triggers the first global rule in Figure 1.16. The goal

**atr_focus( Origin, regular, between_100_250)**

is evaluated, using the local relation **atr_focus**. This succeeds and the new assertion is added to the database:

**permanent( atr_focus: form( unifocal, regular, between_100_250))**

(3) After summing together the atrial impulses we get the asertion:

**permanent( atria: form( unifocal, regular, between_100_250))**

(4) This assertion triggers the second global rule in Figure 1.16. The Prolog goal to be evaluated is now:

**av_conduct( progress_delayed, regular, Rhythm1,**
**              between_100_250, Rate1)**

This can be satisfied in two ways, by either **Rate1 = between_100_250** or by **Rate1 = between_60_100**. So two hypotheses are indicated:

**permanent( av_conduct:**
**              form( progress_delayed, irregular, between_100_250))**
or
**permanent( av_conduct:**
**              form( progress_delayed, irregular, between_60_100))**

Depending on the search strategy used, the system may now assert one of the above hypotheses into the database, and consider the second one on backtracking which corresponds to a depth-first style search; or, it may assert both which corresponds to a breadth-first style search.

**Figure 1.17** Fragments of the qualitative simulation trace for the combination of arrhythmias atrial tachycardia and Wenckebach. Some steps were omitted from the actual trace.

that corresponds to the arrhythmia with which the simulation process was started.

As an example, Figure 1.17 shows part of a simulation run when the state of the heart is a combination of two simple arrhythmias: atrial tachycardia and Wenckebach.

## 1.3.4   Implementation of the simulation algorithm

The easiest way of implementing the simulation algorithm outlined above is to use the depth-first search strategy. This is straightforward and suitable for single simulation runs, that is, for answering questions of the prediction type: given an arrhythmia, what are its corresponding ECGs? If several ECGs are possible, they are simply generated through backtracking. Also, an execution trace obtained in such a simulation run can be used as the basis for generating an explanation of what is going on in the heart. This is suitable since the simulation steps follow the causal chains of events in the heart, according to the global rules of the model. These rules essentially describe the causal relations between objects and events in the heart.

In a Prolog implementation of depth-first simulation on various machines, ranging from Edinburgh Prolog on DEC-10 (Pereira, Pereira, and Warren 1978) to Arity Prolog on IBM PC/XT/AT (Arity 1986), each simulation run takes a few CPU seconds, producing all alternative ECGs.

This straightforward method, however, is not as effective in answering questions of the diagnostic type. Diagnostic-type questions are of the form: given an ECG, what arrhythmias could have caused it? To answer such questions, we could run the model in the opposite direction. Start with a given ECG and end with possible functional states of the heart that may cause this ECG.

We can in fact run the model in this direction by the backward chaining of the rules in the model. In order to do that we can reverse the global rules and use the simple depth-first search again. However, the practical problem of efficiency now arises because the branching factor (nondeterminism) in the backward direction is much higher than that in the forward direction. This entails much more backtracking and rather complex search, thus rendering this approach to diagnosis impractical. Efficiency can be improved by rewriting the model so as to introduce more constraints into the rules, which would help the system recognize contradictive branches at an earlier stage. An attempt at reformulating rules, however, revealed two drawbacks. The size of the model increases considerably, and the transparency is greatly affected. This, in turn, mars the explanation of the heart's behavior based on the execution trace.

An alternative way to achieve efficient diagnosis is to *compile the model*. That is to generate from the deep model of the heart a complete surface level representation of the arrhythmia—ECG relation (Figure 1.12) as a set of pairs of the form:

**(Combined_arrhythmia, ECG_description)**

In principle this can be done by executing the depth-first simulation (forward chaining) for each possible combined arrhythmia, and storing all its ECG manifestations. It would be necessary to repeat this for all possible alternative execution paths in order to obtain all possible ECGs for each arrhythmia. This is again rather inefficient for two reasons. First, for each disjunctive solution the simulator has to backtrack to some previously used rule in the model and restore its previous state. Second, the final resulting ECG descriptions have the form of disjunctions of terms about ECG. These disjunctive terms can be more complex than necessary and can be simplified later. This posterior simplification, however, is again a complex operation. Each disjunct is the result of an alternative execution path. The simplification can be carried out much more economically at the very moment that a disjunct (or, typically, part of it) is generated, before it gets further expanded and mixed in the expression with other not closely related terms.

These two factors (saving the restoration of previous states, and immediate simplification of disjunctive expressions) motivated the implementation of another type of simulation algorithm that handles alternative execution paths in a breadth-first fashion. This algorithm develops alternatives essentially in parallel and currently simplifies disjunctions. The simplification rules actually used were rather model dependent in the sense that they do not preserve logical equivalence in general but only in the special case of the properties of the heart model. So the breadth-first simulation is not general and we would possibly have to modify the simplification rules in the case of a change in the model.

This specialized simplification method proved to be rather powerful. As a typical example of the reduction effect consider the combined arrhythmia atrial fibrillation and ventricular ectopic beats. The depth-first simulation generates 72 ECG descriptions which is equivalent to one ECG description with 72 disjunctive terms. The breadth-first simulation results in a description comprising four disjunctive terms. There was a similar factor of improvement in general, which can be seen from the results of generating the complete arrhythmia-ECG base.

Full details of the simulation algorithm, its implementation, and results of generation of the complete surface level representation from the deep model are in Chapter 3.

## 1.3.5 Compilation of deep model into surface representation

The breadth-first simulation algorithm was executed on all mathematically possible combinations of simple arrhythmias. The majority of these combined arrhythmias were eliminated by the legality constraints over the states of the heart. The complete arrhythmia-ECG knowledge base was thus automatically generated (see Chapter 3 for details). Results of the generation reveal some interesting points. The most complicated arrhythmias are combinations of seven simple disorders. There are altogether 2,419 "legal" combined arrhythmias within the level of detail of the heart model. These arrhythmias are related to the large number of 140,966 generated ECG manifestations. This is indicative of the difficulty in ECG diagnosis of cardiac arrhythmias. On average, each arrhythmia has almost 60 different corresponding ECG manifestations. The relation between arrhythmias and their ECG manifestations is represented by 8,314 Prolog clauses generated as a result of the compilation of the deep model into its surface representation. Each clause represents a pair: **(Combined_arrhythmia, ECG_description)**. Each ECG description specifies a number of possible ECGs, about 20 on average. This is the reduction factor due to the simplification technique used in the breadth-first simulation.

The set of 140,966 ECG patterns (the right hand sides of the arrhythmia-ECG rules) are not unique. The same ECG patterns can occur at several places which means that several arrhythmias can have the same ECG manifestation. Consequently, arrhythmias cannot be unambigously diagnosed from a given ECG. Empirical probing showed that for a given ECG there are typically between two and four possible combined arrhythmias in the arrhythmia knowledge-base. From the medical point of view, however, these alternative diagnoses are not significantly different from the point of view of treatment. They would typically all require the same treatment.

The arrhythmia-ECG base generated from the model is complete in two ways. First, it comprizes all physiologically possible arrhythmias at the level of detail of the model. Second, each arrhythmia is associated with all its possible ECG manifestations. In principle, the problem of diagnosing is now simple. As the rules in the knowledge base are logical implications, we can apply the *modus tollens* rule of inference on them. Consider a rule of the form

**Combined_arrhythmia   $\Longrightarrow$   ECG_description**

where **ECG_description** is the disjunction of *all* possible ECGs that **Combined_arrhythmia** can cause. Then, if a given ECG does not match **ECG_description** it follows that **Combined_arrhythmia** is eliminated as a diagnostic possibility. All arrhythmias that are not thus eliminated are possible diagnoses with respect to the given ECG data. Any further discrimination between the so obtained set of arrhythmias can be done only on the basis of some additional evidence (e.g., clinical data). Also, as the knowledge base is complete (with respect to the level of detail in the model) the empty set of possible arrhythmias would imply that the given ECG is physiologically impossible.

## 1.3.6     Compression of the arrhythmia-ECG base using inductive learning tools

As discussed, the arrhythmia-ECG base can be used for efficient ECG diagnosis based on a simple pattern-matching rule. However, it is rather bulky for some practical application requirements. If stored as a text file, the 8,314 Prolog clauses that represent the arrhythmia-ECG relation, occupy more than 5 MB of store. Also this mere complexity renders the contents of this knowledge base difficult to compare with the conventional medical codifications of the electrocardiographic knowledge. Therefore an attempt was made to find a more compact representation of the arrhythmia-ECG base that would still allow efficient ECG diagnosis. This corresponds to the induction step in the knowledge-acquisition cycle of Figure 1.5.

As explained in section 1.2, the main idea was to use the compiled representation as a source of examples and to use an inductive learning program to obtain their compact descriptions. Various inductive learning programs were used for this purpose, all of them belonging to the AQ family of learning programs (e.g., Michalski 1983). The programs GEM (Reinke 1984) and EXCELL (Becker 1985) were used in earlier experiments reported in (Mozetič 1985a, 1986) and (Bratko, Mozetič, and Lavrač 1986). The final results, reported in this book, were obtained with NEWGEM (Mozetič 1985b). Taking the complete arrhythmia-ECG base as the set of examples, the number of examples for these learning programs would be too high. Therefore we had first to generate a subset of the knowledge base that would retain its completeness to the greatest possible extent. Some domain-specific factorization properties facilitated the selection of a considerably reduced subset for learning whereby the information thus lost can be recovered by a small set of additional rules. The subset thus obtained was substantially smaller than the original arrhythmia-ECG base. There are 943 combined arrhythmias and 5,240 ECGs in the subset compared to 2,419 arrhythmias and 140,966 ECGs in the complete knowledge base.

Roughly, the compresssion procedure was as follows. The learning subset of the arrhythmia-ECG base comprised 943 rules (corresponding to 943 combined arhythmias) of the form:

**Combined_arrhythmia $\implies$ ECG_description**

The goal of learning was to convert this information into rules of two forms:

(1) Compressed *prediction rules* that answer the question: What ECGs may be caused by a given disorder in a heart's component?

(2) Compressed *diagnostic rules* that answer the question: What heart disorders are indicated by a given ECG feature?

Learning programs of the the AQ family generate class descriptions as VL1 expressions (Variable-Valued Logic 1, Michalski and Larson 1975). Before such programs could have been used, the learning subset had to be converted into rules of yet two other forms in order to get the right input for the learning programs required, i.e., examples of objects that belong to classes being learned. The principle of how to do that was indicated in section 1.2. For synthesizing prediction rules, the proper starting point were pairs of the form:

**(Selected_disorder,  ECG_description)**

where a "selected disorder" is for example: atrial focus is in the tachycardic state. For the learning program, the disorder is the class, and the ECG description is the vector of attribute values.

The starting point for the synthesis of diagnostic rules were pairs of the form:

**(Selected_ECG_feature,  Combined_arrhythmia)**

where a "selected ECG feature" is for example: P wave has abnormal shape.

In general, as shown in section 1.2, rules of these forms are not logically equivalent to the original rules, so they have to be used with care. Mozetič (1985a, 1986; see also Chapter 4) states the conditions under which both the original rules and the transformed ones produce equivalent diagnostic results. So this additional request had to be verified in our case as well.

Figure 1.12 shows the compression effects achieved in terms of storage space needed when storing different representations simply as text files. The figure 25 KB associated with the corresponding representations includes both the induced descriptions plus the extra information needed to attain logical equivalence with the extensional representation. Notice the compression factor of about 200. The similarity in size between the deep model and the compressed representations is co-incidental.

Figure 1.18 shows a prediction rule generated by the induction algorithms and some corresponding descriptions from the medical literature. Some of the synthesized descriptions correspond very well to the descriptions in the medical literature, as Figure 1.18 illustrates. On the other hand, some of the synthesized descriptions are considerably more complex than those in the medical literature. The computer generated descriptions in such cases give much more detailed specification which may not be necessary for an intelligent reader with the physiological background. Such a reader can usually infer the missing detail from his or her background knowledge. However, the additional details must still be made explicit in the case of a computer application in the form of a diagnostic expert system. Otherwise a lot of background knowledge and inference would have to be added which would be extremely difficult and its correctness hard to verify.

---

[av_conduct = avb3]  ⇒
  [rhythm_QRS = regular] &
  [relation_P_QRS = independent_P_QRS]

Goldman (1976): In this condition the atria and ventricles beat entirely *independently* of one another. ... The ventricular *rhythm* is usually quite *regular* but at much slower *rate (20–60)*.

Phibbs (1973): 1. The atrial and ventricular *rates are different*: the atrial rate is faster; the ventricular rate is slow and *regular*. 2. There is *no consistent relation between P waves and QRS complexes*.

---

**Figure 1.18** A synthesized prediction rule (above) and some corresponding descriptions from the medical literature (Goldman 1976 and Phibbs 1973).

Here is an example of synthesized diagnostic rule:

**[relation_P_QRS = after_P_some_QRS_miss]** ⇒
   **[av_conduct = wen ∨ mob2]**
   **∨**
   **[atr_focus = afl ∨ af] & [av_conduct = normal]**

This rule corresponds to a particular diagnostic feature in the ECG, characterized by that some P waves are not followed (as normally) by the corresponding QRS complexes. The rule states that this feature is indicative of the defects called Wenckebach or Mobitz 2, or, when the AV conductance is normal, of the atrial flutter or fibrillation. The rule thus clearly indicates what kinds of disorders a diagnostic system should be looking for in the case that this abnormality is detected in the ECG. Such rules thus suggest a goal-oriented strategy for investigating ECG features in the ECG interpretation.

Details of the knowledge compression procedure, the compression results and a comparison of compressed rules with medical descriptions are in Chapter 4.

## 1.3.7 Summary of representations and AI techniques in KARDIO

In KARDIO, various representations of the ECG knowledge are used. The main three representations are at different knowledge levels:
- deep level: the qualitative causal model of the heart
- surface level: the complete arrhythmia-ECG base
- surface level compressed: compact diagnostic and prediction rules

Table 1.1 compares these representations from the following points of view:
- nature of knowledge
- method of construction
- representational formalism
- size as text file (in kilo bytes)
- direction of inference the representation supports
- the functional role

| | I<br>Causal model<br>of the heart | II<br>Arrhythmia-<br>ECG base | III<br>Compressed<br>diagnostic<br>knowledge |
|---|---|---|---|
| Nature of<br>knowledge | deep<br>causal | surface<br>operational | surface<br>operational |
| Method of<br>construction | manual | automatic<br>synthesis<br>from I | automatic<br>compression<br>from II |
| Represent.<br>formalism | first-order<br>logic | propositional<br>logic | propositional<br>logic |
| Size | 27 KB | 5 MB | 25 KB |
| Direction of<br>inference | Arr → ECG<br>forward | Arr ↔ ECG<br>both | Arr ← ECG<br>backward |
| Role | qualitative<br>simulation,<br>generate II | diagnosis,<br>provide<br>examples for III | diagnosis |

**Table 1.1** Comparison of different representations of electrocardiographical knowledge.

The size of the compressed diagnostic knowledge of 25 KB accounts for both the compressed rules plus some necessary additional information. The compressed rules themselves are not sufficient for the diagnosis because of loss of information in the selection of the learning subset of the arrhythmia-ECG base. To attain the full diagnostic equivalence with the extensional shallow representation we have to add descriptions of arrhythmias and ECG features that were eliminated in selecting the learning subset. Furthermore, "legality" constraints and related testing procedures have to be included as well. After adding all of these, the size of the compressed diagnostic knowledge becomes 25 KB.

The main vehicles for implementing various knowledge representations and transformations were the following tools and techniques of Artificial Intelligence:

- logic programming, Prolog in particular
- qualitative modeling
- inductive learning tools

It should be noted, of course, that the inductive learning programs were until this stage used as tools for compression of a representation and not for actual learning. Since the input information to the learning programs was complete no generalization could have occurred. however, the next section overviews actual learning of the heart model when generalization takes place.

## 1.3.8   Introducing abstraction hierarchy into and learning of qualitative models

Chapter 5 describes further developments (Mozetič 1987a, b) in respect to automating the model design process by means of machine learning. A system for semi-automatic construction of deep knowledge bases is presented, that supports the representation of a model on several levels of abstraction. The system can be viewed as a prototype of a second generation expert system shell.

A hierarchy, introduced into the heart model, is based on hierarchical relations between components of the heart and qualitative values. Such a hierarchy is used in various ways. The system that is used interactively by the model designer takes advantage of hierarchical model representation to speed up the automatic learning of the model. A substantial submodel of the KARDIO heart model was reconstructed semi-automatically using this system. Further, the hierarchy is also employed to improve the efficiency of diagnostic reasoning (Mozetič, Bratko, and Urbančič 1987). Results obtained at a simpler, more abstract level, are used to guide the reasoning on a more detailed level, thereby reducing the search complexity. Finally, the hierarchy also has a role in generating good and concise explanation of the heart providing a means of flexibly focusing the explanation on points selected by the user.

## 1.3.9 Completeness assessment and clinical applicability

The ECG knowledge of this study is in various forms used in the KARDIO expert system for ECG interpretation (Lavrač et al. 1985). The automatically synthesized surface level electrocardiographical knowledge base is complete with respect to the level of detail of the model. In an assessment study of KARDIO (Grad and Čerček 1984), cardiologists made the following estimates based on clinical tests of KARDIO described below: the knowledge base covers 90–95 % of patients in a population suffering from cardiac arrhythmias. In a "selected" population (especially difficult cases referred to a specialist cardiologist on account of previous examinations) KARDIO would correctly handle 75 % of arrhythmia cases. Here "corrected handling" means that KARDIO's diagnosis would imply correct treatment. In an actual test with KARDIO-E (the version of KARDIO used in this assessment study) on 36 randomly selected arrhythmia cases from internal medical practice the arrhythmia knowledge base was suffficient in 34 cases (94 %). The failed cases are due to some incompleteness of the deep model, such as the present model's incapability of handling artificial pacemakers.

Another validation study was made to assess the *correctness* of the deep model of the heart (and thus also the derived surface representations). For this purpose a subset of 105 combined arrhythmias was selected from the complete set of 2,419 arrhythmias in the arrhythmia-ECG base. The subset was selected randomly in a way to best represent the complete problem domain with respect to both the nature of the arrhythmias and the complexity of arrhythmias, ranging from simple disorders up to most complex combinations of seven disorders. Of course, this selection does not in any way correspond to statistical distribution of cases in the medical practice.

For each of the selected arrhythmias, a form was prepared containing one of the possible ECG descriptions associated with this arrhythmia. Additional alternative diagnoses of the same ECG were also given. The evaluating cardiologists were then asked to comment on these diagnoses. To minimize locality effects, three cardiologists from three different countries participated in the evaluation (Great Britain, The Netherlands, and Yugoslavia).

The following paragraphs summarize the most critical conclusions of this evaluation experiment:

(1) The knowledge contents was assessed as correct, although there were several specialists' comments, mainly prompted by misinterpretation of particular features in the ECG description language and variations in the medical terminology.

(2) The ECG description language can be improved to alleviate terminological problems referred to above. (Concrete suggestions were implemented in a later version of the heart model.)

(3) The level of detail in the heart model could be more suitably balanced for practical application. In some respects the present model is unnecessarily detailed, whereas it would be useful to cover a few additional disorders. However there was no general agreement among the cardiologists on this question.

(4) The changes in the description language and the fine adjustments in the level of detail can be easily introduced within the present framework. All the representation formalisms, associated algorithms and programs can be used without change.

The problems mentioned above eventually made it difficult to obtain from this validation study any significant quantitative results regarding the completeness and correctness of the KARDIO model.

In respect to clinical application of KARDIO, the cardiologists felt that a significant limitation is that KARDIO accepts as input symbolic ECG descriptions rather than the actual ECG signal. Thus the user is at present required to translate the patient's ECG waveform into the corresponding symbolic description. Although our own experience with medical doctors—nonspecialists—showed that they are quite capable of such a translation, the feeling was that this puts the user into an unusual or unnatural situation. In some practical situations, such manual translation is indeed unfeasible and it has to be mechanized. Available ECG analysis machines could be used to automate this translation step. Most obviously, KARDIO would then be added as a diagnostic expert system to such a machine. Some cardiologists expressed hesitation regarding this architecture because KARDIO seemed in a way too powerful for such a combination in the view of difficulties in extracting qualitative description features from ECG waveforms. In presently available ECG analyzers, these difficulties lead to unreliable recognition of some of the ECG features. However, the integration of a model of KARDIO type into the low-level recognition process would be beneficial also at the low end: it should help to eliminate those low-level interpretations that are impossible with respect to the model. In such a system, KARDIO would then not only serve as a diagnostic expert system, but would also facilitate model-based low-level processing of the ECG signal. This idea has not been developed.

## 1.4  Comparison with other approaches to qualitative modeling

We will here briefly review three other approaches to and make a short comparison with respect to their application to medical diagnosis and application in physiology. The three approaches are Kuipers (1986), de Kleer and Brown (1984), and Forbus (1984).

Kuipers' approach, called QSIM, can be viewed as an abstraction of ordinary differential equations. A model is defined by a set of *functions* of time and a set of *constraints* on these functions. For each function we have an ordered set of distinguished symbolic values, called *landmarks*. The current value of a function is expressed in terms of these values: the value of a function can be either a landmark or an interval between two adjacent landmarks. Constraints on functions formalize their interdependences in terms of usual mathematical operations: arithmetic operations and time derivatives. In addition to these we can also state a more interesting relation: *monotonically increasing (decreasing) function*. Using this type of constraint it is possible to express the qualitative relation between two functions when the exact relationship between them is not known. Time in QSIM is treated as a sequence of symbolic time points whose existence is associated with "interesting events." Such events occur when a function crosses its landmark value or the derivative of a function becomes equal to zero. A distinguishing feature of QSIM is that during qualitative simulation new landmarks are discovered.

QSIM has been applied in modeling of physiological processes: hormone control of water balance in the body (Kuipers and Kassirer 1985; Kuipers 1987) and compartmental systems (Nicolosi and Leaning 1988). QSIM is very attractive because of its solid mathematical basis. It is straightforward to define a QSIM model when a traditional mathematical model based on differential equations is already known. There are two serious limitations of QSIM, however. First, it seems to be very difficult to express in QSIM models which are not susceptible to differential equations. This is often the case in medicine and it seems that a QSIM model of the heart that would correspond to the KARDIO model would be extremely complex. Second, even when a QSIM model is derived from corresponding differential equations, the QSIM qualitative simulation algorithm may nondeterministically generate numerous behaviors. Some of the generated behaviors can be justified simply by lack of information in a qualitative model. Unfortunatelly QSIM also generates unreal behaviors that are not justified by lack of information. This problem with QSIM is known as excessive branching which generates spurious behaviors and has been studied for example by Lee, Chiu, and Kuipers (1987), and Struss (1988).

The approach to qualitative simulation by de Kleer and Brown (1984) is centered on the concept of a *confluence* i.e., a qualitative differential equation. It seems that it would, as a candidate for physiological modeling, suffer from similar limitations as QSIM. Similar to KARDIO, and unlike QSIM, the approach of de Kleer and Brown explicitly involves the structure of a model. The structure consists of components and their interconnections. As in KARDIO, the qualitative behavior of the system is derived from the behavior of the components and their interconnections.

The third approach in this short comparison, QPT (Qualitative Process Theory, by Forbus 1984), is the most complicated of all three and its execution requires substantial computation. QPT has not been applied to physiological domains although it does offer some valuable concepts that cannot be found in any other approach. In particular, QPT explicitly formalizes the concept of *process*. This clearly offers a novel way of diagnostic reasoning about a system whose normal or abnormal behavior can be explained in terms of what processes are going on, or should be going on.

Other studies in qualitative modeling of cardiac arrhythmias are (Shibahara 1985) and (Hunter, Gotts, and Hamlet 1988). Their work was mainly concerned with a more restricted problem, namely the behavior of the AV node. In comparison with KARDIO, their models are more detailed (and deeper) with respect to the AV node, but do not cover other arrhythmias. The KARDIO model level was chosen mainly with the view to practical diagnostic needs, and in this respect the other two model levels are probably unnecessarily detailed. They can, on the other hand, explain some interesting physiological phenomena that are beyond the level of detail in KARDIO.

Comparison of several approaches to qualitative modeling in the view of their applicability in physiology indicates circumstances under which the KARDIO approach is the most practical. The main feature in the KARDIO approach is the use of logic as the representation formalism. KARDIO is not rooted in any tradional theory used in modeling, such as numerical techniques and differential equations. In comparison with other approaches to qualitative modeling, the main advantage of KARDIO applied to physiology lies in the potential power of the description language used. The model designer has the freedom to choose the most suitable description language and define the laws of the domain in a most natural way. The description language is thus hardly constrained by any traditional mathematical notions. In general, this has of course, the disadvantage that no existing mathematical theory is assumed and automatically available to the model designer. Instead, if such a mathematical theory is useful it has to be explicitly stated in the model. It really depends on the problem of whether the freedom to choose is more precious than the availability of some established mathematical theory. The latter is probably more important when the problem is susceptible to some traditional approach, such as differential equations, but in physiology the freedom is probably more valuable. This is illustrated by representations used in KARDIO. It is hard to imagine the complexity of equivalent representations in the formalisms of other, more traditional methods. One example is the representation of time. Although the modeling of the electrical activity of the heart involves processes in time, time is not explicitly mentioned in the KARDIO model at all. Instead, repetitive processes in time are described in terms of features, such as the rate of a repetitive event,

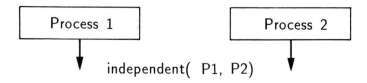

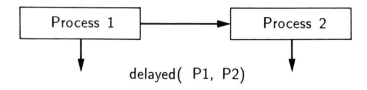

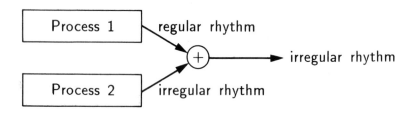

**Figure 1.19** Describing relations between processes in KARDIO, and a law for summation. Examples in this figure define the following laws: (1) if two unrelated processes generate two signals, P1 and P2 respectively, then the two signals P1 and P2 are independent; (2) if process 1 generates signal P1 and process 2 generates signal P2, and process 2 accepts some (triggering) input from process 1, then P2 is delayed with respect to P1; (3) the sum of two signals, one with regular and one with irrregular rhythm, is a process with irregular rhythm. Notice that these laws are domain specific—they are not generally valid.

regularity of its rhythm, and the shape of a waveform. The qualitative values of these features can be for example as follows:

rate: slow, normal, fast
rhythm: regular, irregular
shape: normal, distorted

Figure 1.19 illustrates how relations between processes are typically defined in KARDIO. For two sequences of events, generated by two asynchronous processes, we simply say that they are "independent"; or if two periodic processes are synchronized, we may say that one of them is delayed with respect to the other which may reflect their causal interdependence.

The domains of variables in KARDIO can contain structured values, whereas in other approaches to qualitative modeling the elements of "quantity spaces" are unstructured. We also define the operations on such descriptions so as to best suit the domain. For example, we can define a law that the sum of one process with regular rhythm and another one with irregular rhythm will give a process with irregular rhythm.

On the other hand, the freedom to choose a powerful description language and define your own laws (to be used as constraints in the model) in the style of KARDIO would usually require the programming of a new interpreter for a new model. In other approaches, the model designer can usually apply a ready-to-use implementation. But as our experience showed convincingly, Prolog as an implementation language greatly facilitates the programming of specialized interpreters needed for any chosen description language and corresponding user-defined operations or laws of inference. In the case of KARDIO at least, the programming itself occupied a very minor part of the total effort in the project.

One broad strategy of qualitative modeling in medicine aiming to combine the representational flexibility of the KARDIO approach with the qualitative versions of other approaches to modeling in physics could be to use logic as a description language in the style of KARDIO, use the concepts of *process* and *individual view* from Qualitative Process Theory for structuring the model and for generating explanations, and use an improved QSIM-like theory as a basis for qualitative differential equations in cases that the physiological process is amenable to such a description.

# Chapter 2

# Qualitative Model of the Heart

This chapter is a detailed description of a model of electrical activity of the heart, represented in qualitative terms. First, cardiac arrhythmias and their relation to ECG are described from the medical point of view, and a description language is defined. Then, all ingredients of the model are described: structure of electrical network in the heart, relations between arrhythmias and heart disorders, legality constraints over the states of the heart, and finally global and local rules.

## 2.1    Describing arrhythmias

In this section the physiology of the electrical activity of the heart and its influence on the ECG curve is described. We define a language for a qualitative description of ECG and a dictionary of cardiac arrhythmias. We conclude with several examples of simple cardiac arrhythmias and describe the corresponding ECG curves with the chosen language.

### 2.1.1    Electrophysiology of the heart

The heart is unique among the muscles of the human body in that it possesses the property of autonomous rhythmic contraction. The electrical impulses that cause each contraction arise in the electrical control system of the heart. The contraction of the muscle is accompanied with electrical polarization and repolarization of the muscle which cause changes in electrical potential on the surface of the body. By applying electrodes to various positions on the body and connecting these electrodes to an electrocardiographic apparatus, the electrocardiogram (ECG) is recorded. The ECG is a graphic recording of the electrical potentials produced in association with the heartbeat.

The heart consists of two atria and two ventricles. The essential anatomy of the conducting system of the heart is shown in Figure 1.11. It consists of only six major components (Phibbs 1973):

(1) Sino-atrial (SA) node, located in the upper part of the right atrium, is the regular impulse generator of the heart.

(2) In the atria there are several conduction pathways that lead to the AV node.

(3) Atrio-ventricular (AV) node, lying in the upper portion of the interventricular septum is the beginning of the specialized conducting system that leads to the ventricles. However, sometimes there are additional, congenital pathways that lead directly from the atria to the ventricles, thus bypassing the AV node.

(4) Bundle of His is a continuation of the AV node into the interventricular septum. The part between the AV node and the bundle of His is called the junction.

(5) Left and right bundle branches are a continuation of the bundle of His, going down each side of the interventricular septum to the ends of the ventricles.

(6) In the ventricles a specialized conduction system is spread in a network of the Purkinje fibers that represent the last link in the chain of excitation.

Changes in electrical potentials that are recorded on the ECG are primarily caused by the following factors (Goldman 1976):

(1) initiation of impulse formation (discharging) at some pacemaker of the heart,

(2) transmission of the impulse through the specialised conduction system of the heart,

(3) activation (depolarization) of the atrial and ventricular myocardium, and

(4) recovery (repolarization) of all the above areas.

Figure 1.15 (a) introduces a terminology of waves on the ECG curve.

In the normal heart the SA node is the pacemaker that regularly discharges impulses. The impulse traverses the atrial pathways and causes the contraction of the atria, producing the P wave (Figure 2.1-1). Then it reaches the AV node, where it is delayed. In the ECG this delay is manifested in the flat part of the PR interval (Figure 2.1-2). Passing on to the bundle of His, the right and left bundle branches, and the ramification of the Purkinje system, it reaches the ventricles. Conduction down this electrical pathway produces the ventricular activation that is seen on the ECG as the QRS complex (Figure 2.1-2,3,4). Depolarization is so completed and after a short delay (ST segment) the myocardium is repolarized which is reflected by the T wave (Figure 2.1-5).

Electrical activity of the heart can be disturbed by different abnormalities that are called cardiac arrhythmias. Cardiac arrhythmia is the abnormality in the rate, regularity, or site of origin of the cardiac impulse or a disturbance in conduction of the impulse so that the normal sequence of activation of atria and ventricles is altered.

Cardiac arrhythmias are reflected on the ECG by irregular beat sequences, abnormal shapes of waves or changed interval lengths. A normally shaped P wave and normal PR interval suggest that the excitation originated in the SA node and that it traversed the atrium through the ordinary conduction system. Changes in shape or absence of the P wave and PR interval changes suggest that the excitation originates in an ectopic focus either in the atria or in the AV node. A wide and bizarre QRS complex is always a result of a ventricular impulse or an aberrant conduction down the left or right bundle branch.

## 2.1.2 Qualitative description of ECG

It turns out that for the description of a large majority of ECG curves that are produced by cardiac arrhythmias it suffices to describe the P wave, PR interval, QRS complex, the relation between them, rhythm, and rate. The ST segment and T wave do not help in diagnosing

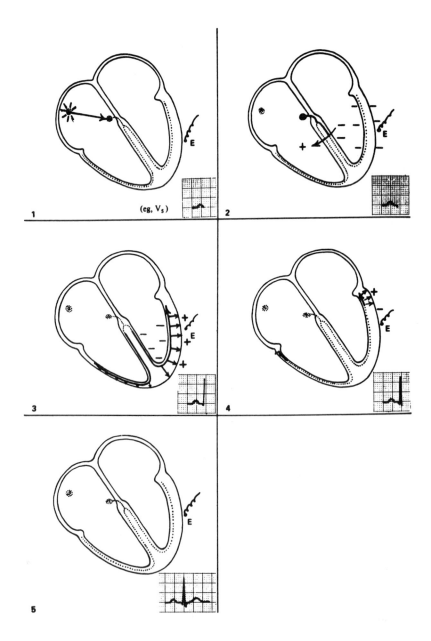

**Figure 2.1** Formation and transmission of the electrical impulse in the heart and its reflexion in the ECG (Goldman 1976, Figure 5-8).

cardiac arrhythmias, but are relevant in diagnosing muscle disorders (e.g. infarcts).

The language for the qualitative description of the ECG, used in this work, describes ECG patterns that result from dominant and from ectopic beats. In a particular ECG description, there can be at most one type of dominant beats and any number of different ectopic beats. Dominant and ectopic beats are described with different attributes. First, we give a definition of dominant beat attributes. The following Prolog clause (stretching down many lines) defines all the attributes and their possible values. The attributes are arranged into a list in which each attribute is accompanied by the list of its possible values. Attribute values are mutually exclusive. Comments are on the right hand side.

**dominant_desc( [**

| | |
|---|---|
| **rhythm_QRS :**<br>**[ regular,**<br>**irregular ],** | regularity of dominant beats |
| **dominant_P :**<br>**[ normal,**<br>**abnormal,**<br>**changing,**<br>**absent ],** | morphology of dominant P waves |
| **rate_of_P :**<br>**[ zero,**<br>**under_60,**<br>**between_60_100,**<br>**between_100_250,**<br>**between_250_350,**<br>**over_350 ],** | number of dominant P waves<br>per minute |
| **relation_P_QRS :**<br>**[ meaningless,**<br>**after_P_always_QRS,**<br>**after_P_some_QRS_miss,**<br><br>**independent_P_QRS ],** | relation between dominant P waves<br>and QRS complexes<br>– P always accompanied by QRS<br>– P sometimes not accompanied<br>by QRS<br>– P and QRS are independent |

| | |
|---|---|
| **dominant_PR :** | duration of dominant PR intervals |
| **[ meaningless,** | |
| **normal,** | — between 0.12 and 0.22 second |
| **prolonged,** | — longer than 0.22 second |
| **shortened,** | — shorter than 0.12 second |
| **changing,** | — within normal limits |
| **after_QRS_is_P ],** | — P waves follow QRS complexes |
| **dominant_QRS :** | shape of dominant QRS complexes |
| **[ normal,** | — not wider than 0.12 second |
| **wide_LBBB,** | — wider than 0.12 second, with positive deflection in leads above the left ventricle: D1, V5, V6, aVL. Abbreviation LBBB stands for left bundle branch block. |
| **wide_RBBB,** | — wider than 0.12 second, with positive deflection in leads above the right ventricle: D3, V1, V2, aVF. Abbreviation RBBB stands for right bundle branch block. |
| **wide_non_specific,** | — wider than 0.12 second, and of different types than above |
| **delta_LBBB,** | — wide of LBBB type, with delta wave |
| **delta_RBBB,** | — wide of RBBB type, with delta wave |
| **absent ],** | — bizzare or absent QRS |
| **rate_of_QRS :** | number of dominant QRS |
| **[ zero,** | complexes per minute |
| **under_60,** | |
| **between_60_100,** | |
| **between_100_250,** | |
| **between_250_350,** | |
| **over_350 ]       ] ).** | |

Each ECG description contains at least seven attributes with corresponding values. For each type of ectopic beat another triple of attributes is added. As the attributes for different ectopic beats are equal, each ectopic attribute is indexed by I to connect ectopic attributes in triples. The description of an ectopic beat consists of only three attributes, because rhythm and rate are of no interest here:

**ectopic_desc( I, [**

| | |
|---|---|
| **ectopic_P(I) :**<br>  **[ abnormal,**<br>    **absent ],** | morphology of ectopic P wave |
| **ectopic_PR(I) :**<br>  **[ meaningless,**<br>    **normal,**<br>    **prolonged,**<br>    **shortened,**<br>    **after_QRS_is_P ],** | duration of ectopic PR interval |
| **ectopic_QRS(I) :**<br>  **[ normal,**<br>    **wide_LBBB,**<br>    **wide_RBBB,**<br>    **wide_non_specific,**<br>    **delta_LBBB,**<br>    **delta_RBBB,**<br>    **absent ]      ] ).** | shape of ectopic QRS complex |

Note that the value of some attributes can also be **meaningless**. This value is possible only when the P wave is absent (for PR interval and relation P-QRS) and when the rate of P is over 250 (for PR interval).

As an example we give an if-then rule that defines the normal ECG corresponding to sinus rhythm without ectopic beats:

**[sinus_rhythm]   $\Longrightarrow$**
  **[rhythm_QRS = regular] &**
  **[dominant_P = normal] &**
  **[rate_of_P = between_60_100] &**
  **[relation_P_QRS = after_P_always_QRS] &**
  **[dominant_PR = normal] &**
  **[dominant_QRS = normal] &**
  **[rate_of_QRS = between_60_100]**

### 2.1.3   Simple cardiac arrhythmias

We talk about a simple cardiac arrhythmia when only one disturbance of the electrical activity of the heart is present. It should be stressed that an arrhythmia is not necessarily a pathological defect of the heart. It can also be an abnormal functional state of some part of the heart as a normal reaction to abnormal conditions.

World Health Organization recommends the classification of cardiac arrhythmias according to impulse origin, discharge sequence, rate, and impulse conduction (WHO 1978, 1979). We have tried to follow these recommendations as much as possible when constructing a dictionary of cardiac arrhythmias. The name of an arrhythmia should indicate impulse origin, discharge rate, etc.

The set of simple arrhythmias dealt with in this study forms the arrhythmia dictionary, defined by the following set of Prolog clauses. Each clause states an abbreviation of an arrhythmia and the corresponding full term, separated by the operator "..".

```
arrhythmia( sr..sinus_rhythm ).
arrhythmia( sa..sinus_arrhythmia ).
arrhythmia( sb..sinus_bradycardia ).
arrhythmia( st..sinus_tachycardia ).
arrhythmia( sad..sa_node_disorders ).

arrhythmia( wp..wandering_pacemaker ).
arrhythmia( at..atrial_tachycardia ).
arrhythmia( mat..multi_atrial_tachycardia ).
arrhythmia( afl..atrial_flutter ).
arrhythmia( af..atrial_fibrillation ).
arrhythmia( aeb..atrial_ectopic_beats ).

arrhythmia( avb1..av_block_1 ).
arrhythmia( wen..wenckebach ).
arrhythmia( mob2..mobitz_2 ).
arrhythmia( avb3..av_block_3 ).
arrhythmia( wpw..wpw_syndrome ).
arrhythmia( lgl..lgl_syndrome ).
```

**arrhythmia( jr..junctional_rhythm ).**
**arrhythmia( ajr..accelerated_junctional_rhythm ).**
**arrhythmia( jt..junctional_tachycardia ).**
**arrhythmia( jeb..junctional_ectopic_beats ).**

**arrhythmia( lbbb..left_bundle_branch_block ).**
**arrhythmia( rbbb..right_bundle_branch_block ).**

**arrhythmia( vr..ventricular_rhythm ).**
**arrhythmia( avr..accelerated_ventricular_rhythm ).**
**arrhythmia( vt..ventricular_tachycardia ).**
**arrhythmia( vfl..ventricular_flutter ).**
**arrhythmia( vf..ventricular_fibrillation ).**
**arrhythmia( veb..ventricular_ectopic_beats ).**
**arrhythmia( mveb..multi_ventricular_ectopic_beats ).**

Notice that sinus rhythm (the normal state of the heart) is treated as an arrhythmia for uniformity. The reason is that the activity of the heart has to be completely specified even in the cases when it is normal. This is also the reason why some simple cardiac arrhythmias in our description language cannot occur alone, but always in combination with sinus rhythm or other arrhythmias. This holds for all conduction disturbances (AV blocks, bundle branch blocks) and ectopic beats (atrial, junctional and ventricular).

Definitions of all simple arrhythmias in terms of the state of the heart are in section 2.2.2

## 2.1.4 Examples

In this section we present some examples of simple cardiac arrhythmias. Each arrhythmia is presented in three forms:

(1) a scheme of the heart showing its electrical activity and possibly an associated failure,

(2) a corresponding ECG curve, and

(3) a qualitative ECG description.

The schemes and ECG curves are taken from (Goldman 1976). The ECG descriptions were derived by qualitative simulation using our model of the heart. The examples are presented as Figures 2.2–2.8.

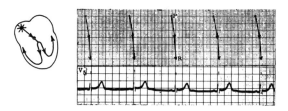

[sinus_bradycardia]    ⟹
   [rhythm_QRS = regular] &
   [dominant_P = normal] &
   [rate_of_P = under_60] &
   [relation_P_QRS = after_P_always_QRS] &
   [dominant_PR = normal] &
   [dominant_QRS = normal] &
   [rate_of_QRS = under_60]

**Figure 2.2**   Sinus bradycardia with the rate of 50/min (Goldman 1976, Figure 12-7).

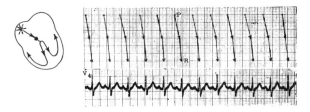

[sinus_tachycardia]    ⟹
   [rhythm_QRS = regular] &
   [dominant_P = normal] &
   [rate_of_P = between_100_250] &
   [relation_P_QRS = after_P_always_QRS] &
   [dominant_PR = normal] &
   [dominant_QRS = normal] &
   [rate_of_QRS = between_100_250]

**Figure 2.3**   Sinus tachycardia with the rate of 125/min (Goldman 1976, Figure 12-6).

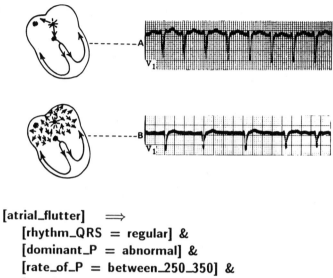

[atrial_flutter]   $\Longrightarrow$
  [rhythm_QRS = regular] &
  [dominant_P = abnormal] &
  [rate_of_P = between_250_350] &
  [relation_P_QRS = after_P_some_QRS_miss] &
  [dominant_PR = meaningless] &
  [dominant_QRS = normal] &
  [rate_of_QRS = between_100_250]

[atrial_fibrillation]   $\Longrightarrow$
  [rhythm_QRS = irregular] &
  [dominant_P = absent] &
  [rate_of_P = zero] &
  [relation_P_QRS = meaningless] &
  [dominant_PR = meaningless] &
  [dominant_QRS = normal] &
  [rate_of_QRS = between_60_100]

**Figure 2.4** Atrial flutter with 2:1 AV block (A). The atrial rate is 272/min and the ventricular rate is 136/min. After using digitalis (antiarrhythmic drug) we get atrial fibrillation (B). The ventricular rate is slowed down to 80/min and no P waves are seen (Goldman 1976, Figure 12-33A,B).

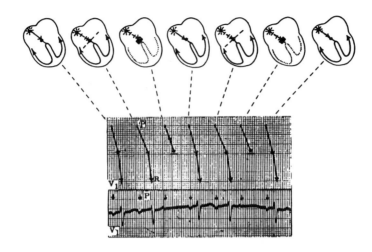

[sinus_rhythm, wenckebach]  $\Longrightarrow$
   [rhythm_QRS = irregular] &
   [dominant_P = normal] &
   [rate_of_P = between_60_100] &
   [relation_P_QRS = after_P_some_QRS_miss] &
   [dominant_PR = prolonged] &
   [dominant_QRS = normal] &
   [rate_of_QRS = between_60_100]

**Figure 2.5** Second degree AV block of the Wenckebach type. The PR interval is progressively longer (the first lasts for 0,16 sec, and the second 0,28 sec) until every third atrial beat fails to produce ventricular response (Goldman 1976, Figure 13-7).

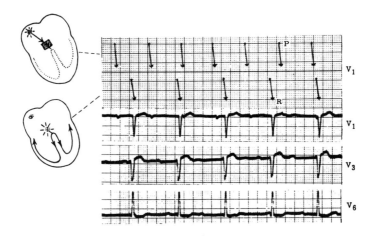

[sinus_rhythm, av_block_3, accelerated_junctional_rhythm]  ⟹
    [rhythm_QRS = regular] &
    [dominant_P = normal] &
    [rate_of_P = between_60_100] &
    [relation_P_QRS = independent_P_QRS] &
    [dominant_PR = meaningless] &
    [dominant_QRS = normal] &
    [rate_of_QRS = between_60_100]

**Figure 2.6** Complete AV block. The atrial rhythm is regular at the rate of 82/min. Since all impulses are blocked, there is a second independent pacemaker near the AV node that gives regular rhythm to the ventricles at the rate of 60/min (Goldman 1976, Figure 13-12).

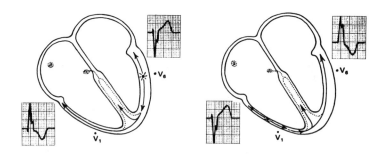

[sinus_rhythm, ventricular_ectopic_beats]    ⟹
    [rhythm_QRS = regular] &
    [dominant_P = normal] &
    [rate_of_P = between_60_100] &
    [relation_P_QRS = after_P_always_QRS] &
    [dominant_PR = normal] &
    [dominant_QRS = normal] &
    [rate_of_QRS = between_60_100] &
    [ectopic_P(vf) = absent] &
    [ectopic_PR(vf) = meaningless] &
    [ectopic_QRS(vf) = wide_RBBB ∨ wide_LBBB]

**Figure 2.7**  Ventricular ectopic beats. Ectopic focus in the left ventricle results in a wide QRS complex, of the RBBB type. Ectopic focus in the right ventricle produces a wide QRS complex of the LBBB type (Goldman 1976, Figures 14-10, 14-11).

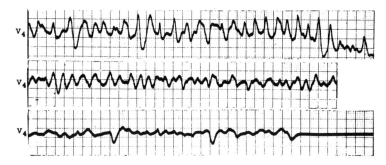

[ventricular_fibrillation]    $\Longrightarrow$
    [rhythm_QRS  =  irregular]  &
    [dominant_P  =  absent]  &
    [rate_of_P  =  zero]  &
    [relation_P_QRS  =  meaningless]  &
    [dominant_PR  =  meaningless]  &
    [dominant_QRS  =  absent]  &
    [rate_of_QRS  =  over_350]

**Figure 2.8**  Ventricular fibrillation.  The ventricular complexes are rapid, irregular and bizarre (Goldman 1976, Figure 14-28).

## 2.2    The model

We start this section with an overview of the program for automatic derivation of ECG descriptions and with a scheme of the model of the heart. We define a language for describing the state of the heart. All simple cardiac arrhythmias are defined with abnormal states of particular heart components. Then we describe constraints over the states of the heart. The section is concluded with a detailed description of rules in the model of the heart.

### 2.2.1    Overview of the model

When developing an expert system for ECG diagnosis of cardiac arrhythmias, the problem of diagnosing combinations of simple cardiac arrhythmias arose. We talk about a *combined arrhythmia* when there are several abnormalities in the electrical activity of the heart at the same time. As there are few thousand combinations of arrhythmias it was impossible to acquire all the corresponding ECG descriptions manually in consultation with cardiologists. So the main goal in developing a qualitative model of the heart was automatic derivation of ECG descriptions for all possible combinations of cardiac arrhythmias.

Each simple arrhythmia corresponds to a state of some heart component. A combination of arrhythmias defines the state of several heart components, and we get a complete state of the heart by assuming the remaining components to be normal. Completed state of the heart is checked against constraints that eliminate physiologically impossible and medically uninteresting combinations. In the medical practice, an arrhythmia is assumed uninteresting if it is not identifiable, even theoretically, from the ECG taken from surface ECG leads.

The model of the heart can be represented as a network consisting of: impulse generators, , impulse conduction pathways and summation elements for impulses. These are called *heart components*. In Figure 2.9 impulse generators are denoted by ovals:

- SA_NODE is the sino-atrial node,
- ATR_FOCUS is a pacemaker anywhere in the atria,
- AV_JUNCTION is a pacemaker between the AV node and the junction,

- REG_VENT_FOCUS is a pacemaker anywhere in the ventricles that permanently discharges impulses,
- ECT_VENT_FOCUS is a pacemaker anywhere in the ventricles that discharges impulses from time to time.

Conduction pathways in Figure 2.9 are denoted by rectangles:

- AV_CONDUCT is conduction from the atria to the ventricles,
- BUNDLE_BRANCHES is conduction through bundle branches.

Summators for impulses in Figure 2.9 are denoted by + , and lower case words denote the names of impulses. Some impulses are reflected on the ECG by corresponding ECG features.

The model of the heart is formally represented by logical formulae that define relations between objects in the heart. There are four types of objects in the model:

(1) heart (heart components)

(2) permanent (permanent impulses)

(3) occasional (occasional impulses)

(4) ecg (ECG descriptions)

Objects have attributes. The model deals with assertions about such objects. Each assertion consists of the type of an object, an attribute and its value. Assertions take the form:

**Object( Attribute : Value )**

For the heart components the attributes are the names of impulse generators or conduction pathways (as in Figure 2.9), and their values denote functional states, such as "normal" or "quiet." For impulses, both permanent and occasional, the attributes are the names of impulses (as in Figure 2.9), and the values denote forms, described in qualitative terms. ECG descriptions have attributes and values as defined in section 2.1.2.

The complete *state of the heart* is defined by the states of all the heart components. By qualitative simulation permanent and occasional impulses are generated, conducted through pathways and summed together. At the end an ECG description is derived, depending on the origin and conduction of particular impulses.

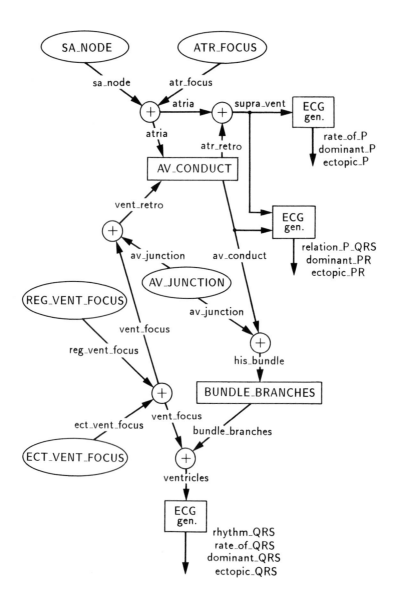

**Figure 2.9** A scheme of the model of the heart. This is a refinement of Figure 1.13.

## 2.2.2 Qualitative state of the heart

The model of the heart consists of five impulse generators impulse generator (Figure 2.9):

- sa_node
- atr_focus
- av_junction
- reg_vent_focus
- ect_vent_focus

and two conduction pathways:

- av_conduct
- bundle_branches

The state of an impulse generator is specified by the mode in which it discharges impulses. This can be:

- permanent
- occasional

Permanent discharging of impulses is, in addition, specified by the rhythm and rate. The rhythm can be:

- quiet
- regular
- irregular

The rate of discharging can be:

- zero
- under_60
- between_60_100
- between_100_250
- between_250_350
- over_350

Occasional discharging of impulses is additionally specified by their type, i.e., the number of foci that from time to time discharge impulses in some part of the heart:

- unifocal
- multifocal

The state of av_conduct is defined by the conduction mode from the atria to the ventricles. This can be:

- normal
- delayed
- progress_delayed
- partially_blocked
- blocked
- james
- kent

James and Kent denote extra pathways from the atria to the ventricles that bypass the AV node. The state of bundle_branches is defined by the conduction mode through the left and right bundle branches:

- normal
- left_blocked
- right_blocked

According to tradition in cardiology, the specification of an arrhythmia only mentions some of the heart's components whereas the others, unmentioned, are assumed to be in their normal or "default" states. The state of the heart is then properly completed by these default values. We here give the state of the heart which is used to complete the states of those components that are not explicitly specified by an arrhythmia:

```
rest_heart( [sa_node: permanent( quiet, zero ),
            atr_focus: permanent( quiet, zero ),
            av_conduct: normal,
            av_junction: permanent( quiet, zero ),
            bundle_branches: normal,
            reg_vent_focus: permanent( quiet, zero ),
            ect_vent_focus: permanent( quiet, zero )] ).
```

It should be noted that this is not a definition of the normal heart, as there is no active impulse generator. In the normal heart, which corresponds to the "arrhythmia" sinus_rhythm, the SA node is permanently discharging impulses, with regular rhythm and the rate between 60 and 100 per minute.

Each simple cardiac arrhythmia is defined as a state (or a disjunction of states) of one heart component. In the program, these definitions are specified as the binary relation **arr_heart** between arrhythmias and states of the heart components. The following Prolog code is a complete definition of this relation.

Disturbances of sinus rhythm:

```
arr_heart( sinus_rhythm,
    sa_node: permanent( regular, between_60_100 ) ).

arr_heart( sinus_arrhythmia,
    sa_node: permanent( irregular, between_60_100 ) ).
arr_heart( sinus_arrhythmia,
    sa_node: permanent( irregular, under_60 ) ).

arr_heart( sinus_bradycardia,
    sa_node: permanent( regular, under_60 ) ).

arr_heart( sinus_tachycardia,
    sa_node: permanent( regular, between_100_250 ) ).

arr_heart( sa_node_disorders,
    sa_node: permanent( irregular, between_60_100 ) ).
arr_heart( sa_node_disorders,
    sa_node: permanent( irregular, under_60 ) ).
```

Comment: In this specification there is no difference between sinus_arrhythmia and sa_node_disorders. This difference is handled by the user interface as explained later in this section.

Disturbances of atrial rhythm:

```
arr_heart( wandering_pacemaker,
    atr_focus: permanent( irregular, between_60_100 ) ).

arr_heart( atrial_tachycardia,
    atr_focus: permanent( regular, between_100_250 ) ).

arr_heart( multi_atrial_tachycardia,
    atr_focus: permanent( irregular, between_100_250 ) ).

arr_heart( atrial_flutter,
    atr_focus: permanent( regular, between_250_350 ) ).
```

arr_heart( atrial_fibrillation,
    atr_focus: permanent( irregular, over_350 ) ).

arr_heart( atrial_ectopic_beats,
    atr_focus: occasional( unifocal ) ).

Disturbances of AV conduction:

arr_heart( av_block_1,
    av_conduct: delayed ).

arr_heart( wenckebach,
    av_conduct: progress_delayed ).

arr_heart( mobitz_2,
    av_conduct: partially_blocked ).

arr_heart( av_block_3,
    av_conduct: blocked ).

arr_heart( wpw_syndrome,
    av_conduct: kent ).

arr_heart( lgl_syndrome,
    av_conduct: james ).

Disturbances of junctional rhythm:

arr_heart( junctional_rhythm,
    av_junction: permanent( regular, under_60 ) ).

arr_heart( accelerated_junctional_rhythm,
    av_junction: permanent( regular, between_60_100 ) ).

arr_heart( junctional_tachycardia,
    av_junction: permanent( regular, between_100_250 ) ).

arr_heart( junctional_ectopic_beats,
    av_junction: occasional( unifocal ) ).

Disturbances of conduction through bundle branches:

arr_heart( left_bundle_branch_block,
    bundle_branches: left_blocked ).

arr_heart( right_bundle_branch_block,
    bundle_branches: right_blocked ).

Disturbances of ventricular rhythm:

arr_heart( ventricular_rhythm,
    reg_vent_focus: permanent( regular, under_60 ) ).

arr_heart( accelerated_ventricular_rhythm,
    reg_vent_focus: permanent( regular, between_60_100 ) ).

arr_heart( ventricular_tachycardia,
    reg_vent_focus: permanent( regular, between_100_250 ) ).

arr_heart( ventricular_flutter,
    reg_vent_focus: permanent( regular, between_250_350 ) ).

arr_heart( ventricular_fibrillation,
    reg_vent_focus: permanent( irregular, over_350 ) ).

arr_heart( ventricular_ectopic_beats,
    ect_vent_focus: occasional( unifocal ) ).

arr_heart( multi_ventricular_ectopic_beats,
    ect_vent_focus: occasional( multifocal ) ).

As we see from above, only disturbances of ventricular rhythm are defined by the states of two different heart components (reg_vent_focus and ect_vent_focus). The introduction of two foci in ventricles is necessary for combinations of regular ventricular rhythms (e.g. ventricular tachycardia) with ectopic ventricular rhythms. The same ventricular focus cannot be in two different states at the same time, i.e., it cannot discharge both permanent and occasional impulses at the same time.

We do not have this problem with atrial or junctional focus, as the area of potential foci in the atria is much smaller than in the ventricles. A focus that permanently discharges impulses disables any other electrical activity near it, including occasional. The reason for that is the time necessary for repolarization of myocardium after its depolarization.

The arrhythmia **sa_node_disorders** denotes several basic cardiac arrhythmias:

- sino-atrial arrest,
- sino-atrial block of type Wenckebach,
- sino-atrial block of type Mobitz II.

The three arrhythmias differ only in the rhythm of impulse discharging and are combined with other arrhythmias according to the same principles. For their differentiation we would have to introduce different values for rhythm in the language for ECG description and in the language for describing the state of the heart. We chose another solution that leaves this problem to the user interface. When it determines that among possible arrhythmias there is also **sa_node_disorders** it requires additional specification of the rhythm and accordingly selects one of the three possibilities.

Something similar is true for "ectopic beats," either atrial, junctional or ventricular. Ectopic beats result from occasional impulses and type of their discharging is defined only by the number of foci in some part of the heart (unifocal, multifocal). Additional specification about their relation to permanent impulses would be needed. An additional attribute in the ECG description (e.g. type_of_ectopic_beat) would define the relation between ectopic and regular beats. In this way, it would be possible to distinguish between the following types of ectopic beats:

- premature beats
- escape beats
- bigeminy
- R on T phenomenon
- couplets
- salvos
- parasystolia

  . . .

This problem is also left to the user interface.

## 2.2.3   Constraints over states

In this section we precisely define constraints over the states of the heart. But first let us outline basic assumptions regarding the system for the ECG diagnosis of cardiac arrhythmias. Our qualitative description of an ECG curve refers only to the surface ECG leads.

This is the reason that neither ECG descriptions nor arrhythmia definitions include phenomena that can be identified only by deep leads (e.g. ezofageal). Moreover, the arrhythmias refer only to a relatively short ECG tracing during which the arrhythmia does not change. The result of an analysis of a longer tracing is a sequence of diagnoses of short tracings.

A state of the heart that corresponds to a combination of arrhythmias can be logically contradictory, physiologically impossible, or medically uninteresting. This is it is checked against constraints that eliminate all states, senseless for the reasons above. These constraints are precisely defined in the following paragraphs.

A combination of arrhythmias is *logically contradictory* if it violates the rule:

(1) The same heart component cannot be in two different states.

*Physiologically impossible* are those combined arrhythmias in which more than one impulse generator in the heart permanently discharges impulses and the generators are not "protected" against each other by a complete conduction block. A pacemaker that permanently discharges impulses disables all other pacemakers with lower discharging rates. After the depolarization of myocardium, some time is needed for the repolarization, during which no excitation can take place. This assumption mutual exclusion of pacemakers requires additional qualification. In principle, it is possible for two pacemakers to be simultaneously active. However, in such a case one of them only has a very limited local effect, and it cannot be seen on the surface ECG leads. It is unimportant from the practical view point of treatment. Therefore, according to the cardiologists' suggestion, the assumption of mutual exclusion of pacemakers was adopted in the model. There are three possible cases:

(1) In the atria there cannot be two permanent impulse generators (sa_node and atr_focus).

(2) For the same reason there cannot be two permanent impulse generators in the ventricles (av_junction and reg_vent_focus).

(3) If the AV conduction is not completely blocked, there cannot be a permanent impulse generator in both the atria and the ventricles.

Combinations of arrhythmias are *medically uninteresting* when they cannot be identified from the surface ECG leads, not even in principle. There can even be examples of physiological malfuntions that are not important because of specific conditions:

(1) If there is no permanent activity in the heart at all or in the ventricles because of complete AV block, this is called cardiac arrest. Medically, it does not make sense to combine this state with any other disturbance.

(2) If there is no permanent impulse generator in the atria it is medically uninteresting to talk about AV conduction disturbance.

(3) If in the atria there is only an occasional impulse generator and no permanent activity, the only medically interesting AV conduction disturbance is the WPW syndrome. In this case impulses are conducted directly to the ventricles, bypassing the AV node and bundle branches, producing differently shaped QRS complexes.

(4) When the rate of an atrial pacemaker is over 250/min (atrial flutter or fibrillation) AV conduction disturbance should not be considered (with the exception of the WPW syndrome). In this case the blocking of impulses in the AV node is a physiologically normal reaction that protects the ventricles against too high a rate.

(5) When the rate of the atrial pacemaker is over 250/min and WPW syndrome is present as well, the ventricles take the rate of the atria. With such a high rate they absolutely dominate over any other activity in the heart and therefore it is uninteresting to combine this with any other disturbance.

(6) For the same reason it is uninteresting to combine ventricular flutter or fibrillation with any other arrhyhtmia.

(7) If there is no impulse transmission through bundle branches (e.g., there is conduction through the bundle of Kent, or there is a pacemaker in ventricles) it is uninteresting to consider any kind of bundle branch block.

## 2.2.4 Rules in the model

The processes in the heart are in the model defined by 35 global rules and a number of auxiliary relations. Each global rule is a triple of the form:

**Cause** $\implies$ **Consequence** & **Condition**

**Cause** and **Consequence** are sets of assertions about the objects in the model, and **Condition** is a logical statement. Precise interpretation of the rules in predicate calculus is given in the next chapter. For the purpose of this section the rules can be interpreted as follows:

IF **Cause** THEN **Consequence** WHERE **Condition**

In the model of the heart there are four types of objects: **heart** (generators and conduction pathways), **permanent** (permanent impulses), **occasional** (occasional impulses), and **ecg** (ECG descriptions).

There are four types of rules in the model as well. They define processes in the heart and relations between objects as follows:

(1) impulse generation

(2) impulse conduction

(3) summation of impulses

(4) producing ECG

The syntax of assertions about heart components was defined in section 2.2.2. The language for ECG description was defined in section

2.1.2. It remains to define the syntax for assertions about impulses, both permanent and occasional:

**permanent( Location : Val_permanent )**
**occasional( Location : Val_occasional )**

**Location** denotes the location of an impulse in the model of the heart as in Figure 2.9. Exactly one permanent impulse and (in principle) arbitrary number of occasional impulses are associated with each location in the model. The value of **Val_permanent** or **Val_occasional** describes an impulse in qualitative terms. Permanent impulses are described by a compound term of the form:

**Val_permanent  =   form( Shape, Rhythm, Rate )**

Here **Shape** corresponds to the origin or to the way of impulse conduction. **Rhythm** and **Rate** are the same as in the language for the state of the heart description. Occasional impulses are described by:

**Val_occasional  =   form( Shape, Origin, Type )**

**Shape** has the same meaning as for permanent impulses, and **Origin** is the name of an impulse generator. **Type** is not used in the present version of the model. It could be used to specify the relation between permanent and occasional impulses, which would enable the differentiation between various types of ectopic beats.

In the rules, **Condition** has the syntax of Prolog goal clause. For compact definition of rules it is useful to define some auxiliary relations. One such relation is "member," defined as predicate **in**, using infix notation:

**X in [X | _].**
**X in [_ | List]  :-   X in List.**

Two other useful relations are "greater than" and "successor" over the qualitative values of rates. They are denoted by ">–" and **succ**, respectively:

```
succ( zero,              under_60         ).
succ( under_60,          between_60_100   ).
succ( between_60_100,    between_100_250  ).
succ( between_100_250,   between_250_350  ).
succ( between_250_350,   over_350         ).
```

```
A >— B  :—  succ( B, A ).
A >— B  :—  succ( B, C ), A >— C.
```

The definition of the relation "less than" over rates, that uses symbol "—<", is similar. Definitions of other auxiliary relations are given together with the rules.

The complete set of 35 rules of the model and auxiliary relations follows below, written as they are used by the qualitative simulation program. Rule numbers and comments are added. The syntax of rules is Prolog where the symbols "⟹", "&", ">—", "—<", and ":" are declared as infix operators so that "⟹" bind weakest and ":" strongest. The cause part and the consequence part of a rule are stated as lists of assertions, so that rules have the form:

[Cause$_1$, Cause$_2$, ...]
⟹ [Cons$_1$, Cons$_2$, ...]
& Condition.

The assertions in a list are interpreted as a conjunction, so that the rule above is read:

IF   Cause$_1$ AND Cause$_2$ AND ...
THEN   Cons$_1$ AND Cons$_2$ AND ...
WHERE   Condition

The following is the complete listing of the heart model:

Permanent impulse generation.

Rule 1

[heart( sa_node: permanent( Rhythm, Rate ))]
⟹ [permanent( sa_node: form( sa_node, Rhythm, Rate ))].

Rule 2

[heart( atr_focus: permanent( Rhythm, Rate ))]
⟹ [permanent( atr_focus: form( Origin, Rhythm, Rate ))]
& atr_focus( Origin, Rhythm, Rate ).

Rule 3

[heart( av_junction: permanent( Rhythm, Rate ))]
 $\Longrightarrow$ [permanent( av_junction:
                    form( av_junction, Rhythm, Rate ))].

Rule 4

[heart( reg_vent_focus: permanent( Rhythm, Rate ))]
 $\Longrightarrow$ [permanent( reg_vent_focus:
                    form( reg_vent_focus, Rhythm, Rate ))].

Rule 5

[heart( ect_vent_focus: permanent( Rhythm, Rate ))]
 $\Longrightarrow$ [permanent( ect_vent_focus:
                    form( ect_vent_focus, Rhythm, Rate ))].

Comment: All generators that are in the "permanent" mode generate permanent impulses. An impulse simply adopts the rhythm and the rate of a generator, and the shape of an impulse is characterized by the name of the generator. This is true for all generators except for the atrial focus, where **Origin** is more precisely defined with the rhythm and the rate of discharging:

```
%  atr_focus(  Origin,       Rhythm,    Rate              )

    atr_focus(  atr_focus,    quiet,     zero              ).
    atr_focus(  atr_focus,    regular,   between_60_100   ).
    atr_focus(  atr_focus,    regular,   between_100_250 ).
    atr_focus(  wandering,    irregular, between_60_100   ).
    atr_focus(  wandering,    irregular, between_100_250 ).
    atr_focus(  flutter,      regular,   between_250_350 ).
    atr_focus(  fibflut,      irregular, over_350          ).
    atr_focus(  fibrill,      irregular, over_350          ).
```

Occasional impulse generation.

Rule 6

[heart( atr_focus: occasional( unifocal ))]
 $\Longrightarrow$ [permanent( atr_focus: form( quiet, quiet, zero )),
      occasional( atr_focus: form( atr_focus, af, _ ))].

Rule 7

[heart( av_junction: occasional( unifocal ))]
 ⟹ [permanent( av_junction: form( quiet, quiet, zero )),
     occasional( av_junction: form( av_junction, jf, _ ))].

Rule 8

[heart( ect_vent_focus: occasional( unifocal ))]
 ⟹ [permanent( ect_vent_focus: form( quiet, quiet, zero )),
     occasional( ect_vent_focus: form( ect_vent_focus, vf, _ ))].

Rule 9

[heart( ect_vent_focus: occasional( multifocal ))]
 ⟹ [permanent( ect_vent_focus: form( quiet, quiet, zero )),
     occasional( ect_vent_focus: form( ect_vent_focus, vf, _ )),
     occasional( ect_vent_focus: form( ect_vent_focus, vf1, _ ))].

Comment: Generators that are in the "occasional" mode generate both occasional impulses and permanent impulses with the rate of zero. The generation of fictitious permanent impulses is needed because on each location in the model there must be exactly one permanent impulse. This is required by rules that involve the summation of impulses, as will became clear later. The shape of occasional impulses is simply denoted by the name of a generator. If the type of the ventricular focus is **multifocal** it designates two foci anywhere in the ventricles. In principle there can be an arbitrary number of occasional generators in the ventricles or anywhere in the heart, producing arbitrary number of occasional impulses. The only requirement is that they differ in the second parameter, i.e., in the origin.

Summation of impulses:
    sa_node + atr_focus ⟶ atria.

Rule 10

[permanent( sa_node: Impulse1 ),
 permanent( atr_focus: Impulse2 )]
 ⟹ [permanent( atria: Impulse )]
     & sum( Impulse1, Impulse2, Impulse ).

Rule 11

**[occasional( atr_focus: Impulse )]**
**⟹ [occasional( atria: Impulse )].**

Comment: "Summation" of occasional impulses is trivial as they are only renamed. Since the SA node does not discharge any occasional impulse there is no rule for its renaming. For the summation of permanent impulses there must always be two impulses. This is the reason for the introduction of fictitious permanent impulses. If both impulses have the rate of zero, their sum also has the rate of zero:

> **sum( form(Conduct, quiet, zero),**
> **form(_,          quiet, zero),**
> **form(Conduct, quiet, zero) ) :− !.**

Otherwise the sum of two impulses adopts the shape denoted by **Conduct**, the rhythm **Rhythm** and the rate **Rate** from the active impulse. Two clauses are needed because of commutativity of summation:

> **sum( form(Conduct, Rhythm, Rate),**
> **form(_,          quiet,    zero),**
> **form(Conduct, Rhythm, Rate) ).**

> **sum( form(_,          quiet,    zero),**
> **form(Conduct, Rhythm, Rate),**
> **form(Conduct, Rhythm, Rate) ).**

Summation of impulses:
> reg_vent_focus + ect_vent_focus ⟶ vent_focus.

Rule 12

**[permanent( reg_vent_focus: Impulse1 ),**
**permanent( ect_vent_focus: Impulse2 )]**
**⟹ [permanent( vent_focus: Impulse )]**
**&    sum( Impulse1, Impulse2, Impulse ).**

Summation of impulses:
> av_junction + vent_focus ⟶ vent_retro.

Rule 13

[permanent( av_junction: Impulse1 ),
 permanent( vent_focus: Impulse2 )]
 $\implies$ [permanent( vent_retro: Impulse )]
 &    sum( Impulse1, Impulse2, Impulse ).

Rule 14

[occasional( av_junction: Impulse )]
 $\implies$ [occasional( vent_retro: Impulse )].

Rule 15

[occasional( ect_vent_focus: Impulse )]
 $\implies$ [occasional( vent_retro: Impulse )].

Comment: The summation of the junctional and ventricular impulse.

Retrograde impulse conduction:
       vent_retro $\longrightarrow$ AV_CONDUCT $\longrightarrow$ atr_retro.

Rule 16

[permanent( vent_retro: form( Focus, Rhythm0, Rate0 )),
 heart( av_conduct: Conduct )]
 $\implies$ [permanent( atr_retro: form( Retro_cond, Rhythm, Rate ))]
 &    retrograd( Conduct, Focus, Rhythm0, Rate0,
                 Retro_cond, Rhythm, Rate ).

Rule 17

[occasional( vent_retro: form( Focus, Origin, Type )),
 heart( av_conduct: Conduct )]
 $\implies$ [occasional( atr_retro: form( Retro_cond, Origin, Type ))]
 &    retrograd( Conduct, Focus, Retro_cond ).

Comment: Retrograde conduction from the ventricles to the atria. The conduction is possible if the AV conduct is not completely blocked, i.e., if it is in any other state than blocked:

```
%  not_blocked(  Conduct         )
   not_blocked(  normal          ).
   not_blocked(  kent            ).
   not_blocked(  james           ).
   not_blocked(  delayed         ).
   not_blocked(  progress_delayed ).
   not_blocked(  partially_blocked ).
```

If the rate of permanent impulses from the ventricles is over 250/min or zero, there is no retrograde conduction. Otherwise the impulse can be conducted in the atria faster, equally fast or slower than in the ventricles, depending on the origin:

```
%  retrograd(  Conduct, Focus, Rhythm0, Rate0, Retro_cond,
               Rhythm, Rate )

   retrograd(  blocked, _, _, _, equal, quiet, zero ).
   retrograd(  _, _, _, zero, _, quiet, zero ).
   retrograd(  _, _, _, Rate0, _, quiet, zero ) :-
      Rate0 >- between_100_250.
   retrograd(  Conduct, Focus, Rhythm0, Rate0, Retro_cond,
               Rhythm0, Rate0 ) :-
      not_blocked( Conduct ),
      Rate0 >- zero, Rate0 -< between_250_350,
      retrograd( Focus, Retro_cond ).

%  retrograd(  Conduct,  Focus,  Retro_cond  )

   retrograd(  blocked,   _,        equal        ).
   retrograd(  Conduct, Focus, Retro_cond ) :-
      not_blocked( Conduct ),
      retrograd( Focus, Retro_cond ).

%  retrograd(  Focus,                Retro_cond  )

   retrograd(  av_junction,      faster      ).
   retrograd(  av_junction,      slower      ).
   retrograd(  av_junction,      equal       ).
   retrograd(  reg_vent_focus, equal       ).
   retrograd(  reg_vent_focus, slower      ).
   retrograd(  ect_vent_focus, equal       ).
   retrograd(  ect_vent_focus, slower      ).
```

Summation of impulses:

    atria + atr_retro ⟶ supra_vent.

Rule 18

[permanent( atria: Impulse1 ),
 permanent( atr_retro: Impulse2 )]
  ⟹ [permanent( supra_vent: Impulse )]
     &    sum( Impulse1, Impulse2, Impulse ).

Rule 19

[occasional( atria: Impulse )]
  ⟹ [occasional( supra_vent: Impulse )].

Rule 20

[occasional( atr_retro: Impulse )]
  ⟹ [occasional( supra_vent: Impulse )].

Comment: The summation of the atrial impulse and the retrogradely conducted impulse.

Impulse conduction through AV conduct:

    atria ⟶ AV_CONDUCT ⟶ av_conduct.

Rule 21

[permanent( atria: form( _, Rhythm0, Rate0 )),
 heart( av_conduct: Conduct )]
  ⟹ [permanent( av_conduct: form( Conduct, Rhythm, Rate ))]
    & av_conduct( Conduct, Rhythm0, Rhythm, Rate0, Rate ).

Rule 22

[occasional( atria: form( _, Origin, Type )),
 heart( av_conduct: Conduct )]
  ⟹ [occasional( av_conduct: form( Conduct, Origin, Type ))].

Comment: The conduction from the atria to the ventricles depends on the state of the AV conduction. The shape of an impulse is denoted by the state of the AV conduction **Conduct**. The rhythm and the rate of the permanent impulse are transformed depending on the state of the AV conduction:

% av_conduct(  Conduct, Rhythm0, Rhythm, Rate0, Rate )

av_conduct( normal, Rhythm, Rhythm, Rate, Rate ) :–
  Rate –< between_250_350.
av_conduct( delayed, Rhythm, Rhythm, Rate, Rate ) :–
  Rate in [under_60, between_60_100, between_100_250].
av_conduct( progress_delayed, regular, irregular,
              Rate0, Rate ) :–
  poss_reduced( Rate0, Rate ).
av_conduct( progress_delayed, irregular, irregular,
              Rate0, Rate ) :–
  poss_reduced( Rate0, Rate ).
av_conduct( partially_blocked, Rhythm, Rhythm,
              Rate0, Rate ) :–
  poss_reduced( Rate0, Rate ).
av_conduct( blocked, _, quiet, Rate, zero ) :–
  Rate >– zero.
av_conduct( kent, Rhythm, Rhythm, Rate, Rate ) :–
  Rate >– zero.
av_conduct( james, Rhythm, Rhythm, Rate, Rate ) :–
  Rate in [under_60, between_60_100, between_100_250].
av_conduct( normal, irregular, irregular, over_350, Rate ) :–
  Rate in [under_60, between_60_100, between_100_250].
av_conduct( normal, regular, irregular,
              between_250_350, Rate ) :–
  Rate in [under_60, between_60_100, between_100_250].
av_conduct( normal, regular, regular,
              between_250_350, Rate ) :–
  Rate in [under_60, between_60_100, between_100_250].

When there is the second degree of AV block (Wenckebach or Mobitz II)
the rate of the impulse can possibly be reduced:

poss_reduced( Rate,              Rate ) :–
  Rate >– zero, Rate –< between_250_350.
poss_reduced( between_60_100,  under_60           ).
poss_reduced( between_100_250, between_60_100 ).

Summation of impulses:
  av_conduct + av_junction ⟶ his_bundle.

Rule 23

[permanent( av_conduct: Impulse1 ),
 permanent( av_junction: Impulse2 )]
 $\Longrightarrow$ [permanent( his_bundle: Impulse )]
 & sum( Impulse1, Impulse2, Impulse ).

Rule 24

[occasional( av_conduct: Impulse )]
 $\Longrightarrow$ [occasional( his_bundle: Impulse )].

Rule 25

[occasional( av_junction: Impulse )]
 $\Longrightarrow$ [occasional( his_bundle: Impulse )].

Comment: The impulse, conducted from the atria is summed with the junctional impulse and passed to the bundle of His.

Impulse conduction through bundle branches:
      his_bundle $\longrightarrow$ BUNDLE_BRANCHES $\longrightarrow$ bundle_branches.

Rule 26

[permanent( his_bundle: form( HB_cond, Rhythm, Rate )),
 heart( bundle_branches: Conduct )]
 $\Longrightarrow$ [permanent( bundle_branches:
                  form( BB_cond, Rhythm, Rate ))]
 & bb_conduct( HB_cond, Conduct, BB_cond ).

Rule 27

[occasional( his_bundle: form( HB_cond, Origin, Type )),
 heart( bundle_branches: Conduct )]
 $\Longrightarrow$ [occasional( bundle_branches:
                  form( BB_cond, Origin, Type ))]
 & bb_conduct( HB_cond, Conduct, BB_cond ).

Comment: When the impulse is conducted through the bundle branches its rhythm and rate do not change. If the atrial impulse is completely blocked in the AV node, or if it is conducted through the bundle of Kent, then it is not conducted through the bundle branches. In this case its shape denoted by **BB_cond** remains unchanged. Otherwise it adopts for its shape the state of the bundle branches conduction **Conduct**:

```
%  bb_conduct(  HB_cond,   Conduct,   BB_conduct  )
   bb_conduct( blocked,    _,         blocked      ).
   bb_conduct( kent,       _,         kent         ).
   bb_conduct( HB_cond,  Conduct,  Conduct        ) :-
      HB_cond in [normal, james, delayed, progress_delayed,
                  partially_blocked, av_junction].
```

Summation of impulses:

bundle_branches + vent_focus ⟶ ventricles.

Rule 28

```
[permanent( bundle_branches: Impulse1 ),
 permanent( vent_focus: Impulse2 )]
 ⟹ [permanent( ventricles: Impulse )]
      &    sum( Impulse1, Impulse2, Impulse ).
```

Rule 29

```
[occasional( bundle_branches: Impulse )]
 ⟹ [occasional( ventricles: Impulse )].
```

Rule 30

```
[occasional( ect_vent_focus: Impulse )]
 ⟹ [occasional( ventricles: Impulse )].
```

Comment: The impulse conducted through the bundle branches and the impulse from the ventricular focus are summed to the ventricular impulse.

Producing ECG description:

Rule 31

```
[permanent( supra_vent: form( SV_cond, _, Rate )),
 permanent( av_conduct: form( AV_cond, _, _ ))]
 ⟹ [ecg( dominant_P: P_wave ),
     ecg( rate_of_P: P_rate ),
     ecg( dominant_PR: PR_interval ),
     ecg( relation_P_QRS: P_QRS_relation )]
      &  atr_ecg( Rate, SV_cond, AV_cond,
             P_wave, P_rate, PR_interval, P_QRS_relation ).
```

Rule 32

[occasional( av_conduct: form( AV_cond, af, _ ))]
$\Longrightarrow$ [ecg( ectopic_P( af ): P_wave ),
    ecg( ectopic_PR( af ): PR_interval )]
    &    atr_ecg( atr_focus, AV_cond, P_wave, PR_interval ).

Rule 33

[occasional( atr_retro: form( SV_cond, Origin, _ ))]
$\Longrightarrow$ [ecg( ectopic_P( Origin ): P_wave ),
    ecg( ectopic_PR( Origin ): PR_interval )]
    &    atr_ecg( SV_cond, normal, P_wave, PR_interval ).

Comment: The permanent supraventricular impulse causes P wave. The rate of P waves is equal to the rate of the impulse. The shape of P wave depends on supraventricular conditions, i.e. on the impulse origin or on the retrograde conduction:

```
%  atr_ecg(  Rate, SV_cond, AV_cond,
%            P_wave, P_rate, PR_interval, P_QRS_relation )
   atr_ecg( zero, _, _,
            absent, zero, meaningless, meaningless ).
   atr_ecg( Rate, SV_cond, AV_cond,
            P_wave, P_rate, PR_interval, P_QRS_relation ) :-
      Rate >- zero,
      supra_vent( SV_cond, P_wave, Rate, P_rate ),
      his_bundle( AV_cond, SV_cond, PR_interval,
                  P_QRS_relation ).

%  atr_ecg(  SV_cond, AV_cond, P_wave, PR_interval )
   atr_ecg( SV_cond, AV_cond, P_wave, PR_interval ) :-
      supra_vent( SV_cond, P_wave, _, _ ),
      his_bundle( AV_cond, SV_cond, PR_interval, _ ).

%  supra_vent(  SV_cond,    P_wave,    Rate,   P_rate)
   supra_vent( sa_node,    normal,    Rate, Rate ).
   supra_vent( atr_focus,  abnormal, Rate, Rate ).
   supra_vent( wandering,  changing, Rate, Rate ).
   supra_vent( flutter,    abnormal, Rate, Rate ).
   supra_vent( fibflut,    abnormal, Rate, Rate ).
   supra_vent( fibrill,    absent,    _,      zero ).
```

```
supra_vent( faster,      abnormal, Rate, Rate ).
supra_vent( equal,       absent,   _,    zero ).
supra_vent( slower,      abnormal, Rate, Rate ).
```

Comment: PR interval and P-QRS relation depend both on the conduction from the atria to the ventricles **AV_cond** and on the supraventricular conduction **SV_cond**:

```
%  his_bundle(  AV_cond, SV_cond, PR_interval, P_QRS_relation )
   his_bundle( delayed, _, prolonged, after_P_always_QRS).
   his_bundle( progress_delayed, _, prolonged,
               after_P_some_QRS_miss).
   his_bundle( partially_blocked, _, normal,
               after_P_some_QRS_miss).
   his_bundle( james, _, shortened, after_P_always_QRS).
   his_bundle( blocked, _, meaningless, independent_P_QRS).
   his_bundle( kent, sa_node, shortened, after_P_always_QRS).
   his_bundle( kent, atr_focus, shortened, after_P_always_QRS).
   his_bundle( kent, wandering, shortened, after_P_always_QRS).
   his_bundle( kent, flutter, meaningless, meaningless).
   his_bundle( kent, fibflut, meaningless, meaningless).
   his_bundle( kent, fibrill, meaningless, meaningless).
   his_bundle( normal, sa_node, normal, after_P_always_QRS).
   his_bundle( normal, fibrill, meaningless, meaningless).
   his_bundle( normal, fibflut, meaningless, meaningless).
   his_bundle( normal, fibflut, meaningless, independent_P_QRS).
   his_bundle( normal, fibflut, meaningless,
               after_P_some_QRS_miss).
   his_bundle( normal, flutter, meaningless,
               after_P_some_QRS_miss).
   his_bundle( normal, wandering, normal, after_P_always_QRS).
   his_bundle( normal, wandering, changing, after_P_always_QRS).
   his_bundle( normal, atr_focus, normal, after_P_always_QRS).
   his_bundle( normal, atr_focus, shortened, after_P_always_QRS).
   his_bundle( normal, atr_focus, prolonged, after_P_always_QRS).
   his_bundle( normal, faster, shortened, after_P_always_QRS).
   his_bundle( normal, equal, meaningless, meaningless).
   his_bundle( normal, slower, after_QRS_is_P,
               after_P_always_QRS).
```

Producing ECG description:

Rule 34

[permanent( ventricles: form( VENT_cond, Rhythm, Rate ))]
$\Longrightarrow$ [ecg( rhythm_QRS: Rhythm ),
    ecg( rate_of_QRS: Rate ),
    ecg( dominant_QRS: QRS_complex )]
&      ventricles( VENT_cond, Rate, QRS_complex ).

Rule 35

[occasional( ventricles: form( VENT_cond, Origin, _ ))]
$\Longrightarrow$ [ecg( ectopic_QRS( Origin ): QRS_complex )]
&      ventricles( VENT_cond, QRS_complex ).

Comment: The ventricular impulse defines the rhythm, the rate and the shape of QRS complexes. The shape depends on the bundle branches conduction, the ventricular origin or the AV conduction **VENT_cond**:

% ventricles(   VENT_cond,   Rate,   QRS_complex   )

    ventricles( VENT_cond, Rate, absent          ) :–
       Rate in [zero, over_350].
    ventricles( VENT_cond, Rate, QRS_complex ) :–
       Rate >– zero, Rate –< over_350,
       ventricles( VENT_cond, QRS_complex ).

% ventricles(   VENT_cond,     QRS_complex     )

| | | |
|---|---|---|
| ventricles( normal, | normal | ). |
| ventricles( left_blocked, | wide_LBBB | ). |
| ventricles( right_blocked, | wide_RBBB | ). |
| ventricles( reg_vent_focus, | wide_RBBB | ). |
| ventricles( reg_vent_focus, | wide_LBBB | ). |
| ventricles( reg_vent_focus, | wide_non_specific | ). |
| ventricles( ect_vent_focus, | wide_RBBB | ). |
| ventricles( ect_vent_focus, | wide_LBBB | ). |
| ventricles( ect_vent_focus, | wide_non_specific | ). |
| ventricles( kent, | delta_LBBB | ). |
| ventricles( kent, | delta_RBBB | ). |
| ventricles( blocked, | absent | ). |

# Chapter 3

# Model Interpretation and Derivation of Surface Knowledge

In this chapter algorithms for qualitative simulation using the heart model are developed. Detailed results of the execution of the model of the heart are given. The model was used to automatically generate ECG descriptions for all possible combinations of cardiac arrhythmias, distinguishable within the detail level of the model.

## 3.1 Formalization and implementation of the model

Rules in the model of the heart are defined as formulas of the first order predicate calculus. We here present the qualitative simulation, based on the model, as theorem proving and generation. An implementation of three inference mechanisms is described: derivation of ECG descriptions from given arrhythmias applying depth-first search and breadth-first search with space optimization, and derivation of possible arrhythmias from a given ECG description. The inference mechanism is illustrated with an example trace of the qualitative simulation that can also be used for causal explanation of the heart activity. Finally, we prove the soundness of the inference rules used.

### 3.1.1   Formalization in predicate calculus

The rules in the model can be viewed as a set of axioms expressed in the first order predicate calculus. Each combination of arrhythmias defines a state of the heart that is added to the axioms as a set of hypotheses. The hypotheses are verified using inference rules of predicate calculus, and a set of theorems is derived. Among the proven theorems there are also assertions about the corresponding ECG descriptions.

The syntax of a first order predicate language is defined by a vocabulary and formation rules. We adopt the formation rules from (Nilsson 1980) and specify only the symbols used. An atomic formula is of the form $p(X)$. We use lower case letters for predicate symbols and function symbols, and capital letters for variables (or tuples of variables). A term is a variable, a constant or it has the form $f(t)$, where $f$ is a functional symbol, and $t$ is a tuple of terms. The following symbols are used as connectives:

| | |
|---|---|
| $\neg$ | negation |
| & | conjunction |
| $\vee$ | disjunction |
| $\Longrightarrow$ | implication |
| $\Longleftrightarrow$ | equivalence |

The precedence of the operators is increasing in the following order: negation, conjunction, disjunction, implication, and equivalence. We assume that operators with lower precedence bind stronger. We use the following notation for quantifiers:

| | |
|---|---|
| $(\forall\ X)$ | universal quantifier |
| $(\exists\ X)$ | existential quantifier |

We assume that both quantifiers have higher precedence than the connectives.

The global rules in the model of the heart are formulas of the form:

$$(\forall\ X)(\exists\ Y)\ a(X)\ \Longrightarrow\ b(Y)\ \&\ c(X,Y) \tag{1}$$

where $X$ and $Y$ are tuples of variables, and $a(X)$ and $b(Y)$ are conjunctions of atomic formulas and $c(X,Y)$ is an atomic formula.

In this section we outline the algorithm by which these rules are used in the system in order to:

(1) check the consistency of a hypothesized state of the heart, and in the case of consistency,

(2) derive the ECG descriptions that correspond to this state.

In section 3.1.5 we prove the soundness of the simulation algorithm.

"Cause" $a(X)$ and "consequence" $b(Y)$ are assertions about states of objects in the model. $c(X, Y)$ has the role of "condition," and is used for checking consistency of both $a(X)$ and $b(Y)$, and for instantiation of variables in consequences proved. In the rules, the condition is written as a goal clause, that is, as a call to a Prolog procedure. All condition parts $c(X, Y)$ of global rules are defined in pure Prolog as a set of Horn clauses of the form:

$$(\forall\ X, Y)\ c(X, Y)\ \Longleftarrow\ P \tag{2}$$

where $P$ stands for a conjunction of atomic formulas.

For a given or a generated hypothesis:

$$a(t) \tag{3}$$

where $t$ stands for a tuple of ground terms, we can derive from (1) by modus ponens:

$$(\exists\ Y)\ b(Y)\ \&\ c(t, Y) \tag{4}$$

Then we check if the condition $c(t, Y)$ is satisfiable:

$$(\exists\ Y)\ c(t, Y) \tag{5}$$

This check is carried out by the Prolog interpreter directly. The Prolog interpreter proves whether this goal clause is a logical consequence of the Prolog program or not. Let us assume for example that the intepreter has found exactly two instances, $s_1$ and $s_2$, of the variable $Y$, for which formula (5) is true:

$$c(t, s_1)\ \&\ c(t, s_2)$$

Because of existential quantification in formula (4) the atomic formula $b(Y)$ must be true for at least one instance of $Y$:

$$b(s_1)\ \vee\ b(s_2)$$

This is the consequence we wanted to prove. From the rule (1) and the hypothesis (3) we can derive disjunctive assertions. These are conjunctively related to assertions, derived from other rules and hypotheses.

If the Prolog interpreter cannot derive any solution for $c(t, Y)$ then the formula (4) is also false. Now, as the axioms (1) are always true, the hypothesis (3) cannot be true. We have found a contradiction: the state of the heart is inconsistent with the model, which means that this state of the heart is impossible. If a hypothesis is not found to be inconsistent with the model (that is, axioms), we conclude that it is true. The conditions in the rules act as constraints over the truth of given and derived hypotheses.

## 3.1.2    Depth-first forward simulation

The implementation in Prolog of the inference mechanism, applying depth-first search, is simple as the Prolog interpreter itself uses the depth-first strategy. Backtracking need not be programmed explicitly.

Here we give the top level of the program that derives all ECG descriptions for a given combination of arrhythmias. These Prolog clauses precisely define relations in Figure 2.9:

```
derive_ecg_df( Arr_comb, ECG, Trace ) :-
    heart_state_df( Arr_comb, Hypos, Trace ),
    model_of_the_heart( RuleList ),
    forward_df( RuleList, Hypos, Facts, Trace ),
    collect_ecg( Facts, ECG ).

heart_state_df( Arr_comb, Hypos, Trace ) :-
    abnormal_heart( Arr_comb, Hypos0 ),
    rest_heart( Hypos1 ),
    complete_state( Hypos1, Hypos0, Hypos2 ),
    legality_constraints( Hypos2, Trace ),
    heart_facts( Hypos2, Hypos ).
```

The variable **Arr_comb** denotes a combination of arrhythmias, **ECG** is the corresponding ECG description, and **Trace** is used for explanation. For a given combination of arrhythmias, initial hypotheses (the state of the heart) are determined. Then the rules from the model are taken (**model_of_the_heart**), and applying inference mechanism (**forward_df**) on them, new assertions are derived, some of which denote ECG descriptions. The state of the heart is derived by successively determining the states of the heart components for each simple arrhythmia, and then completed with the definition of the normal states. Completed state is then checked by legality constraints and transformed to a form required by the inference mechanism.

The depth-first search generates, for a hypothesis and a rule, only one new hypothesis and ignores the rest of disjunctive hypotheses for the moment. If after applying all the rules no contradiction is found, we end with a set of conjunctive assertions. Another solution is found by backtracking to rules where the conditions can be resatisfied in some other way, thus generating alternative hypotheses. Having applied all the rules again, we get another set of conjunctive assertions, disjunctively connected to the first set. Using this algorithm repeatedly, all possible consequences can be derived from the initial set of hypotheses.

The procedure above is easily stated in Prolog as the relation

**forward_df( RuleList, Hypos, Facts, Trace )**

where **forward_df** stands for "forward depth-first." "Forward" refers to forward chaining, that is, application of rules in the forward direction. The relation should be read: applying all rules in **RuleList** in the depth-first forward fashion on some set of hypotheses **Hypos**, results in the set **Facts** of proved assertions.

```
forward_df( [], Hypos, Hypos, _ ).
forward_df( [Rule | Rules], Hypos, Result, Trace ) :-
    forw_trans( Rule, Rule1 ),
    modus_ponens( Rule1, Hypos, Hypos1, Trace ),
    forward_df( Rules, Hypos1, Result, Trace ).

forw_trans( Left  ⟹ Right & Condit,
            Left  ⟹ Right & Condit ).
forw_trans( Left  ⟹ Right,
            Left  ⟹ Right & true ).

modus_ponens( Rule, Hypos, Hypos1, Trace ) :-
    apply_rule( Rule, Hypos, List, Trace ), !,
    prove_conseq( List, Hypos, Hypos1, Trace ).
modus_ponens( _, Hypos, Hypos, Trace ) :-
    write_not_applied( Trace ).
```

Procedure **forward_df** is called from the procedure **derive_ecg_df**. As input parameters it has a list of rules **Rules**, a state of the heart **Hypos** and **Trace**. If **Trace** has value **trace** then the program will, during the execution, output trace information. The procedure takes the first rule **Rule** from the list, transforms it into the appropriate form **Rule1** and derives from it and the current set of assertions **Hypos** some new set of assertions **Hypos1**. A recursive call for the rest of the rules and new assertions is made until there is no more rules. All derived theorems are returned by the output parameter **Result**. Notice the following characteristics of this execution strategy: the rules are applied in the order in which they appear in the model; each rule is applied to all occurences of the rule's "cause pattern" in the current set of hypotheses.

### 3.1.3    Breadth-first forward simulation

The implementation of the inference mechanism applying depth-first search is simple, but relatively inefficient. For each disjunctive solution the mechanism has to backtrack to some rule in the model and restore its previous state. Besides that, we get the disjunction of different ECG descriptions that can be very complex. Simplification of such a disjunctive expression is not simple and may require a lot of computation.

These two drawbacks of depth-first search motivate the implementation of an inference mechanism that would simultaneously derive *all* disjunctive theorems (breadth-first search), add them to initial assertions, and at the same time simplify new expressions. We give a simple example. Let a previously generated assertion be:

$$a(t_1) \ \lor \ a(t_2)$$

We assume that from the rule:

$$(\forall \ X)(\exists \ Y) \quad a(X) \ \implies \ b(Y) \ \& \ c(X, Y)$$

we can derive $b(s_1)$ from $a(t_1)$ and $b(s_2)$ from $a(t_2)$. By adding new assertions to the initial ones, we get:

$$a(t_1) \ \& \ b(s_1) \ \lor \ a(t_2) \ \& \ b(s_2)$$

which can possibly be simplified. If we want to avoid future complicated simplification of such expressions (possibly much more complex
than this), we must simplify it now and not wait until the end of
the derivation process. For example, $B(Y)$ might be a conjunction of
atomic formulas:

$$b(s_1) = b_1(u) \ \& \ b_2(v)$$
$$b(s_2) = b_1(u) \ \& \ b_2(w)$$

Then simplified expression would be:

$$b_1(u) \ \& \ (a(t_1) \ \& \ b_2(v) \ \lor \ a(t_2) \ \& \ b_2(w))$$

However, the actually implemented simplification of logical expressions, used by the inference mechanism at the time of derivation, is for
efficiency reasons domain dependent. It only producces correct results
if the initial assertions ($a(t_1)$ and $a(t_2)$ above) are not used in subsequent derivations. This is true in this model of the heart so that all
thus produced ECG descriptions are logical consequences of the model
and the initial hypotheses. Any change of a rule in the model can result
in producing additional ECG descriptions that do not logically follow
from the assumptions.

The breadth-first simulation and the simplification of logical expressions is illustrated by the following example. The rules that were
not used during the simulation or are of little interest are omitted.
Comments and enumeration of rules are added to the program output.
The program output is in bold face. The numbers preceded by the
underscore character, such as _209, are names of variables internally
generated by Prolog.

---

**Input combination of arrhythmias:**

**[atrial_fibrillation, ventricular_ectopic_beats]**

**State of the heart:**

**sa_node:permanent(quiet,zero),**
**atr_focus:permanent(irregular,over_350),**
**av_conduct:normal,**
**av_junction:permanent(quiet,zero),**
**bundle_branches:normal,**

**reg_vent_focus:permanent(quiet,zero),**
**ect_vent_focus:occasional(unifocal)**

**Legality constraints succeeded!**

Comment: For arrhythmias atrial fibrillation and ventricular ectopic beats, the state of the heart is derived and checked against the legality constraints.

---

Rule 2

**heart(atr_focus:permanent(_194,_195))**   $\Longrightarrow$
  **permanent(atr_focus:form(_196,_194,_195))**

**Consequent proved:**
  **[permanent([atr_focus:**
    **[form(fibflut,irregular,over_350),**
    **form(fibrill,irregular,over_350)]])]**

Comment: The derived assertions about two disjunctive permanent impulses are simplified into an assertion about one permanent atrial impulse that can have two disjunctive forms.

---

Rule 8

**heart(ect_vent_focus:occasional(unifocal))**   $\Longrightarrow$
  **permanent(ect_vent_focus:form(quiet,quiet,zero)),**
  **occasional(ect_vent_focus:form(ect_vent_focus,vf,unifocal))**

**Consequent proved:**
  **[permanent([ect_vent_focus:[form(quiet,quiet,zero)]]),**
    **occasional([ect_vent_focus:**
    **[form(ect_vent_focus,vf,unifocal)]])]**

Comment: The ventricular ectopic focus discharges the fictitious permanent impulse and the occasional impulse.

---

Rule 10

**permanent(sa_node:_205),**
**permanent(atr_focus:_206)**   $\Longrightarrow$
  **permanent(atria:_207)**

**Consequent proved:**
  [permanent([atria:
      [form(fibflut,irregular,over_350),
        form(fibrill,irregular,over_350)]])]

Comment: After the summation, the simplified form of disjunctive assertions is preserved.

---

**Rule 15**

occasional(ect_vent_focus:_216)  $\Longrightarrow$
  occasional(vent_retro:_216)

**Consequent proved:**
  [occasional([vent_retro:[form(ect_vent_focus,vf,unifocal)]])]

**Rule 17**

occasional(vent_retro:form(_224,_225,_226)),
heart(av_conduct:_227)  $\Longrightarrow$
  occasional(atr_retro:form(_228,_225,_226))

**Consequent proved:**
  [occasional([atr_retro:[form( equal,vf,unifocal),
                          form(slower,vf,unifocal)]])]

Comment: The retrograde conduction of the occasional ventricular impulse. Again, the impulse can take two disjunctive forms.

---

**Rule 18**

permanent(atria:_229),
permanent(atr_retro:_230)  $\Longrightarrow$
  permanent(supra_vent:_231)

**Consequent proved:**
  [permanent([supra_vent:
      [form(fibflut,irregular,over_350),
        form(fibrill,irregular,over_350)]])]

Comment: Summation of impulses into the permanent supraventricular impulse.

---

---

Rule 20

occasional(atr_retro:_233)      ⟹
   occasional(supra_vent:_233)

Consequent proved:
   [occasional([supra_vent:[form(equal,vf,unifocal),
                           form(slower,vf,unifocal)]]))]

Comment: Renaming of the retrograde occasional impulse.

---

Rule 21

permanent(atria:form(_234,_235,_236)),
heart(av_conduct:_237)      ⟹
   permanent(av_conduct:form(_237,_238,_239))

Consequent proved:
   [permanent([av_conduct:
      [form(normal,irregular,under_60),
       form(normal,irregular,between_60_100),
       form(normal,irregular,between_100_250)]])]

Comment: The AV conduction. Note the simplified form of disjunctive assertions.

---

Rule 23

permanent(av_conduct:_244),
permanent(av_junction:_245)      ⟹
   permanent(his_bundle:_246)

Consequent proved:
   [permanent([his_bundle:
      [form(normal,irregular,under_60),
       form(normal,irregular,between_60_100),
       form(normal,irregular,between_100_250)]])]

Rule 26

permanent(his_bundle:form(_249,_250,_251)),
heart(bundle_branches:_252)       ⟹
    permanent(bundle_branches:form(_253,_250,_251))

**Consequent proved:**
    [permanent([bundle_branches:
            [form(normal,irregular,under_60),
              form(normal,irregular,between_60_100),
              form(normal,irregular,between_100_250)]])]

Rule 28

permanent(bundle_branches:_259),
permanent(vent_focus:_260)       ⟹
    permanent(ventricles:_261)

**Consequent proved:**
    [permanent([ventricles:
            [form(normal,irregular,under_60),
              form(normal,irregular,between_60_100),
              form(normal,irregular,between_100_250)]])]

Comment: A few summations of impulses.

---

Rule 31

permanent(supra_vent:form(_264,_265,_266)),
permanent(av_conduct:form(_267,_268,_269))       ⟹
    ecg(dominant_P:_270),
    ecg(rate_of_P:_271),
    ecg(dominant_PR:_272),
    ecg(relation_P_QRS:_273)

**Consequent proved:**
    [ecg([dominant_P:[abnormal],
          rate_of_P:[over_350],
          dominant_PR:[meaningless],
          relation_P_QRS:[meaningless,independent_P_QRS,
                          after_P_some_QRS_miss]])],

```
[ecg([dominant_P:[absent],
      rate_of_P:[zero],
      dominant_PR:[meaningless],
      relation_P_QRS:[meaningless]])]
```

Comment: Now the derived ECG descriptions cannot be simplified into less than two expressions. The inference is continued with two sets of disjunctive assertions and therefore each subsequent rule that fires, is applied twice.

---

Comment: From now on two execution branches produce identical results. Here the duplicated output is omitted.

Rule 33

```
occasional(atr_retro:form(_281,_282,_283))        ⟹
   ecg(ectopic_P(_282):_284),
   ecg(ectopic_PR(_282):_285)
```

Consequent proved:
```
   [ecg([ectopic_P(vf):[absent],
         ectopic_PR(vf):[meaningless]])],
   [ecg([ectopic_P(vf):[abnormal],
         ectopic_PR(vf):[after_QRS_is_P]])]
```

Comment: Again, a simplification to less than two expressions is not possible. Together with the first two, we now have four sets of disjunctive assertions. As from here on, each rule will be applied four times. However, we omit multiplicated outputs.

---

Rule 34

```
permanent(ventricles:form(_289,_290,_291))        ⟹
   ecg(rhythm_QRS:_290),
   ecg(rate_of_QRS:_291),
   ecg(dominant_QRS:_292)
```

Consequent proved:
```
   [ecg([rhythm_QRS:[irregular],
         rate_of_QRS:[under_60,between_60_100,
                      between_100_250],
         dominant_QRS:[normal]])]
```

Rule 35

occasional(ventricles:form(_293,_294,_295))    $\implies$
   ecg(ectopic_QRS(_294):_296)

**Consequent proved:**
   [ecg([ectopic_QRS(vf):[wide_RBBB,wide_LBBB,
                        wide_non_specific]])]

Comment: Production of ECG description.

---

Comment: In the alternative descriptions that follow, those attribute values in which alternatives differ are in italic.

[rhythm_QRS = irregular] &
[dominant_P = *abnormal*] &
[rate_of_P = *over_350*] &
[relation_P_QRS = *meaningless* ∨ *independent_P_QRS* ∨
                        *after_P_some_QRS_miss*] &
[dominant_PR = meaningless] &
[dominant_QRS = normal] &
[rate_of_QRS = under_60 ∨ between_60_100 ∨
                        between_100_250] &
[ectopic_P(1) = *absent*] &
[ectopic_PR(1) = *meaningless*] &
[ectopic_QRS(1) = wide_RBBB ∨ wide_LBBB ∨
                        wide_non_specific]

**For another ECG press "RETURN", else "no":** ⟨CR⟩

[rhythm_QRS = irregular] &
[dominant_P = *abnormal*] &
[rate_of_P = *over_350*] &
[relation_P_QRS = *meaningless* ∨ *independent_P_QRS* ∨
                        *after_P_some_QRS_miss*] &
[dominant_PR = meaningless] &
[dominant_QRS = normal] &
[rate_of_QRS = under_60 ∨ between_60_100 ∨
                        between_100_250] &
[ectopic_P(1) = *abnormal*] &
[ectopic_PR(1) = *after_QRS_is_P*] &

[ectopic_QRS(1) = wide_RBBB ∨ wide_LBBB ∨
                  wide_non_specific]

**For another ECG press "RETURN", else "no":** ⟨CR⟩

[rhythm_QRS = irregular] &
[dominant_P = absent] &
[rate_of_P = zero] &
[relation_P_QRS = meaningless] &
[dominant_PR = meaningless] &
[dominant_QRS = normal] &
[rate_of_QRS = under_60 ∨ between_60_100 ∨
               between_100_250] &
[ectopic_P(1) = absent] &
[ectopic_PR(1) = meaningless] &
[ectopic_QRS(1) = wide_RBBB ∨ wide_LBBB ∨
                  wide_non_specific]

**For another ECG press "RETURN" else "no":** ⟨CR⟩

[rhythm_QRS = irregular] &
[dominant_P = absent] &
[rate_of_P = zero] &
[relation_P_QRS = meaningless] &
[dominant_PR = meaningless] &
[dominant_QRS = normal] &
[rate_of_QRS = under_60 ∨ between_60_100 ∨
               between_100_250] &
[ectopic_P(1) = abnormal] &
[ectopic_PR(1) = after_QRS_is_P] &
[ectopic_QRS(1) = wide_RBBB ∨ wide_LBBB ∨
                  wide_non_specific]

**For another ECG press "RETURN", else "no":** ⟨CR⟩

**No more solutions!**

Comment: At the end of simulation, ECG descriptions are selected
from all four disjunctive sets of assertions. The complicated expression
with 72 conjuncts was, in effect, simplified into the disjunction of 4 conjuncts. The 72 conjuncts are expressed by combinations of alternative
values of some attributes (called *internal* disjunctions).

## 3.1.4   Backward simulation

From the very beginning of the development of the model of the heart we had an ambition to use the model directly for diagnosis, and not only for the simulation. For diagnosis, the natural use of rules is in the opposite direction (backward chaining) thereby reasoning from consequences to causes. We give the top level of the corresponding procedure that finds all possible arrhythmias (causes) for a given ECG description (consequences):

```
derive_arr( ECG, Arr_comb, Trace ) :-
    ecg_facts( ECG, Hypos ),
    model_of_the_heart( Rules ),
    backward( Rules, Hypos, Facts, Trace ),
    collect_heart( Facts, Heart ),
    legality_constraints( Facts, Trace ),
    heart_arrhythm( Heart, Arr_comb, Trace ).
```

First, an ECG description **ECG** is transformed into the form of assertions **Hypos** that is required by the rules in the model. Then the inference mechanism for backward simulation finds all possible causes **Facts** of the specified ECG description. The state of the heart **Heart** is selected from them, then checked against legality constraints and the corresponding combination of arrhythmias **Arr_comb** is found.

The rules in the model were specifically designed with the intention to allow, in addition to their normal interpretation as in the previous two sections, also the "inverse" interpretation. As will be explained later, only part of the rules in the model has straightforward inverse interpretation. The rest of the model would require some modifications. The rules in the model, straightforwardly inverted for reasoning from "consequences" to "causes," have the form:

$$(\forall\ Y)(\exists\ X)\ b(Y)\ \Longrightarrow\ a(X)\ \&\ c(X, Y)$$

This formula is similar to the original; only "cause" $a(X)$ and "consequence" $b(Y)$ are interchanged. The role of "condition" $c(X,Y)$ remains the same, except that input and output modes of variables are inverted. As this makes no difference to the Prolog interpreter, the procedure **backward** (backward simulation) is only slightly different from the procedure **forward_df** (forward, depth-first simulation, see section 3.1.2):

> **backward( [], Hypos, Hypos, _ ).**
>
> **backward( [Rule | Rules], Hypos, Result, Trace ) :–**
>     **backward( Rules, Hypos, Hypos1, Trace ),**
>     **back_trans( Rule, Rule1 ),**
>     **modus_ponens( Rule1, Hypos1, Result, Trace ).**
>
> **back_trans( Left $\Longrightarrow$ Right & Condit,**
>             **Right $\Longrightarrow$ Left  & Condit ) :– !.**
>
> **back_trans( Left $\Longrightarrow$ Right,**
>             **Right $\Longrightarrow$ Left  & true ).**

We must apply the list of the rules **Rules** in the reverse order. Therefore the procedure first calls itself recursively and only then the selected rule **Rule** is applied. The rule is transformed into the required form **Rule1** where "cause" and "consequence" are interchanged. The procedure, the same as for forward simulation, then derives from the current assertions **Hypos1** new assertions **Result**.

Clearly the inversion of rules above is not truth preserving in general. In spite of this, it was shown that part of the inverted rules of the heart model still produces correct pairs **(Arrhythmia, ECG)**. Problems arise in the case of ectopic beats in the specified ECG description. The inverted rules describing conduction of occasional impulses and production of ectopic beats in the ECG description are not correct. The location of an occasional impulse in the heart alone is not sufficient for its complete identification. There can be several impulses from different foci at the same location in the heart. Let us consider two rules from the model (section 2.2.4) as an example:

Rule 29

[occasional( bundle_branches: Impulse )]
  $\Longrightarrow$ [occasional( ventricles: Impulse )].

Rule 30

[occasional( ect_vent_focus: Impulse )]
  $\Longrightarrow$ [occasional( ventricles: Impulse )].

The first rule says that each occasional impulse from the **bundle_branches** is conducted to the **ventricles**. The second rule states that each occasional impulse from an ectopic ventricular focus **ect_vent_focus** is also conducted to the **ventricles**. This is correct. However, when the second rule is simply inverted (in the non-truth preserving way) it becomes incorrect. It states that *each* occasional impulse in the ventricles is coming from the ectopic ventricular focus. Obviously, this is not always true, as the impulse may come from the bundle branches as well.

This defect can be patched up by restating rules in such a way that the impulses are precisely identified by their origin. The simplest solution is to augment the location of all occasional impulses with their origin. The rules above would have to be rewritten as:

Rule 29a

[occasional( bundle_branches(af): Impulse )]
  $\Longrightarrow$ [occasional( ventricles(af): Impulse )].

Rule 29b

[occasional( bundle_branches(jf): Impulse )]
  $\Longrightarrow$ [occasional( ventricles(jf): Impulse )].

Rule 30a

[occasional( ect_vent_focus(vf): Impulse )]
  $\Longrightarrow$ [occasional( ventricles(vf): Impulse )].

Rule 30b

[occasional( ect_vent_focus(vf1): Impulse )]
  $\Longrightarrow$ [occasional( ventricles(vf1): Impulse )].

Such rewriting of the rules would also simplify the implementation of the inference mechanism for forward simulation, as each rule is used at most once. On the other hand, the number of rules would increase by a factor of almost two and the transparency of explanation would be considerably worse.

Another problem with backward simulation is its inefficiency. Backward reasoning is less efficient than forward reasoning because of the particular properties of the heart model. First, the nondeterministic branching in the backward direction is higher than in the forward direction. Second, the legality constraints are applied to the state of the heart, which is the earliest stage in forward reasoning and the latest stage in backward reasoning. Therefore the legality constraints will immediately prune unfeasible lines of forward reasoning before they are actually started. On the other hand, the legality constraints will in backward reasoning detect impossible results at the end of the reasoning process when all the time has already been wasted in deriving these impossible results.

Already during the backward derivation of new assertions, the mechanism could know that the same heart subsystem cannot be in two different states. Besides that, because of the exclusive disjunction connecting values of the same attribute in an ECG description, negative assertions could also be used. For example, if dominant P waves are abnormal, they can be neither normal, nor absent, nor changing. From the negative assertion $\neg b(Y)$ and the original rule:

$$(\forall\ X)(\exists\ Y)\ a(X)\ \implies\ b(Y)\ \&\ c(X,Y)$$

assertions $\neg a(X)$ can be derived for some instances of $X$, applying *modus tollens* rule of inference. However, this kind of reasoning was neither formalized nor tested.

## 3.1.5   Soundness proof of the simulation algorithm

Here we formally prove the soundness of the foregoing simulation algorithm. This section can be skipped.

First we sketch the simulation algorithm which corresponds to breadth-first forward simulation of section 3.1.3:

Start with a given set of initial hypotheses $H_0$;
$S := \{H_0\}$;
**repeat** select a rule $(\forall X)(\exists Y)\ a(X) \implies b(Y)\ \&\ c(X,Y)$;
      select a set of hypotheses $H \in S$;
      select a hypothesis $a(t) \in H$, such that this pair
      rule-hypothesis has not yet been selected;
      **if**   the rule fires ($a(X)$ can be unified with $a(t)$)
      **then** derive $(\exists Y)\ b(Y)\ \&\ c(t,Y)$
            $S := S - \{H\}$;
            **if**   $(\exists Y)\ c(t,Y)$ is true, e.g. for $Y = s_1,\ s_2$
            **then** derive $b(s_1) \lor b(s_2)$;
                $S := S \cup \{H \cup \{b(s_1)\},\ H \cup \{b(s_2)\}\}$;
**until**  all pairs rule-hypothesis are exhausted;
**if**   $S = \{\}$
**then** return $\neg\ H_0$
**else** return $H_0 \implies \bigvee_i H_i$ over all $H_i \in S$.

The set $S$ thus represents the derived consequences in disjunctive form.

Now we formulate a theorem that supports the reasoning described in previous sections.

*Soundness theorem:*

    If the set of derived consequences is empty then the initial hypotheses $H_0$ are inconsistent with the rules in the model $M$. Otherwise, if the set of derived consequences is nonempty then (a) $H_0$ is consistent with $M$ and (b) the derived consequences do logically follow from $H_0$ and $M$.

*Proof:*

    The skeleton of the proof is as follows. First we show how logical consistency of $H_0$ and $M$ can be demonstrated; the treatment is based on resolution. Second, we show how the simulation algorithm for establishing consistency corresponds to finding contradiction using resolution. More precisely: we consider a complete set of ways contradiction can be detected with resolution; then we show that the algorithm performs all the corresponding actions for detecting contradiction.

*Step 1: Logical consistency of $H_0$ and $M$*

The model $M$ is defined by a set of global rules $G$ and a set of local rules $L$. Under the closed world assumption the local rules can be taken as *completed* (Lloyd 1984). First we transform the model $M$ into clausal form.

A global rule of the form:

$$(\forall X)(\exists Y)\; a(X) \implies b(Y) \;\&\; c(X,Y)$$

is transformed into two clauses $G_1$ and $G_2$:

$$
\begin{aligned}
G_1: \quad & \neg\; a(X) \;\vee\; b(f(X)) \\
G_2: \quad & \neg\; a(X) \;\vee\; c(X,f(X))
\end{aligned}
$$

where $f$ is a Skolem function. All variables above are universally quantified and local to the clauses.

Next, we apply the *completion* of a logic program (Lloyd 1984) to local rules in the model. Let

$$c(t_i, s_i) \;\Longleftarrow\; P_i$$

be one of the clauses that define predicate $c$ in the model. $t_i$ and $s_i$ are tuples of partially instantiated terms, and $P_i$ is a conjunction of atomic formulas. All variables are universally quantified, and predicate symbol "=" denotes equality relation. First step of the completion yields

$$c(X,Y) \;\Longleftarrow\; (\exists Z)\; X = t_i \;\&\; Y = s_i \;\&\; P_i$$

where $X$ and $Y$ are tuples of variables not occuring in the clause, and $Z$ is a tuple of variables from the original clause. The completed definition of the predicate $c$ is the formula:

$$(\forall X, Y)\; c(X,Y) \;\Longleftrightarrow\; Q_1 \;\vee\; Q_2 \;\vee \ldots \vee\; Q_k$$

where each $Q_i$ is in general of the form:

$$(\exists Z)\; X = t_i \;\&\; Y = s_i \;\&\; P_i$$

After the transformation to the clausal form we get the set of clauses

$$
\begin{aligned}
L_1: \quad & c(X,Y) \;\vee\; \neg\; Q_1 \\
L_2: \quad & c(X,Y) \;\vee\; \neg\; Q_2 \\
& \ldots \\
L_k: \quad & c(X,Y) \;\vee\; \neg\; Q_k
\end{aligned}
$$

for the implication to the left (the original formula). Further we get a clause

$$L_0 : \quad \neg\ c(X,Y)\ \lor\ Q_1\ \lor\ Q_2\ \lor \ldots \lor\ Q_k$$

for the implication to the right (the completed part of the formula).

Without loss of generality we here assume that the set of initial hypotheses $H_0$ consists of only one atom:

$$H_0 : \{a(t)\}$$

$H_0$ is consistent with the model $M$ if contradiction cannot be demonstrated. We can apply resolution principle to test for inconsistency. Since we can assume that the model $M$ itself is consistent (inconsistent model is of no practical value), to derive empty clause it is sufficient to consider only resolution steps that involve atom $a(t)$. This is the only possible source of contradiction.

By resolution, from $a(t)$ and $G_1$ and $G_2$ follow these two clauses:

$$b(f(t))$$
$$c(t, f(t))$$

Now we check the consistency of $c(t, f(t))$ with local rules $L$. We distinguish between two cases, A and B.

*Case A: $c(t, f(t))$ is inconsistent with $L$*

The inconsistency of $c(t, f(t))$ with $L$ can be demonstrated only by using the completed part of the definition of $c$. By resolution, from $c(t, f(t))$ and $L_0$ we get:

$$Q_1\ \lor\ Q_2\ \lor \ldots \lor\ Q_k$$

Empty clause can be derived only if for all $Q_i$, that is for all formulas:

$$t = t_i\ \&\ f(t) = s_i\ \&\ P_i$$

contradiction can be demonstrated. Therefore, the following must hold:

$$(\forall\ i)\ t \neq t_i\ \lor\ f(t) \neq s_i\ \lor\ \neg\ P_i$$

*Case B: $c(t, f(t))$ is consistent with $L$*

If $c(t, f(t))$ cannot be shown to be inconsistent with $L_0$ then the negation of the above statement must hold:

$$(\exists\ i)\ t = t_i\ \&\ f(t) = s_i\ \&\ P_i$$

Let us assume for example that this holds for $i = 1, 2$, which means that $c(t, Y)$ is satisfiable in two ways by using clause $L_1$ or clause $L_2$. Therefore:

$$f(t) = s_1 \quad \vee \quad f(t) = s_2$$

From this, $b(f(t))$ and the equality axioms (see Lloyd (1984) for equality axioms for logic programs) it follows:

$$b(s_1) \quad \vee \quad b(s_2)$$

There is now no other way to prove inconsistency apart from deriving empty clause from $b(s_1) \vee b(s_2)$. If now

$$M \ \& \ H_0 \ \& \ (b(s_1) \ \vee \ b(s_2))$$

is inconsistent then $H_0$ must be false. Otherwise

$$M \ \& \ H_0$$

is consistent (claim (a) of the soundness theorem). Further

$$\vee_i \ b(s_i) \quad \text{over all } i \text{ such that } M \ \& \ b(s_i) \text{ is consistent}$$

logically follows from $H_0$ (claim (b) of the soundness theorem).

*Step 2: Soundness of reasoning steps by the simulation algorithm*

We have to show that the simulation algorithm checks all the above possible ways of demonstrating contradiction. We will therefore consider the actions of the algorithm that correspond to cases A and B above.

Algorithm:
$H_0 = \{a(t)\}; \ S := \{\{a(t)\}\};$
the rule fires, i.e. $a(t)$ matches $a(X)$

Resolution:
unify $a(t)$ with $a(X)$

Algorithm:
derive $(\exists Y)b(Y) \ \& \ c(t, Y)$
$S := S - \{H_0\} = \{\}$

Resolution:
add clauses $b(f(t))$ and $c(t, f(t))$

Algorithm:
is $c(t, Y)$ satisfiable?

Case A: $c(t, Y)$ is unsatisfiable

Algorithm:
Prolog fails with the goal $c(t, Y)$. Do not update $S$; notice that $H_0$ was deleted from $S$ and thus it is eliminated as a candidate set of consistent hypotheses. It will not appear in the resulting set $S$ returned by the algorithm.

Resolution:
$H_0$ found to contradict $M$.

Case B: $c(t, Y)$ is satisfiable

Algorithm:
Prolog returns one or more solutions for $c(t, Y)$, e.g. $Y = s_1, s_2$. Hypothesize $b(s_1) \vee b(s_2)$ and update $S$ with $H_0 \cup \{b(s_1)\}$ and $H_0 \cup \{b(s_2)\}$.

Resolution:
Add clause $b(s_1) \vee b(s_2)$.

Algorithm:
Continue firing rules on the updated set $S$.

Resolution:
Check consistency of $M \& H_0 \& (b(s_1) \vee b(s_2))$.

When all the rules have been exhausted then all the sets in $S$ are consistent with $M$.

*This completes the proof.*

The selection of a pair hypothesis-rule, from which new hypotheses are derived is, in principle, arbitrary. If on each hypothesis all rules are applied, the derivation of all possible consequences is ensured. But the efficiency and transparency of the derivation critically depends on the strategy for selecting pairs. As all the rules in the heart model are nonrecursive, i.e., the consequence effects the cause neither directly nor indirectly, they can be ordered. Therefore the rules in the actual implementation are ordered in a list according to the following principle.

Let there be two rules,

Rule$_1$:    $A_1 \implies B_1$ & $C_1$
Rule$_2$:    $A_2 \implies B_2$ & $C_2$

If $B_1$ and $A_2$ share the same atomic formula then Rule$_1$ must precede Rule$_2$. The nonrecursiveness property of the rule set ensures that $A_1$ and $B_2$ in this case cannot share any atomic formula.

Such an ordering allows the simulation algorithm to consider each rule in the list only once. From a selected rule and a current set of hypotheses all consequences are derived. The rule can then be discarded, as no consequence derived later will trigger this rule again.

The ordering of the rules also affects the transparency of explanation. A chain of causes and consequences can provide a good causal account of mechanisms in any device. This is not always possible to achieve and is not completly sufficient for explanation by itself, but it provides a good basis for a user interface with explanatory capabilities.

## 3.2    Derivation of arrhythmia-ECG knowledge base

The model of the heart was executed on all mathematically possible combinations of simple cardiac arrhythmias. The majority of these combinations was eliminated by constraints over the states of the heart. For the rest of them, the corresponding ECG descriptions were derived by qualitative simulation of the heart. The surface arrhythmia-ECG knowledge base was thus automatically generated. Results of the generation are summarized in Table 3.1.

Note that in Table 3.1 the number of generated arrhythmias for combinations of single arrhythmias (18) is less than the number of all simple arrhythmias (30) because some arrhythmias (conduction disturbances and ectopic beats) cannot occur on their own, but only in combination with other arrhythmias (e.g., "sinus rhythm").

We can see that the largest number of possible arrhythmias are combinations of 4 simple arrhythmias. The number of arrhythmias

| Simple arr. | Mathematical combinations | Generated | | Prolog clauses | KB of store |
|---|---|---|---|---|---|
| | | Arr. | ECGs | | |
| 1 | 30 | 18 | 63 | 27 | 8 |
| 2 | 435 | 118 | 2,872 | 286 | 119 |
| 3 | 4,060 | 407 | 17,551 | 1,207 | 609 |
| 4 | 27,405 | 759 | 45,939 | 2,679 | 1,583 |
| 5 | 142,506 | 717 | 52,707 | 2,867 | 1,948 |
| 6 | 593,775 | 340 | 20,322 | 1,164 | 892 |
| 7 | 2,035,800 | 60 | 1,512 | 84 | 69 |
| Totals | 2,804,011 | 2,419 | 140,966 | 8,314 | 5,228 |

Table **3.1** Results of generating the arrhythmia-ECG knowledge base. The store occupancy in this table is measured on the DEC-10 machine, where the results were originally generated. When moving data to other machines these figures are slightly changed (5.1 MB for the complete knowledge base on SUN 2).

then decreases. There is no combination of eight or more simple arrhythmias. Note the very large number of the generated ECG descriptions—140,966. This indicates the difficulty of the problem of ECG diagnosis of cardiac arrhythmias. On the average, each arrhythmia has almost 60 different corresponding ECG descriptions.

The knowledge base was generated by the inference mechanism in the breadth-first fashion, which turned out to be much more efficient compared to depth-first search. Besides that, the derived ECG descriptions are represented in compact and simplified form. If an ECG description corresponding to some arrhythmia cannot be simplified into a single conjunctive expression with internal disjunctions, a Prolog clause about the same arrhythmia is multiplicated for each expression in the knowledge base. From Table 3.1 we can see that arrhythmias are defined by 4 clauses on the average.

The whole model of the heart and its interpreter are implemented in Prolog (Edinburgh Prolog for DEC-10; Pereira, Pereira, and Warren 1978) in approximatly 1200 lines of Prolog code. The compiled program generated the arrhythmia knowledge base in one hour of CPU time on a DEC-10 KL processor. The whole knowledge base requires over 5 MB of storage on a disk.

Here we give a few examples of combinations of arrhythmias, with derived ECG descriptions. More examples are in Appendix A. Some examples are accompanied by ECG waveforms from (Goldman 1976) when Goldman gives them. From the set of all generated ECG descriptions, only the one that describes the corresponding waveform from Goldman is selected.

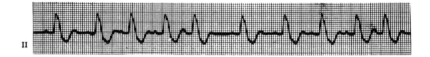

[sa_node_disorders, left_bundle_branch_block]   $\Longrightarrow$
  [rhythm_QRS = irregular] &
  [dominant_P = normal] &
  [rate_of_P = between_60_100] &
  [relation_P_QRS = after_P_always_QRS] &
  [dominant_PR = normal] &
  [dominant_QRS = wide_LBBB] &
  [rate_of_QRS = between_60_100]

Figure 3.1 The SA block of the Wenckebach type with left bundle branch block. In the model, the SA block is contained under more abstract arrhythmia: the SA node disorders. The problem of more precise differentiation between the SA node disorders is left to the user interface (for details see section 2.2.2). With an additional specification of the rhythm, sinus arrhythmia that has the same ECG description would be eliminated as well (Goldman 1976, Figure 12-10).

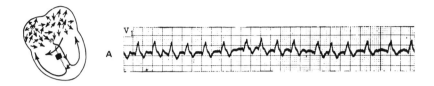

[atrial_fibrillation, right_bundle_branch_block]   ⟹
    [rhythm_QRS = irregular] &
    [dominant_P = absent] &
    [rate_of_P = zero] &
    [relation_P_QRS = meaningless] &
    [dominant_PR = meaningless] &
    [dominant_QRS = wide_RBBB] &
    [rate_of_QRS = between_100_250]

**Figure 3.2**  Atrial fibrillation with right bundle branch block. The irregular ventricular rhythm is at the rate of 170/min, QRS complexes are wide. Ventricular tachycardia has similar ECG, but with the regular rhythm (Goldman 1976, Figure 14-22A).

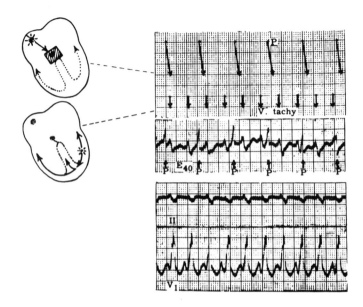

[sinus_rhythm, av_block_3, ventricular_tachycardia] $\Longrightarrow$
 [rhythm_QRS = regular] &
 [dominant_P = normal] &
 [rate_of_P = between_60_100] &
 [relation_P_QRS = independent_P_QRS] &
 [dominant_PR = meaningless] &
 [dominant_QRS = wide_RBBB] &
 [rate_of_QRS = between_100_250]

**Figure 3.3** This arrhythmia would be abbreviated as ventricular tachy-cardia by the majority of physicians. However, our system requires the complete specification of the heart's functional state (see section 2.2.2), so sinus rhythm and complete AV block are added. The ventricular rhythm originates in a focus in the left ventricle, at the rate of 173/min. There is a completly independent sinus rhythm, at the rate of 95/min (Goldman 1976, Figure 14-19).

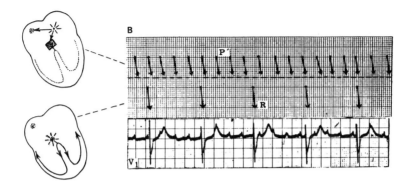

[atrial_tachycardia, av_block_3, junctional_rhythm]  ⟹
    [rhythm_QRS = regular] &
    [dominant_P = abnormal] &
    [rate_of_P = between_100_250] &
    [relation_P_QRS = independent_P_QRS] &
    [dominant_PR = meaningless] &
    [dominant_QRS = normal] &
    [rate_of_QRS = under_60]

**Figure 3.4** Complete AV block with atrial tachycardia and junctional rhythm. The rate of the ventricular beats is 55/min. The rate of the atrial beats is 230/min which is close to atrial flutter. The complete AV block is present (and not only flutter with normal 4:1 block) which causes the independent relationship between QRS complexes and P waves (compare with the ECG description in Figure 2.4 (A)), (Goldman 1976, Figure 13-13B).

[multi_atrial_tachycardia,
 wenckebach,
 junctional_ectopic_beats,
 left_bundle_branch_block]    $\Longrightarrow$
    [rhythm_QRS = irregular] &
    [dominant_P = changing] &
    [rate_of_P = between_100_250] &
    [relation_P_QRS = after_P_some_QRS_miss] &
    [dominant_PR = prolonged] &
    [dominant_QRS = wide_LBBB] &
    [rate_of_QRS = between_100_250 ∨ between_60_100] &
    [ectopic_P(1) = abnormal] &
    [ectopic_PR(1) = shortened ∨ after_QRS_is_P] &
    [ectopic_QRS(1) = wide_LBBB]

**Figure 3.5** Multifocal atrial tachycardia, AV block of type Wenckebach, junctional ectopic beats, and left bundle branch block. Although it is physiologicaly quite possible, for this arrhythmia and the majority of combinations of four or more arrhythmias, we could not find corresponding ECG curves or systematic ECG descriptions in medical literature.

[sinus_bradycardia,
 atral_ectopic_beats,
 av_block_3,
 junctional_ectopic_beats,
 left_bundle_branch_block,
 accelerated_ventricular_rhythm,
 multi_ventricular_ectopic_beats]  $\Longrightarrow$
   [rhythm_QRS = regular] &
   [dominant_P = normal] &
   [rate_of_P = under_60] &
   [relation_P_QRS = independent_P_QRS] &
   [dominant_PR = meaningless] &
   [dominant_QRS = wide_RBBB ∨ wide_LBBB ∨
                   wide_non_specific] &
   [rate_of_QRS = between_60_100] &
   [ectopic_P(1) = absent] &
   [ectopic_PR(1) = meaningless] &
   [ectopic_QRS(1) = wide_RBBB ∨ wide_LBBB ∨
                   wide_non_specific] &
   [ectopic_P(2) = absent] &
   [ectopic_PR(2) = meaningless] &
   [ectopic_QRS(2) = wide_RBBB ∨ wide_LBBB ∨
                   wide_non_specific] &
   [ectopic_P(3) = absent] &
   [ectopic_PR(3) = meaningless] &
   [ectopic_QRS(3) = wide_LBBB] &
   [ectopic_P(4) = abnormal] &
   [ectopic_PR(4) = meaningless] &
   [ectopic_QRS(4) = absent]

**Figure 3.6** One of the most complicated combinations of 7 simple arrhythmias: sinus bradycardia, atrial ectopic beats, complete AV block, junctional ectopic beats, accelerated ventricular rhythm, and multifocal ventricular ectopic beats. From the medical point of view, this is a curiosity of course. In principle, such disturbance in the heart electrical activity is possible, but most likely a corresponding ECG was never recorded.

# Chapter 4

# Knowledge Base Compression by Means of Machine Learning

This chapter describes the compression of the arrhythmia-ECG base. A method is presented that takes the knowledge base as a source of examples of particular features (heart disorders or ECG features) and uses an inductive learning algorithm to obtain their compact descriptions in the form of prediction and diagnostic rules. We present the inductive learning tools, describe the necessary transformations of the arrhythmia-ECG base, give results of the knowledge base compression and compare the compressed rules with knowledge in medical literature.

## 4.1 Learning from examples

We briefly introduce the problem of learning from examples and associated terminology for the purpose of this chapter. The inductive learning program AQ, used for knowledge compression in KARDIO, is described in detail.

### 4.1.1 Definition of the learning task

Machine learning is one of the central and most active areas of research in artificial intelligence (Michalski, Carbonell, and Mitchell 1983, 1986;

Mitchell, Carbonell, and Michalski 1986; Bratko and Lavrač 1987; Kodratoff 1988). The field is concerned with developing methods, techniques and tools for automatic learning, as well as finding the sound
theoretical background for the developed methods.

The techniques and tools used in KARDIO belong to the field of
learning from examples. Here the task is to induce general rules, or
a theory, from a given set of examples. Usually examples are objects
of a known class described in terms of attributes and their values.
The final product of learning are symbolic descriptions of concepts.
It is desired that these descriptions be expressed in high-level, human
understandable terms and forms. Induced descriptions of concepts,
representing different classes of objects, can be used for classification
and prediction, and can account for new observations.

Let us define the problem of learning concepts from examples formally by defining concepts as sets.

Let $U$ be the universal set of *objects* that the learner may en-
counter. There is in principle no limitation on the size of $U$. A *concept*
$C$ can be defined as a subset of objects in $U$:

$$C \subset U$$

To learn concept $C$ means to recognize objects in $C$. In other
words, once $C$ is learned the system is able for any object $X$ in $U$ to
recognize whether $X$ is in $C$. Once we have an object and a concept
description we need a rule, or a procedure, to establish whether the
object belongs to the concept. Such a rule will determine whether
the object satisfies, or matches, the concept description. This can be
formalized as a matching predicate of two arguments:

*match( object, concept_description )*

The definition of matching depends on the learning system.

The source of information for learning are *examples*. An example
for learning concept $C$ is a pair

*(class, object)*

where *object* is an object description and *class* is either "+" or "-". If
*object* belongs to $C$ then *class* = "+" otherwise *class* = "-". We say

that *object* is either a *positive example* or a *negative example* of concept $C$, respectively.

The problem of learning concept $C$ from examples can now be stated formally as follows: Given set $S$ of examples, find formula $F$ such that:

for all objects $X$:
(1) if $X$ is a positive example in the training set $S$
then $X$ matches $F$
(2) if $X$ is a negative example in $S$
then $X$ does not match $F$

As the result of learning, $F$ is the "system's understanding" of concept $C$ as learned from examples. Formula $F$ is called a *concept description* or a *cover*. According to the above definition $F$ and $C$ "agree" on all the given example objects in $S$. We say that concept description $F$ is complete and consistent with regard to the set of learning examples $S$. $F$ is *complete* if it covers all positive examples, i.e. if all positive examples match $F$. $F$ is *consistent* if it does not cover any negative examples, i.e. if no negative example matches $F$.

According to the above definition, the task of learning is to find formula F that is consistent and complete with respect to all the learning examples. However, there is no a priori guarantee that F will correctly classify other objects as well. A major aim of learning is to learn to classify unseen objects (that is, those contained in $U$ but not contained in $S$). Therefore one important criterion of success of learning is the classification accuracy of $F$ on unseen objects.

Sometimes we allow the construction of formula $F$ which misclassifies some objects in $S$. This is sensible in cases when it is known that the learning data contains errors or other kind of uncertainty. These properties of data are usually referred to as *noise*. Noise is typical of some application domains such as medicine. Since the learning data is unreliable, the exact agreement between formula $F$ and concept $C$ on learning set $S$ does not guarantee correctness, and it can therefore be abandoned in favour of some other advantage such as conceptual simplicity of $F$. Although this sort of simplification in learning from noisy data is extremely important and typical of medical applications (e.g. Bratko and Kononenko 1987; Cestnik, Kononenko, and Bratko

1987), it will not be further discussed in this chapter since this feature was not significant for our experiments. There is no noise in the arrhythmia-ECG base. More about reasons for and coping with noise can be found in (Brazdil and Clark 1988).

The usual criteria for measuring the success of a learning system include: classification accuracy, computational complexity, and transparency of induced concept description $F$. In the knowledge compression exercise of this chapter a special attention was paid to the transparency criterion. It is often important that the generated description be understandable by a human in order to tell the user something interesting about the application domain. Such a description can thus also be used by humans directly, without machine help, as an enhancement to humans' own knowledge. This criterion is also very important when the induced descriptions are used in an expert system whose behavior has to be transparent.

Instead of learning a single concept (that is, learning to classify a given object into one of two classes "+" and "-") we may want to classify objects into multiple, disjoint classes. Suppose that objects are described by vectors of attribute values. Let $a_1, a_2, \ldots, a_m$ be attributes and $c_1, c_2, \ldots, c_n$ disjoint concepts. A learning example is again a pair:

*(class, object)*

where *object* is represented by an attribute value vector and *class* is one of the disjoint classes $c_1, \ldots, c_n$. The $i$-th learning example is thus an $(m + 1)$-dimensional vector:

$$(c_j, \ v_{i1}, \ v_{i2}, \ldots, \ v_{im})$$

where $v_{ik}$ is the value of attribute $a_k$ and $c_j$ is the class that the i-th example belongs to. A learning example is a positive example for class $c_j$ and a negative example for all other classes. Now the task is to learn formula $F$ either as a description of all the concepts (typically in the form of a single decision tree) or as a description of particular concepts (typically in the form of separate rules, one for each class).

## 4.1.2 The AQ algorithm

The learning programs used in our experiments belong to the family of programs based on the AQ inductive learning algorithm (Michalski 1969, Michalski and Larson 1975, Michalski 1983). Initial experiments described in (Mozetič 1985a) and (Bratko, Mozetič, and Lavrač 1986) were done with the programs GEM (Reinke 1984) and EXCELL (Becker 1985). Finally, the results of the arrhythmia-ECG base compression, reported in this book, were obtained by more efficient NEWGEM (Mozetič 1985b). NEWGEM was further developed into AQ15 (Hong, Mozetič, and Michalski 1986). This section provides a brief description of NEWGEM and its basic features.

The AQ algorithm learns concept descriptions in the form of if-then rules. Concept descriptions are learned separately for each class. Objects from a given class are considered its positive examples, and all other objects are negative examples of the concept. The algorithm uses attribute descriptions for objects and concepts. Learning examples are vectors of attribute values. Attributes may be of three types: nominal, linear or structured. Concept descriptions in the form of if-then rules are represented in VL1 notation (Variable-valued Logic 1, Michalski and Larson 1975).

In VL1, a *selector* relates an attribute to a value or a "disjunction" of values, for example:

**[weather_type = cloudy ∨ rain]**

Expressions like **cloudy ∨ rain** are called *internal disjunctions*. A *complex* is a conjunction of selectors. The following complex states that the weather is cloudy, the temperature is between 60 and 100 degrees, and the wind blows from the south or west:

**[weather_type = cloudy] & [temperature = 60..100] & [wind_direction = south ∨ west]**

Concept descriptions have the form of if-then rules written as

**Conclusion ⇐ Condition**

It should be noted that "⇐" denotes a relation which is not necessarily implication. Whether the interpretation of "⇐" as implication is correct depends on the learning data (Mozetič and Lavrač 1988). The direction of this arrow "⇐" or "⇒" in this book indicates the natural direction of inference when a rule of this form is used. The conclusion of a rule is a class. The condition of a rule is called a *cover*. A cover is a disjunction of complexes covering all positive examples and none of the negative examples of the concept. The following are two examples of concept descriptions:

> [transport = car]   ⇐   [weather_type = cloudy ∨ rain]
> ∨
> [temperature = 40..60]
>
> [transport = bike]   ⇐   [weather_type = sun] &
> [temperature = 60..100]

The AQ algorithm generates a cover in steps, each step producing one complex of the cover. The algorithm selects a positive example of a class (called a *seed*) and starts with the maximally general complex (one with all possible values for all attributes). The complex is then specialized so that it does not cover any negative example, but still covers the seed. The algorithm keeps several alternative complexes which maximize the number of covered positive examples and are as simple as possible. The set of alternative complexes is called a *star*. When no negative example is covered the algorithm selects the best complex and adds it to the current cover. The algorithm repeats the procedure until all positive examples are covered. The only specialization operation used in the algorithm is removing values from the internal disjunctions of selectors.

The basic learning algorithm is as follows:

Initial cover is empty;
**while** the cover is incomplete (does not cover all
        positive examples)
**do** (1) select an uncovered positive example (a *seed*);
     (2) find a set of alternative complexes that cover the
         seed and no negative example (a *star*);
     (3) select the best complex according to user-defined
         preference criteria;
     (4) add the best complex to the cover.

The algorithm stops when all positive examples are covered. The current cover is then a cover of the class. The algorithm starts with an initial empty cover. In an incremental version of the algorithm the initial cover may be previously learned or supplied by the user.

Generating alternative complexes for a seed in step (2), i.e. generating a star, is as follows:

> Initial set consists of one complex that is maximally
> general complex;
> **while** any complex in the set is inconsistent (does cover
> some negative example)
> **do** (1) select a covered negative example;
> (2) specialize all inconsistent complexes to uncover the
> negative example, but still cover the seed;
> (3) remove those worst complexes that exceed the number
> of permitted alternatives (*maxstar*)

In the initial, maximally general complex, all attributes have all possible values.

*Specialization* of a complex with respect to the seed (that has to be covered) and a negative example (that should not be covered) is done by removing some values from an internal disjunction of values of individual attributes so that the complex remains as general as possible. Notice that alternative specializations are possible, which entails combinatorial complexity of the algorithm. For example, for the complex

**[weather_type = cloudy ∨ rain]**

there are two possible specializations:

**[weather_type = cloudy]**
or
**[weather_type = rain]**

A *measure of quality* for a complex determines a partial order of alternative complexes and is a parameter defined by the user. This constitutes an essential part of the inductive bias used in the system. The measure consists of a list of criteria that are applied to each complex.

When the first criterion cannot discriminate between two complexes the second one is used, and so on. The following is a list of default criteria that order complexes from the best to the worst:

(1) higher number of covered positive examples

(2) lower number of selectors in the complex

(3) lower total number of values in internal disjunctions

The second parameter, definable by the user, is the maximum number of alternative complexes kept by the algorithm at any time (called *maxstar*). Default value for this parameter is 10.

The AQ algorithm enables generating rules of different degrees of generality. Rules may be *general* (selectors having minimum number of attributes, each with maximum number of disjoint values), *minimal* (minimum number of both, attributes and values), or *specific* (maximum number of attributes, each with minimum number of values).

When learning from inconsistent examples, i.e. examples having the same attribute values but belonging to different classes, the AQ algorithm provides three options:

(1) inconsistent examples are treated as positive examples for each class

(2) inconsistent examples are treated as negative examples for each class

(3) inconsistent examples are removed from data

NEWGEM and AQ15 have the incremental learning facility. This was used in machine-aided model construction in Chapter 5. The user may supply rules to be used as initial covers. The programs implement the method of learning with *full memory* (as opposed to learning with *partial memory*). In this type of learning the program remembers all learning examples that were seen so far, as well as the rules it formed. New rules are guaranteed to be correct with respect to all (old and new) learning examples (Reinke 1984, Reinke and Michalski 1988).

NEWGEM and AQ15 are implemented in Berkeley Pascal and run under the Unix operating system on VAX and SUN machines. NEWGEM consists of approximately 6,000 lines of code while AQ15 consists of about 13,000 lines of code. AQ15 is a more complex version of NEWGEM with the *constructive induction* facility where the program's background knowledge is used to construct new attributes not present in input data.

The AQ based programs were earlier applied in the areas of plant disease diagnosis (Michalski and Chilausky 1980, Reinke 1984), chess end-games (Reinke 1984) and others. AQ15 was tested on three medical domains: diagnostics of lymph cancer, prognosis of breast cancer recurrence and diagnostics of the location of primary tumor (Michalski et al. 1986a,b).

## 4.2   Compression of the arrhythmia-ECG base

We describe the compression of the exhaustive arrhythmia-ECG base into a more compact form that is similar to the knowledge found in medical literature and used by experts. We give a motivation and a brief overview of the experiment, describe the necessary transformations of the arrhythmia-ECG base and provide results of the compression. Compressed rules may be used for both, prediction and diagnosis.

### 4.2.1   Motivation and overview

The goal of the arrhythmia-ECG base compression was to extract the essential information from the exhaustive surface knowledge base and to represent it in a compact form that could be used for efficient computer diagnosis as well as to be understood by humans. As such it can also serve as a diagnostic help for experts, even without the use of computers.

The presented method for knowledge base compression (Mozetič 1985a, 1986, 1988) is applicable to any knowledge base with rules where objects are represented by vectors of attribute values, provided that certain conditions are satisfied. The compression method, the needed knowledge base transformations and the conditions for preserving the equivalence of the compressed knowledge with the original knowledge base are described in sections 4.2.2 and 4.2.3.

The main purpose of the arrhythmia-ECG base is ECG diagnosis. As the rules in the knowledge base are logical implications of the form

**Combined_arrhythmia  $\Longrightarrow$  ECG_description**

where **ECG_description** is the disjunction of all possible ECG patterns that **Combined_arrhythmia** can cause, we can apply modus tollens rule of inference on them. Then, if a given ECG does not match **ECG_description** it follows that **Combined_arrhythmia** is eliminated as a diagnostic possibility. All arrhythmias that are not eliminated from the set of possible diagnoses with respect to the given ECG are regarded as possible. Also, as the knowledge base is complete (at the chosen level of detail) the empty set of possible arrhythmias would imply that the given ECG is physiologically impossible.

The exhaustive arrhythmia-ECG base is too bulky for some practical application requirements. If stored as a text file, the 8,314 Prolog clauses that define the arrhythmia-ECG relation, occupy more than 5 MB of store. Also this complexity renders this knowledge base difficult to compare with the standard medical codifications of electrocardiographic knowledge in books. Therefore an attempt has been made to find a more compact representation of the arrhythmia-ECG base that would still allow efficient ECG diagnosis.

The main idea was to use the arrhythmia-ECG base as a source of examples of particular features and to use a learning algorithm to obtain their compact description. Taking the complete arrhythmia-ECG base as a source of examples, the number of examples would be too high for any currently existing inductive learning program. Fortunately it turned out that the complete knowledge base was not necessary for diagnostic purposes. We were able to choose a subset of the knowledge base from which it is relatively easy to reproduce the complete knowledge base using the rules below. In this way the set of learning examples was reduced to a manageable number.

We found a simple combination rule for deriving ECG descriptions for combinations of four simple arrhythmias, namely atrial ectopic beats (**aeb**), junctional ectopic beats (**jeb**), ventricular ectopic beats (**veb**) and multifocal ventricular ectopic beats (**mveb**). The arrhythmia "multifocal ventricular ectopic beats" can be completely omitted also from the set of simple arrhythmias, since it can be represented as a combination of several **veb**. The basis for such a combination rule that enables reducing the learning set is the following: some disorders in the heart are of a permanent nature, while others do not occur regularly. The latter are called ectopic beats. A large number of combined arrhythmias and in particular ECG descriptions are due to the unconstrained combinatorial nature of ectopic beats. If we disregard mutual combinations of different types of ectopic beats we can substantially reduce the number of generated multiple arrhythmias and ECG descriptions. The information thus lost can easily be reconstructed from the remaining rules in the knowledge base. Namely, different types of ectopic beats are both mutually independent and do not affect permanent disorders. The presence or absence of an ectopic beat does not affect the part of the ECG description produced by other disorders.

The learning subset was thus obtained from the original arrhythmia-ECG base by the following reductions:

(1) The subset only deals with 29 simple arrhythmias instead of the original repertoire of 30. We omitted the arrhythmia multifocal ventricular ectopic beats (**mveb**) whose ECG description can be constructed from the description of several ventricular ectopic beats.

(2) Mutual combinations of different types of ectopic beats, namely atrial ectopic beats, junctional ectopic beats, and ventricular ectopic beats, were also discarded.

The reduced arrhythmia-ECG base was obtained by running the model of the heart for all combinations of arrhythmias except the combinations of the above four arrhythmias. The obtained subset containing arrhythmias with at most one ectopic beat was substantially smaller than the original arrhythmia-ECG base having 2,419 combined arrhythmias and 140,966 ECGs: the reduced arrhythmia-ECG base consists of 943 combined arrhythmias related to 5,240 ECG descriptions. Table 4.1 gives characteristics of two different versions of the model of the heart with different complexities.

The reduced arrhythmia-ECG base can be directly used for diag-

| Version of the model of the heart | Simple arr. | Combined arr. | ECG desc. | Store |
|---|---|---|---|---|
| Original model | 30 | 2,419 | 140,966 | 5.1 MB |
| Reduced model | 29 | 943 | 5,240 | 750 KB |

**Table 4.1** Two different versions of the model and the complexity of corresponding knowledge bases, generated by exhaustive simulation of the model (store occupancy is measured on SUN 2/Unix).

nosis, provided that we have a simple combination function mentioned above to handle those cases not explicitly represented in the reduced knowledge base. Although the reduced set of rules is sufficient for diagnostic purposes, an attempt was made towards its transparency and compaction. We used the reduced arrhythmia-ECG base as a source of examples that characterize particular features (heart disorders and ECG features, respectively) and ran the inductive learning program NEWGEM to obtain their compact description in the form of two types of rules:

(1) Compressed *prediction rules* that provide a compact description of selected heart disorders in terms of ECG features. They can be used to answer questions of the prediction-type: given an arrhythmia, what are its corresponding ECGs, i.e., what ECGs may be caused by a given disorder in a heart's component?

(2) Compressed *diagnostic rules* that provide a compact description of causes of individual ECG features. They can be used to answer questions of the diagnostic-type: given an ECG, what arrhythmias could have caused it, i.e., what heart disorders are indicated by given ECG features?

Figure 4.1 gives an overview of the two experiments performed by NEWGEM. First, in the reduced arrhythmia-ECG base, both combined arrhythmias and ECG descriptions have to be represented by attribute value vectors. The transformations into pairs of attribute value vectors and further into the form appropriate for learning, i.e., examples of objects that belong to classes being learned, are described in section 4.2.2. In section 4.2.3 we state the conditions that have to be fulfilled in order to preserve the equivalence of the compressed knowledge with the reduced arrhythmia-ECG base. Section 4.2.4 gives results of the arrhythmia-ECG base compression.

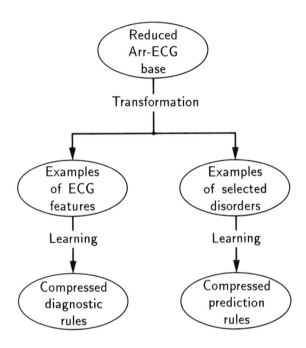

**Figure 4.1** Compression of the reduced arrhythmia-ECG base into two forms: compressed prediction and diagnostic rules.

## 4.2.2 Transformations of the reduced arrhythmia-ECG base into the form appropriate for learning

The reduced arrhythmia-ECG base consists of rules of the form:

**Combined_arrhythmia $\implies$ ECG_description**

We will show how both combined arrhythmias and ECG descriptions can be represented by vectors of attribute values. A combined arrhythmia is a combination of simple arrhythmias. For example, the combined arrhythmia "sinus tachycardia with junctional ectopic beats and wenckebach block" denoted by

**[sinus_tachycardia, wenckebach, junctional_ectopic_beats]**

consists of three simple arrhythmias. As each simple arrhythmia is a disorder of a single heart component and as a particular component cannot be in different states at the same time, we can use the *heart components* as attributes and their *states* as their values. States can either be normal or disordered. Therefore combined arrhythmias such as "sinus tachycardia with junctional ectopic beats and wenckebach block" can be represented by attribute values in the following way:

**[sa_node = st] &**
**[atr_focus = normal] &**
**[av_conduct = wen] &**
**[av_junction = jeb] &**
**[bundle_branches = normal] &**
**[reg_vent_focus = quiet] &**
**[ect_vent_focus = quiet]**

The **quiet** states here are normal states for the two corresponding foci.

In this way rules in the reduced arrhythmia-ECG base may be simply transformed into the form where both combined arrhythmias and ECG descriptions are represented by attribute value vectors. An example of such a rule is the following:

**[sa_node = st] &**
**[atr_focus = normal] &**
**[av_conduct = wen] &**
**[av_junction = jeb] &**
**[bundle_branches = normal] &**
**[reg_vent_focus = quiet] &**
**[ect_vent_focus = quiet]** $\implies$            (1)
    **[rhythm_QRS = irregular] &**
    **[dominant_P = normal] &**
    **[rate_of_P = between_100_250] &**
    **[relation_P_QRS = after_P_some_QRS_miss] &**
    **[dominant_PR = prolonged] &**
    **[dominant_QRS = normal] &**

[rate_of_QRS = between_60_100 ∨ between_100_250] &
[ectopic_P(1) = abnormal] &
[ectopic_PR(1) = shortened ∨ after_QRS_is_P] &
[ectopic_QRS(1) = normal]
∨
[rhythm_QRS = irregular] &
[dominant_P = normal] &
[rate_of_P = between_100_250] &
[relation_P_QRS = after_P_some_QRS_miss] &
[dominant_PR = prolonged] &
[dominant_QRS = normal] &
[rate_of_QRS = between_60_100 ∨ between_100_250] &
[ectopic_P(1) = absent] &
[ectopic_PR(1) = meaningless] &
[ectopic_QRS(1) = normal]

In the arrhythmia-ECG base there is one rule for each combined arrhythmia. The corresponding ECG description may be a disjunction of several ECGs. Whenever possible the internal disjunction is used to obtain a more compact representation of several disjoint ECGs. Note that the rule above defines six ECG patterns. Adopting the VL1 terminology, the first complex includes two internal disjunctions thus representing four ECGs. The remaining two ECGs are represented by the second complex having one internal disjunction.

|  | Combined arrhythmias | ECG descriptions |
|---|---|---|
| Objects | 943 | 5,240 |
| Attributes | 7 | 10 |
| Total values | 36 | 52 |
| Attribute-values space | 52,920 | 2,871,296 |

Table 4.2 Quantitative characteristics of the reduced arrhythmia-ECG base using the attribute-value language.

The reduced arrhythmia-ECG base consists of 943 rules that relate multiple arrhythmias to 5,240 ECG descriptions. Table 4.2. gives characteristics of the two sets of attributes and corresponding values, one for combined arrhythmias and another for ECG descriptions.

To obtain the right input for a learning program we will consider the arrhythmia-ECG rules as relations and represent them as pairs:

**(Combined_arrhythmia, ECG_description)**

Because of the completeness of the arrhythmia-ECG base, **ECG_description** specifies all possible ECGs for a combined arrhythmia. Therefore the arrhythmia-ECG base can be rewritten in a less compact form, having one arrhythmia-ECG pair for each disjoint ECG pattern, i.e.,

$(Arr_i, ECG_i)$

If we fix the order of attributes then we can omit their names. $Arr_i$ is then represented by a vector of states of the heart components

$$Arr_i = (arr_{1i}, arr_{2i}, \ldots, arr_{7i})$$

for the seven components of the heart: **sa_node, atr_focus, av_conduct, av_junction, bundle_branches, reg_vent_focus, ect_vent_focus.** An example is the combined arrhythmia from rule (1):

**(st, normal, wen, jeb, normal, quiet, quiet)**

$ECG_i$ is a vector of values of ECG features:

$$ECG_i = (ecg_{1i}, ecg_{2i}, \ldots, ecg_{10i})$$

for the ten ECG features: **rhythm_QRS, dominant_P, rate_of_P, relation_P_QRS, dominant_PR, dominant_QRS, rate_of_QRS, ectopic_P(1), ectopic_PR(1), ectopic_QRS(1).** An example is the first disjoint ECG pattern from rule (1):

**(irregular, normal, between_100_250,**
**after_P_some_QRS_miss, prolonged, normal,**
**between_60_100, abnormal, shortened, normal)**

Each pair $(Arr_i, ECG_i)$ will be equivalently written as a vector

$$(arr_{1i}, arr_{2i}, \ldots, arr_{7i}, ecg_{1i}, ecg_{2i}, \ldots, ecg_{10i})$$

If we want these vectors to be used for learning we have to specify what are the objects and what are the classes to which the objects belong. Taking into account only one attribute (one heart component or one ECG feature, respectively) and ignoring others, all objects (ECG patterns and combined arrhythmias, respectively) can be divided into classes that correspond to different values of the selected attribute. If this is done for each attribute then the total number of classes is equal to the total number of attribute values. For each class, all vectors having the selected attribute value are considered its positive examples and all other vectors are considered its negative examples. The learning program is then used to find a logical expression that is satisfied by all positive examples and by no negative ones.

In the first experiment with NEWGEM, we selected one heart component and eliminated the others from vectors $(Arr_i, ECG_i)$. The abstracted 11-dimensional attribute vectors of the form

$$(arr_{ki}, ecg_{1i}, ecg_{2i}, \ldots, ecg_{10i})$$

were then ready to be used as examples for learning the description of selected heart disorder $arr_{ki}$ by NEWGEM. It should be noted that each description characterizes one *selected heart disorder* in terms of ECG features, regardless of the states of other heart components. In other words it characterizes an individual simple arrhythmia whether it occurs alone or in a combination with other arrhythmias. The learning procedure was repeated for all heart components, thus generating descriptions of all simple arrhythmias in terms of their ECG features. The obtained rules have the form

**Selected_disorder  $\Rightarrow$  ECG_description**

and can be used for prediction. The results of compression are given in section 4.2.4.

In the second experiment by NEWGEM, characterizations of individual ECG features in terms of heart disorders were constructed. To do that, other ECG features had to be abstracted, giving 8-dimensional attribute vectors of the form

$$(ecg_{ki}, arr_{1i}, arr_{2i}, \ldots, arr_{7i})$$

These vectors were used as examples for learning the description of selected ECG feature $ecg_{ki}$. Generated descriptions of individual ECG features have the form

**Selected_ECG_feature   ⇒   Arrhythmia_description**

where a combined arrhythmia is given in terms of the states of the heart components. By a *selected ECG feature* we mean a value of an individual ECG attribute. These rules may be used for diagnosis. Results of learning diagnostic rules are also given in section 4.2.4.

### 4.2.3   Conditions for preserving the equivalence of rule sets

In this section we state the conditions that guarantee the equivalence between the compressed knowledge and the reduced surface arrhythmia-ECG base that has served as the original source of examples for learning.

As seen in the previous section, transformations of the surface arrhythmia-ECG base had to be performed in order to obtain the form appropriate for applying an inductive learning program. Both combined arrhythmias and ECG descriptions had to be represented in attribute vector form. To obtain the appropriate form for learning, another transformation had to be performed: attribute vectors had to be properly abstracted by selecting one attribute (a heart component or an ECG feature), and ignoring the others. NEWGEM then generated descriptions of heart disorders in the form of prediction rules and descriptions of ECG features in the form of diagnostic rules.

There is a complication, however. The compressed rule sets may not be completely equivalent to the original ones. Through transformations and through compression by an inductive learning program, some information is possibly lost. Therefore additional rules have to be considered when using the compressed rules.

There are two reasons for the loss of information resulting from the transformation of the surface arrhythmia-ECG base into the form appropriate for learning.

The first reason is that the information about "possible" and "impossible" combined arrhythmias and ECG descriptions is lost. The problem is that any combination can be constructed from the abstracted attribute vectors while the original knowledge base states explicitly what all the possible combinations are.

The second reason results from the selection of just one attribute and abstraction of others. To show what information is lost, let us consider the surface arrhythmia-ECG base in the form of Arr-ECG pairs

$$(Arr_i, ECG_i)$$

Let all vectors of ECG features that correspond to a particular *combined arrhythmia Arr* be collected into a set:

$$
\begin{aligned}
ECG(Arr) = \{ECG_i \mid (Arr, ECG_i) \ \in \\
\text{set of } Arr - ECG \text{ pairs}\}
\end{aligned}
\tag{2}
$$

where $ECG_i = (ecg_{1i}, ecg_{2i}, \ldots, ecg_{10i})$ is a vector of values of ECG features and $Arr$ is a vector of values of heart components. Thus $ECG$ is a mapping that assigns to a combined arrhythmia the set of all its corresponding ECG vectors.

Let the set of all vectors of ECG features that correspond to a *selected heart disorder arr* be denoted by:

$$
\begin{aligned}
ECG(arr) = \{ECG_i \mid (arr, ECG_i) \ \in \\
\text{set of abstracted } Arr - ECG \text{ pairs } \}
\end{aligned}
$$

For example, $ECG(arr_{11})$ is obtained as the union of those subsets of (2) that contain $arr_{11}$ as the first component of the vector $(Arr_i, ECG_i)$, i.e.,

$$ECG(arr_{11}) = \cup \{ECG(Arr) \mid Arr = (arr_{11}, \ldots)\}$$

Here we have denoted two different mappings by the same symbol $ECG$. The first mapping operates on combined arrhythmias and the second on single arrhythmias. We will keep this notation as no ambiguity can arise since the mapping is well determined by the number of arguments.

For the sake of the following argument let us suppose that the vector of heart components $Arr_i$ consists of just two components. We will show what happens to the set of corresponding ECG features when only one heart component is selected from vectors $(Arr_i, ECG_i)$. Let us consider the following sets of ECG vectors:

$$
\begin{aligned}
ECG(arr_{11}) &= \{ECG_i \mid (arr_{11}, ECG_i) \ \text{exist}\} \\
ECG(arr_{22}) &= \{ECG_i \mid (arr_{22}, ECG_i) \ \text{exist}\} \\
ECG(arr_{11}, arr_{22}) &= \{ECG_i \mid (arr_{11}, arr_{22}, ECG_i) \ \text{exist}\}
\end{aligned}
$$

For the combined arrhythmia $(arr_{11}, arr_{22})$ the corresponding set of ECG vectors should be equal to the intersection of the sets of ECG vectors of particular heart disorders, i.e.,

$$ECG(arr_{11}, arr_{22}) \;=\; ECG(arr_{11}) \;\cap\; ECG(arr_{22})$$

On the other hand, the set of all ECG vectors for a selected heart disorder is obtained as the union of sets of ECG vectors of arrhythmias having the particular disorder as their component. In the case of two heart components we may write it as the union of the following two sets:

$$ECG(arr_{11}) \;=\; \{ECG_i \mid (arr_{11}, arr_{22}, ECG_i) \quad \text{exist}\} \cup$$
$$\{ECG_i \mid (arr_{11}, arr_{2j}, ECG_i) \quad \text{for} \quad j \neq 2 \quad \text{exist}\}$$

$$ECG(arr_{22}) \;=\; \{ECG_i \mid (arr_{11}, arr_{22}, ECG_i) \quad \text{exist}\} \cup$$
$$\{ECG_i \mid (arr_{1k}, arr_{22}, ECG_i) \quad \text{for} \quad k \neq 1 \quad \text{exist}\}$$

Intersecting these two sets and using the distribution law

$$(A \cup B) \cap (A \cup C) = A \cup (B \cap C)$$

we obtain:

$$ECG(arr_{11}) \;\cap\; ECG(arr_{22}) \;=$$
$$= \{ECG_i \mid (arr_{11}, arr_{22}, ECG_i)\} \cup \qquad\qquad (3)$$
$$(\; \{ECG_i \mid (arr_{11}, arr_{2j}, ECG_i) \; for \; j \neq 2\} \cap$$
$$\{ECG_i \mid (arr_{1k}, arr_{22}, ECG_i) \; for \; k \neq 1\} \;)$$

The intersection of the two sets of ECG vectors thus gives the original set of ECG vectors $ECG(arr_{11}, arr_{22})$ plus some additional ECG vectors, i.e., all the ECG vectors that are in the intersection in (3).

Therefore, the original set of ECG vectors corresponding to a combined arrhythmia cannot be reconstructed as the intersection of sets of ECG vectors corresponding to the arrhythmia's constituent components. Let us further illustrate this by an example. Suppose we have the surface arrhythmia-ECG base consisting of the following rules:

$$Arr_1 \;\Longrightarrow\; ECG_1 \;\vee\; ECG_2$$
$$Arr_2 \;\Longrightarrow\; ECG_1 \;\vee\; ECG_3$$
$$Arr_3 \;\Longrightarrow\; ECG_4$$

This is the corresponding set of arrhythmia-ECG pairs:

$(Arr_1, ECG_1)$
$(Arr_1, ECG_2)$
$(Arr_2, ECG_1)$
$(Arr_2, ECG_3)$
$(Arr_3, ECG_4)$

Suppose that combined arrhythmias are determined by just two components, the first having two possible values $arr_{11}$ and $arr_{12}$, and the second having the possible values $arr_{21}$ and $arr_{22}$. Suppose the combined arrhythmias are:

$$
\begin{aligned}
Arr_1 &= (arr_{11}, arr_{21}) \\
Arr_2 &= (arr_{12}, arr_{22}) \\
Arr_3 &= (arr_{11}, arr_{22})
\end{aligned}
\tag{4}
$$

The corresponding sets of ECG vectors are then the following:

$$
\begin{aligned}
ECG(arr_{11}, arr_{21}) &= \{ECG_1, ECG_2\} & \text{(5a)} \\
ECG(arr_{12}, arr_{22}) &= \{ECG_1, ECG_3\} & \text{(5b)} \\
ECG(arr_{11}, arr_{22}) &= \{ECG_4\} & \text{(5c)}
\end{aligned}
$$

Abstracting with respect to $arr_{11}$ and $arr_{22}$ gives:

$$
\begin{aligned}
ECG(arr_{11}) &= \{ECG_1, ECG_2, ECG_4\} \\
ECG(arr_{22}) &= \{ECG_1, ECG_3, ECG_4\}
\end{aligned}
\tag{6}
$$

For the combined arrhythmia $(arr_{11}, arr_{22})$, the intersection of sets of ECG vectors corresponding to the constituents $arr_{11}$ and $arr_{22}$ is:

$$
ECG(arr_{11}) \cap ECG(arr_{22}) = \{ECG_1, ECG_4\}
$$

This differs from the original set (5c):

$$
ECG(arr_{11}, arr_{22}) = \{ECG_4\}
$$

What can be done to enable reconstruction of the original $(Arr_i, ECG_i)$ pairs from the abstracted pairs $(arr_j, ECG_j)$? When the abstracted pairs are used for prediction, the following exception rule should be applied:

$$
(arr_{11}, arr_{22}) \quad \Rightarrow \quad not \ ECG_1
\tag{7}
$$

This rule should be added to the prediction rules obtained after the compression of abstracted $(arr_j, ECG_j)$ vectors. Since the vectors

$ECG_1$ and $ECG_4$ are positive examples for learning the description of class $arr_{11}$, since $ECG_1$ and $ECG_4$ are positive examples for $arr_{22}$ and since the derived concept descriptions cover all positive examples, the learned ECG descriptions for $arr_{11}$ and $arr_{22}$ both cover $ECG_1$ and $ECG_4$. When using the induced rules, the exception rule (7) has to be taken into account.

From the foregoing example we may see that ECGs for combined arrhythmias cannot be reliably derived from abstracted vectors $(arr_j, ECG_j)$. The straightforward intersection of ECG sets of the constituent disorders gives excess ECGs if:

(1) there exist two combined arrhythmias with different attribute values in at least two attributes having the same ECG vectors (for example this is the case with [5a] and [5b]), and

(2) there is another combined arrhythmia having these two particular disorders as its constituent components and its set of corresponding ECG vectors contains at least one different ECG vector, e.g., (5c).

A similar argument applies also to the compressed diagnostic rules. However, in the case of the reduced arrhythmia-ECG base it was found that for diagnostic rules the described situation never occurs. In the case of compressed prediction rules this situation does occur. We easily generate exception rules by checking the conditions above. If we do not want to mar the uniformity and explanation power of compressed rules by adding exception rules we may ignore the exceptions, but also be aware that the compressed rules cover some additional problem space.

The discussion above shows that some information may be lost when abstracting Arr-ECG vectors. Some information may further be lost in the induction process. Generalizations performed by the learning program simplify ECG descriptions (and heart state descriptions, respectively) thus covering also a part of the "empty" problem space. Therefore, using the compressed prediction and diagnostic rules, it is no longer possible to distinguish between possible and impossible ECG descriptions (and combined arrhythmias, respectively).

Let us summarize the reasons why the compressed rule sets are not necessarily equivalent to the original ones.

(1) The first reason is that during the transformation when selecting a particular component and abstracting others the information about possible and impossible combined arrhythmias (and ECG descriptions, respectively) is lost. Any combination can be constructed from the transformed rules while the original knowledge base states explicitly what all the possible combinations are.

(2) The second reason, again because of the transformation when selecting a particular component and abstracting others, covers the following situation: when some combined arrhythmias (and ECG descriptions, respectively) defined with different values in at least two components imply equal ECG descriptions (and combined arrhythmias, respectively), those might be incorrectly derived as consequences of some other combined arrhythmias (ECG descriptions, respectively), not stated in the original knowledge base.

(3) The third reason results from the application of an inductive learning program that generates concept descriptions that cover also a part of the "empty" problem space. Therefore it is also not possible to distinguish between possible and impossible consequences (ECG descriptions and combined arrhythmias, respectively) with regard to the original rules.

The compressed knowledge base is thus not equivalent to the original one. However, the conclusions that can be derived from the compressed rules are equivalent to those derivable from the original rules if one is able

- first, to recognize objects not occurring in the original knowledge base, thus solving problems stemming from the first and third reason above;

- second, to compare the compressed rules with the original knowledge base, and, if necessary, add exception rules of the form

**Combined_arrhythmia** $\Longrightarrow$ **not ECG_description**

and

**ECG_description** $\Longrightarrow$ **not Arrhythmia_description**

respectively. The procedure is straightforward. Compressed prediction rules are used to predict ECG features for all possible combined arrhythmias. Compressed diagnostic rules are used to predict combined arrhythmias for all possible ECG patterns. In both cases results are compared with the original knowledge base and the differences between the two are exception rules that are to be added to the compressed rules. This solves problems stemming from the second reason above.

## 4.2.4   Results of knowledge base compression

Having transformed the knowledge base into the appropriate form as described in section 4.2.2, compressed *prediction rules* were derived by selecting heart disorders as classes to be learned. Prediction rules have the form:

**Selected_disorder   ⇒   ECG_description**

where a "selected heart disorder" is, for example, the atrial focus being in the tachycardic state. The learning program NEWGEM was used to find minimal (in length) ECG descriptions that characterize heart disorders. Thus obtained compressed prediction rules answer the question: what ECGs may be caused by a given disorder in a heart's component? Besides, our aim was to investigate the transparency of compressed rules and compare them with the medical literature.

Here are two examples of prediction rules induced by NEWGEM:

**[av_conduct   = mob2]   ⇒**
   **[relation_P_QRS  =  after_P_some_QRS_miss] &**
   **[dominant_PR  =  normal]**

**[av_conduct   = avb3]   ⇒**
   **[rhythm_QRS  =  regular] &**
   **[relations_P_QRS  =  independent_P_QRS]**

The entire prediction rule base (descriptions of selected disorders) with some exception rules is given in Appendix C.

The second experiment with NEWGEM was performed to obtain compressed *diagnostic rules* by selecting individual ECG features as classes to be learned. Diagnostic rules providing a compact description of causes of specific ECG features have the form:

**Selected_ECG_feature ⇒ Arrhythmia_description**

where a "selected ECG feature" is, for example, P wave having an abnormal shape. NEWGEM was used again to find minimal length descriptions. The induced descriptions indicate possible causes of particular ECG features. The rules can answer the question: what heart disorders are indicated by a given ECG feature? These rules can be used for direct diagnosis from the patient's ECG.

As shown in section 4.2.3 the compressed knowledge base is not necessarily equivalent to the original one and has to be used with care. To be used correctly, in general we have to add rules that compensate for the loss of information results from selecting one ECG feature and abstracting the others. Fortunately, in the case of compressed diagnostic rules no exception rule is needed. Of course, the combination rules mentioned in section 4.2.1 have to be considered. These are necessary because the input to learning was the reduced arrhythmia-ECG base.

Here are two examples of diagnostic rules:

**[relation_P_QRS = after_P_some_QRS_miss] ⇒**
    **[av_conduct = wen ∨ mob2]**
    **∨**
    **[atr_focus = afl ∨ af] &**
    **[av_conduct = normal]**

**[relation_P_QRS = independent_P_QRS] ⇒**
    **[av_conduct = avb3]**
    **∨**
    **[atr_focus = af] &**
    **[av_conduct = normal]**

The entire diagnostic rule base with a diagnostic algorithm is given in Appendix B. NEWGEM was run to generate compressed rules of *minimal* length. If NEWGEM was run to obtain the most specific descriptions this would improve the computational efficiency of the diagnostic program, but would increase the representational complexity affect and the transparency of the compressed rules. Here is an example of a compressed rule of the *specific* type.

[relation_P_QRS = after_P_some_QRS_miss] ⇒
   [*av_conduct* = *wen* ∨ *mob2*] &
   [*atr_focus* = *wp* ∨ *at* ∨ *mat* ∨ *aeb* ∨ *normal*] &
   [*av_junction* = *jeb* ∨ *normal*] &
   [*reg_vent_focus* = *quiet*]
   ∨
   [*atr_focus* = afl ∨ af] &
   [*av_conduct* = normal] &
   [*sa_node* = normal] &
   [*av_junction* = jeb ∨ normal] &
   [*reg_vent_focus* = quiet]

This description is the most specific. The terms in italics represent the minimal description equal to the first of the two minimal diagnostic rules above.

We were particularly interested in the complexity of compressed prediction and diagnostic rules. Complexity was measured by the number of complexes, the number of selectors and the number of all values of attributes in all rules.

| Attributes | Rules | Compl. | Sel. | Val. | Time |
|---|---|---|---|---|---|
| sa_node | 6 | 10 | 28 | 34 | 4:58 h |
| atr_focus | 7 | 16 | 51 | 101 | 7:02 h |
| av_conduct | 7 | 11 | 29 | 54 | 6:12 h |
| av_junction | 5 | 36 | 165 | 320 | 10:26 h |
| bundle_branches | 3 | 11 | 33 | 66 | 4:33 h |
| reg_vent_focus | 6 | 9 | 27 | 58 | 3:28 h |
| ect_vent_focus | 2 | 9 | 25 | 54 | 2:37 h |
| Total | 36 | 102 (2.8) | 358 (3.5) | 687 (1.9) | 39 h |

**Table 4.3** Complexity of descriptions of selected heart disorders and times needed for learning.

Complexity of prediction rules describing selected heart disorders and time needed for learning is given in Table 4.3. The last column in Table 4.3 is CPU time (without system time) used for learning by the program NEWGEM on SUN 2/Unix workstation. The last row of the table gives, in addition to the total number, the average number of complexes per rule, selectors per complex, and values per selector. The numbers show that compressed rules are relatively simple.

| Attributes | Rules | Compl. | Sel. | Val. | Time |
|---|---|---|---|---|---|
| rhythm_QRS | 2 | 5 | 12 | 35 | 2:32 h |
| dominant_P | 4 | 4 | 7 | 21 | 3:27 h |
| rate_of_P | 6 | 9 | 23 | 55 | 4:44 h |
| relation_P_QRS | 4 | 7 | 14 | 29 | 4: 8 h |
| dominant_PR | 6 | 9 | 21 | 43 | 4:44 h |
| dominant_QRS | 7 | 10 | 17 | 51 | 4:55 h |
| rate_of_QRS | 6 | 15 | 47 | 124 | 4:42 h |
| ectopic_P(1) | 3 | 6 | 10 | 28 | 2:20 h |
| ectopic_PR(1) | 6 | 10 | 19 | 47 | 3:37 h |
| ectopic_QRS(1) | 8 | 13 | 27 | 47 | 4:57 h |
| Total | 52 | 88 (1.7) | 197 (2.2) | 480 (2.4) | 40 h |

Table 4.4 Complexity of descriptions of individual ECG features and times needed for learning.

Complexity of diagnostic rules describing individual ECG features and time needed for learning are given in Table 4.4. The last column in Table 4.4 is again CPU time used for learning by NEWGEM on SUN 2/Unix workstation. In both experiments the system CPU time was about the same as CPU time for learning. This means that for the entire compression nearly one week of total CPU time was needed (2*40h+39h)! As we had to run the learning program 17 times (10+7 attributes), each time on 5240 learning examples and in average 5 classes ((52+36)/17), this is not surprising. This large computation time is not problematic as the knowledge base compression is to be performed only once to generate simple and efficient diagnostic rules. The diagnostic algorithm, implemented in C-Prolog (this is an interpreter, not a compiler), needs typically just few seconds to find a diagnosis using the compressed rules.

It is also interesting to compare the complexity of the original exhaustive knowledge base and the compressed knowledge bases. Table 4.5 summarizes the complexity of the rules resulting from the compression of the reduced arrhythmia-ECG base. The compression effects are given in terms of the number of rules and their complexity and in terms of storage needed when storing different representations simply as text files.

| | Original arr-ECG base | Reduced arr-ECG base | | Compressed prediction rules | | Compressed diagnostic rules | |
|---|---|---|---|---|---|---|---|
| Rules | 2,419 | 943 | | 36 | | 52 | |
| Complexes | 8,314 | 1,659 | (1.8) | 102 | (2.8) | 88 | (1.7) |
| Selectors | 58,197 | 16,590 | (10.0) | 358 | (3.5) | 197 | (2.2) |
| Values | 986,762 | 19,143 | (1.2) | 687 | (1.9) | 480 | (2.4) |
| Store | 5.1 MB | 750 KB | | 18 KB | | 10 KB | |

**Table 4.5** Comparison of the original knowledge base, the reduced arrhythmia-ECG base and the compressed prediction and diagnostic rules.

In Table 4.5, column 1, a "rule" corresponds to a combined arrhythmia, a "complex" corresponds to a Prolog clause. "Selectors" denote all the references to attributes in a whole rule set. The last row gives the sizes of these representations if stored as text files. Numbers in brackets give average number of complexes per rule, number of selectors per complex and number of values per selector, respectively. By comparing the total number of rules or complexes of both compressed rule bases with the reduced arrhythmia-ECG base, we get the approximate compression factor between 18 (943/52) and 25 (943/36). Comparing the number of selectors and storage needed when saved as text files (which is probably the best measure) we get the approximate compression factor between 40 and 85 (16,590/197, 750/10, 16,590/358, 750/18). Diagnostic rules representing the major part of the rule base needed for diagnosis are about 75 times smaller than the reduced arrhythmia-ECG base.

## 4.3 Comparison of compressed prediction rules with medical literature

In medical literature, knowledge is frequently not presented systematically or explicitly, and a great deal of background knowledge is expected from the reader. We believe that making explicit what is implicitly assumed in literature or by experts is an important contribution to the systematization and formalization of domain knowledge, especially with the view to computer application. Automating this process is a considerable step that may help to overcome the knowledge acquisition bottleneck when developing medical expert systems.

In this view, we here assess prediction rules generated by NEWGEM. It is important that these rules be meaningful from the medical point of view. Some of the generated descriptions correspond very well to the definitions in medical literature (e.g. Goldman 1976, Phibbs 1973, Schamroth 1980) while others are considerably more complex. Each rule is a description of a selected heart disorder, whether combined with other disorders or not. Typically, the extracted rules are more specific than descriptions in the medical literature, which omit many details that are not necessary for an intelligent reader with a background in physiology. Such a reader can usually infer the missing detail from his background knowledge. However, detailed knowledge must be made explicit in the case of computer application. For example, if all the necessary detail is not stated in form of rules of a diagnostic expert system, a great deal of background knowledge and inference would have to be added, which would be extremely difficult and its correctness hard to verify.

In the sequel we present some descriptions of selected disorders and compare them with the descriptions found in medical literature (Goldman 1976, Phibbs 1973). All complexes in rules are accompanied by a pair of numbers $(N_1:N_2)$, where $N_1$ denotes the *total* number of learning examples covered by a complex, and $N_2$ the number of learning examples covered *uniquely* by this and no other complex.

**[sa_node = st]**  ⇒                                  % sinus tachycardia
    **[dominant_P = normal]** &
    **[rate_of_P = between_100_250] (390:390)**

Goldman (1976, p. 205): A regular sinus rhythm with a rate in excess of 100.

Phibbs (1973, p. 10): In sinus tachycardia the rate is over 100. It will rarely exceed 160.

Comment: Both medical definitions describe the same rate of P waves but neither of them mentions the shape of the P wave. Normal shape of the P wave is assumed by an intelligent reader. Notice that the qualitative value **between_100_250** means high rate not necssarily bound exactly by 100 and 250.

**[sa_node = sr]**  ⇒                                  % sinus rhythm
    **[rhythm_QRS = regular]** &
    **[dominant_P = normal]** &
    **[rate_of_P = between_60_100] (324:324)**
    ∨
    **[dominant_P = normal]** &
    **[rate_of_P = between_60_100]** &
    **[relation_P_QRS = after_P_some_QRS_miss]** &
    **[dominant_PR = prolonged] (66:66)**

Goldman (1976, p. 205, 380): The average rate is 60–100 beats/minute. ... Regular and equal atrial and ventricular rates; P waves are normal; the P-R interval is normal.

Phibbs (1973, p. 10): In summary, a normal or "sinus" mechanism is diagnosed when (1) P waves appear at regular intervals. (2) Each P wave is followed at a regular normal interval by a ventricular (QRS) complex. (3) All P waves and ventricular (QRS) complexes have the same contour and configuration.

Comment: The first complex in the description of the sinus rhythm corresponds perfectly with the descriptions in the medical literature. The second (alternative) complex may appear when sinus rhythm is combined with another heart disorder. We must be aware that each rule represents a description of a selected heart disorder, possibly combined with other disorders.

[av_conduct = wen]   ⇒        % AV block of Wenckebach type
[relation_P_QRS = after_P_some_QRS_miss] &
[dominant_PR = prolonged] (543:543)

Goldman (1976, p. 380): Cyclically there is progressive lengthening of the PR interval from beat to beat until a P wave is not followed by a QRS.

Phibbs (1973, p. 71): As a rule of thumb, a changing P-R interval associated with a changing ventricular rhythm makes it likely that the mechanism is a Wenckebach A-V block.

Comment: The generated description of the Wenckebach disorder corresponds to the conventional medical descriptions. The arrhythmia Wenckebach is caused by a distorted state of the atrio-ventricular (AV) pathway in the heart, presented in the model by the state of the heart **av_conduct = wen**. Although more appropriate, it was decided not to introduce a new value **progressive_lengthening** of **dominant_PR** trying to keep the description language as compact as possible but still sufficient to discriminate between different disorders.

[av_junction = jt]   ⇒                      % junctional tachycardia
[rate_of_P = under_60..between_100_250] &
[dominant_PR = meaningless] &
[dominant_QRS = normal ∨ wide_LBBB ∨ wide_RBBB] &
[rate_of_QRS = between_100_250] &
[ectopic_QRS(1) = wide_LBBB ∨ wide_RBBB ∨
            wide_non_specific ∨ absent ∨ none] (141:118)
∨
[rhythm_QRS = regular] &
[dominant_P = abnormal ∨ absent] &
[relation_P_QRS = meaningless ∨ after_P_always_QRS ∨
            independent_P_QRS] &
[dominant_PR = meaningless ∨ shortened ∨
            after_QRS_is_P] &
[dominant_QRS = normal ∨ wide_LBBB ∨ wide_RBBB] &
[rate_of_QRS = between_100_250] &
[ectopic_PR(1) = meaningless ∨ after_QRS_is_P ∨ none] &
[ectopic_QRS(1) = wide_LBBB ∨ wide_RBBB ∨
            wide_non_specific ∨ none] (111:72)

∨

[rhythm_QRS = regular] &
[relation_P_QRS = meaningless ∨ after_P_always_QRS] &
[dominant_PR = meaningless ∨ after_QRS_is_P] &
[dominant_QRS = wide_LBBB] &
[rate_of_QRS = between_100_250] &
[ectopic_QRS(1) = wide_LBBB] (10:6)

∨

[rhythm_QRS = regular] &
[rate_of_P = zero ∨ between_100_250] &
[dominant_PR = meaningless ∨ after_QRS_is_P] &
[dominant_QRS = wide_RBBB] &
[rate_of_QRS = between_100_250] &
[ectopic_QRS(1) = wide_RBBB] (14:6)

∨

[rhythm_QRS = regular] &
[rate_of_P = zero ∨ between_100_250] &
[dominant_PR = meaningless ∨ after_QRS_is_P] &
[dominant_QRS = normal] &
[rate_of_QRS = between_100_250] (37:6)

∨

[dominant_P = abnormal] &
[dominant_PR = shortened] &
[dominant_QRS = normal ∨ wide_LBBB ∨ wide_RBBB] &
[rate_of_QRS = between_100_250] &
[ectopic_PR(1) = normal ∨ prolonged ∨ shortened] (9:9)

Goldman (1976, p. 234): The rate can vary from 120–200. The ventricular rhythm is regular. The P waves may precede, be buried in, or follow the QRS complexes, depending on the site of origin.

Phibbs (1973, p. 29): If the ECG records a perfectly regular rate (160–280) with narrow QRS complexes, the presumptive diagnosis is supraventricular paroxymal tachycardia. ... If no P waves are visible, the rhythm may be either atrial or junctional. ... If abnormally shaped P waves appear just before or just after the QRS complex, the diagnosis is A-V junctional tachycardia.

Comment: The description of junctional tachycardia consists of six complexes. Generated descriptions correspond to the ones in the medical literature regarding the PR interval (it is not **normal**). Where specified, the shape of the P wave is also not normal. In some cases the shape of the P wave is not specified to minimize the length of descriptions (recall that NEWGEM was executed in the "minimal-length mode").

As shown by these examples and further in Appendix C, some descriptions of selected heart disorders are very compact and describe just the most characteristic properties of the disorder that are also the most relevant for discriminating between disorders. Other descriptions are extremely complex, covering the cases when a disorder appears in a combination with other disorders. Such complete descriptions are not particularly useful in the sense of capturing essential physiological mechanisms (e.g. junctional tachycardia given in the example above). Typically, the generated descriptions are more specific than descriptions in the medical literature, which omit many details essential for computer diagnosis.

# Chapter 5

# Further Developments: Hierarchies and Learning of Models

In this chapter we describe more recent research on semi-automatic construction of qualitative models. We present a knowledge acquisition system for the construction of deep knowledge bases, represented by qualitative models. We assume that a model is defined by its structure (a set of components and their connections) and functions of the individual components. The system consists of three subsystems: a *learner* that hypothesizes functions of components from instances of their behavior, a *debugger* that locates faulty functions of components and proposes how to correct them, and an *interpreter* that can use the hypothesized model to derive its behavior. The system supports top-down development of a model, starting with an abstract definition and progressing to more and more detailed ones. A more formal and detailed description of the system appears in (Mozetič 1987a,b, 1988).

## 5.1 Overview of the model learning system

The system described in this chapter is an extension of research presented in previous chapters. We are here concerned with two problems: how to construct a deep knowledge base, and how to make it operational. We restrict ourselves to domains for which a deep knowledge may be conveniently represented by a qualitative model.

We used a subset of the arrhythmia diagnosis problem to test the system for learning of qualitative models. The manually constructed model of the heart described in chapters 2 and 3 played a twofold role in the experiments. First, it provided as an oracle examples of the model behavior from which the system hypothesized and refined the model of the heart. Second, it served as an evaluator of the automatically constructed models, and as a target to be reached through the model refinement cycles. Experiments show that a relatively small number of steps was needed to construct the correct model.

We adopt the reductionist's view to qualitative modeling, namely that the behavior of a model can be derived solely from its structure and the behavior of its components (de Kleer and Brown 1983). The structure of the model is defined by a set of its constituent components and their interconnections. Usually, qualitative physics assumes that a classical model, expressed by a set of differential equations, is already known. The classical model is then translated into qualitative constraints over variables, often using just values +, - and 0 (Kuipers 1985). In contrast, we are concerned with problems where classical models do not exist or are too complicated to be expressed only by such simple constraints.

We assume that only partial knowledge about the model is given — its structure. Further, instances of the behavior of the model and its constituent components are provided from which the learning part of the system hypothesizes functions of the components. The interpreter of the model is then able to derive its behavior and the user may compare it with the intended behavior of the model. When a difference between the derived and the intended behavior of the model occurs, a debugger is invoked. The debugger locates faulty hypotheses defining functions of components; proposes instances of behavior that guarantee the intended behavior of the model, and invokes the learner that incrementally refines the hypotheses. The cycle of deriving the behavior of the model, debugging the model and invoking incremental learning is repeated until the intended behavior of the model is achieved. An overview of the system is outlined in Figure 5.1.

It is important to point out that the system embodies two types of learning: initial data-driven learning that generalizes instances of

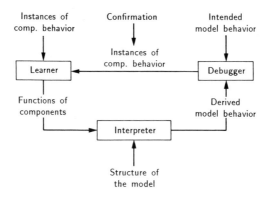

**Figure 5.1** An overview of the system for semi-automatic construction of qualitative models.

components behavior, into rules on the basis of similarities and differences, and does not require any user interaction. This is learning from examples as in the AQ (Michalski 1969) or ID3 (Quinlan 1983) systems, here only enhanced to produce descriptions in a more expressive language. The second type of learning is model-driven, where the debugger actively constructs instances of components' behavior satisfying the intended model behavior and queries the user for confirmation. This part is similar to the MIS (Shapiro 1981) and MARVIN (Sammut and Banerji 1986) systems. Our system therefore offers a ᵤradeoff between the initial amount of knowledge provided by the user and the time he is willing to spend on debugging the model.

The debugging and refinement is completed when the user believes that the knowledge base is correct and complete with respect to the actual system in the real world, i.e., the model behaves as intended. The system then offers the user the possibility to push the level of detail, that is, to develop a qualitative model on a more detailed level of abstraction. There are several advantages if a model is represented on different levels of abstraction. When refining a model on a more detailed level, the debugger makes use of the abstract level to guide the search for corrections to faulty functions of components. Besides that, it enables more efficient use of the model for tasks that are otherwise computationally expensive, e.g., for diagnosing abnormal states of the model.

## 5.2    Knowledge representation

In this section some basic logic programming (Lloyd 1984) and deductive database concepts (Lloyd and Topor 1984, 1985, 1986) are presented. Properties of the deductive nonrecursive database formalism (DNDB) are discussed. The formalism is used to represent qualitative models and provides a sound formal basis to formalize the learning, debugging and interpretation tasks.

### 5.2.1    Deductive nonrecursive database formalism (DNDB)

A *database clause* is a typed first order formula of the form

$$A \quad \leftarrow \quad L_0, \ldots, L_N.$$

where $A$ is an atom and each $L_i$ is a literal (an atom or the negation of an atom). An atom is a predicate applied to a number of terms. A term is either a variable, a constant or a function applied to a number of terms (compound term). An example of atom is $p(X, f(Y))$. $A$ is called the *head* and the conjunction of literals $L_0, \ldots, L_N$ the *body* of the clause. The body may be empty, in which case the clause is called a *fact*. All variables in atoms are assumed to be implicitly universally quantified in front of the clause. A fact with no variables is called a *ground fact*. A *deductive database* is a finite set of database clauses. It will be called *nonrecursive* if its predicates can be partitioned into levels so that the bodies of the clauses in the definitions of higher level predicates contain only lower level predicates. Lloyd and Topor (1985) call such databases "hierarchical"; however, we here use the term "nonrecursive" instead, because in our extension the term "hierarchical" will refer to abstraction hierarchy.

The set of all database clauses with the same predicate in the head forms a predicate definition. As a predicate definition consists of clauses that have the form of implication, the definition of the predicate specifies only the sufficiency condition for A to hold. Such a form allows the system only to infer positive information (i.e., A is true). In order to be able to deduce negative information as well (i.e., not A is true), our databases will be always interpreted under the closed world assumption.

The deductive database formalism uses a typed language. It turns out that types provide a natural way of specifying the domain of a database. We emphasize that, in contrast to the usual restriction in deductive databases, in the proposed formalism compound terms are allowed to appear as arguments of predicates in a database and queries. However, under a reasonable restriction of allowing only nonrecursive types (the same restriction as for a nonrecursive database), we can ensure that each query can have at most a finite number of answers. This restriction bans recursive data types, which means that there are only a finite number of ground terms of each type, and consequently, that each query can have at most a finite number of answers (Lloyd and Topor 1985). This also means that the DNDB formalism is equivalent to propositional calculus in the sense of what can be expressed in the two formalisms. However, having variables, functions and rules, the DNDB form enables more compact representation of concepts.

The use of a database system based on first order logic for knowledge representation has the attractive property that it has a well-developed theory and offers a uniform formalism to represent facts, rules and queries. Further, answering a query may be regarded as a logical deduction and can be efficiently implemented using a Prolog-like system as the query evaluator. The only inference rule used is SLDNF-resolution, which is a linear resolution augmented with the negation as failure rule. To ensure that the negation is handled properly (which is not the case with standard Prolog systems) a *safe* computation rule must be used which only selects negative literals that are ground. In this case it can be shown that the inference rule is *sound*, that is, all answers to a query are logical consequences of a completed database

(Lloyd and Topor 1985). For a nonrecursive database the inference rule is also *complete*, that is all logical consequences can be deduced from the completed database (Lloyd and Topor 1986). Since logical consequence and deduction are equivalent in the case of DNDB, in the sequel we use the symbol "$\models$" to denote both.

## 5.2.2    Representing qualitative models

A qualitative model is represented in a nonrecursive database formalism and can be conveniently divided into three layers of knowledge representation (Mozetič 1987a): the structure of the model, functions of its constituent components, and utility predicates (Figure 5.2).

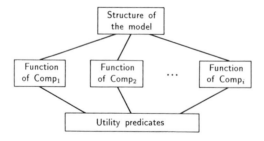

**Figure 5.2** Layers of knowledge representation for qualitative models.

The structure of the model is defined by a set of components and connections between them. A Horn clause (a special case of a database clause, where all the literals in the body are positive) is used to represent the structure of the model. The head of the clause denotes a relation between qualitative state of the model, an input and an output from the model. In the body of the clause (a conjunction of atoms) each predicate denotes a component of the model, and shared variables between atoms represent connections between components.

Each component is denoted by a predicate that relates its qualitative state, an input and an output. The function of a component determines the set of its possible behaviors and is represented by a predicate definition, i.e., a set of database clauses with the same head. Background knowledge in the form of utility predicates may be used in a component definition. Note that a model definition is a special case of a component definition, and that any model may be used as a subcomponent in some super-model.

From the complete definition of a model its behavior can be derived through logical deduction. An instance of the behavior of either a model or a component is represented as a ground fact. Formally, the definition of a model may be regarded as a set of axioms, consisting of axioms that define the structure of the model *Struct*, functions of the individual components *Funct(Comps)* and utility predicates *Util*. Among the derived theorems, some represent instances of the model behavior *Behav(Model)* and instances of the components behavior *Behav(Comps)*:

$$Struct \ \& \ Funct(Comps) \ \& \ Util \ \models$$
$$Behav(Model) \ \& \ Behav(Comps)$$

## 5.2.3    Hierarchy of models

It is useful to represent a qualitative model on several levels of abstraction. In this case a model consists of a hierarchy of single-level models, where the top model is the most abstract (also the simplest), and the bottom model in the hierarchy is the most detailed (also the most complicated). A hierarchy of models helps the learning of a model, and also improves the efficiency of model interpretation when we use the model for diagnosis. Hierarchy can also improve explanation capabilities of the system.

As an example, let us consider a very abstract model of the electrical activity in the heart. From this extremely abstract view, the heart is simply a box consisting of a generator of electrical impulses (giving the pace of the heart). These impulses cause, through another component, some external manifestation, called ECG (see Figure 5.3).

**Figure 5.3** A very abstract model of the heart.

The heart can suffer from an arrhythmia that can be modeled as an internal state of the generator of impulses that affects its behavior. The model consists of only two components: a generator of impulses (**gen_imp**) and a generator of ECG descriptions (**imp_ecg**). The model has no input and relates any state of the heart (**Arrhythmia**) to the output (**ECG**):

**heart( Arrhythmia, ECG )** ←
    **gen_imp( Arrhythmia, Impulse ),**
    **imp_ecg( Impulse, ECG ).**

The function of the impulse generator may be represented by two ground unit clauses:

**gen_imp( slow_rhythm, under_60 ).**
**gen_imp( fast_rhythm, over_60 ).**

A definition of the generator of ECG descriptions completes the example. Note that here **Rate** denotes a universally quantified variable:

**imp_ecg( Rate, Rate ).**

The above model of the heart is extremely coarse. If the user wants to push the level of detail in representation, the system allows him to:

(1) specify more detailed structure, replacing a component in the model by a set of components (Figure 5.4),

(2) refine values of variables by defining hierarchies of values (Figure 5.5),

(3) introduce new variables, not relevant on the more abstract level.

In this more detailed model, the heart consists of the atria, the ventricles and the AV (atrio-ventricular) node that conducts impulses

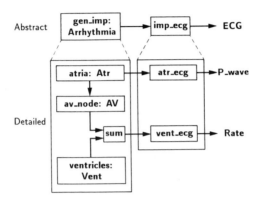

**Figure 5.4** Refinement of the model's structure.

from the atria to the ventricles. Further, in the ECG, not only the rate of the heart beats is of interest, but the presence of the P wave as well.

The more detailed structure of the model is represented by the following clause:

```
heart( arr(Atr, AV, Vent), ecg(P_wave, Rate) )  ←
    atria( Atr, ImpAtr ),
    av_node( AV, ImpAtr, ImpHis ),
    ventricles( Vent, ImpVent0 ),
    sum( ImpVent0, ImpHis, ImpVent ),
    atr_ecg( ImpAtr, P_wave ),
    vent_ecg( ImpVent, Rate ).
```

Types of arguments for all predicates in the model definition must be specified. Each type defines a set of terms, i.e., the domain of some variable. A term is either simple (a constant) or compound (a functor applied to a number of arguments). For example, on the abstract level, there are only two possible states (simple arrhythmias), whereas on the

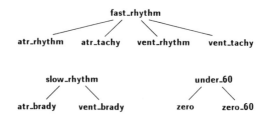

**Figure 5.5** Examples of hierarchies of some domains.

detailed level the state of the heart is defined by the states of the atria, the AV node and the ventricles:

**type( heart( arr, ecg )).**

Abstract:

**domain( arr,    [slow_rhythm, fast_rhythm] ).**

Detailed:

**domain( arr,    arr(atr, av, vent) ).**
**domain( atr,    [quiet, atr_brady, atr_rhythm, atr_tachy] ).**
**domain( av,     [normal, av_block] ).**
**domain( vent, [quiet, vent_brady, vent_rhythm, vent_tachy] ).**

In this example **atr_rhythm** and **vent_rhythm** denote normal atrial and ventricular rates, respectively.

Hierarchies of terms specify relations between values on the abstract and detailed levels. Note that in our example, the abstract level is incomplete with respect to the detailed level since it does not contain it properly (e.g., there is no notion of impulse conduction on the abstract level). Nevertheless, the consistency is required. We say that a model on a detailed level is *consistent* with the abstract level if it does not produce any behavior that contradicts the behavior on the abstract level, with respect to hierarchies of terms. However, a model on an abstract level does not have to account for all possible behaviors at the detailed level, in which case it is said to be *incomplete* with respect to the detailed level.

In the definition of components, background knowledge in the form of utility predicates may be used. For example, the following predicate, defining the ordering of rates, can be part of such background knowledge:

```
succ( zero,     zero_60 ).
succ( zero_60,  60_100 ).
succ( 60_100,   over_100 ).
```

## 5.3   Learning functions of components

The basic motivation for including the learning part into the system for qualitative modeling is that we do not expect an expert to be able to fully articulate his knowledge about the model in the form of rules. Instead, we will have the expert provide only examples of the model behavior. More precisely, we assume that the structure of the model is known, and that the expert is able to provide examples of behavior of the model and its components.

The learning task is to find plausible functions of components from instances of their behavior. Since the function of a component does not depend on other components, learning can be split into several independent tasks, one for each component. In each step, a function of the $i$-th component $Funct(Comp_i)$ must be induced so that all given instances of the component's behavior $Behav(Comp_i)$ can be derived from $Funct(Comp_i)$ and background knowledge $Util$:

$$Funct(Comp_i) \ \& \ Util \ \models \ Behav(Comp_i)$$

Instances of behavior of a component are represented as positive and negative ground facts. A positive fact represents a possible behavior of the component while a negative fact represents an impossible behavior.

Formally, the learning task is to find an inductive hypothesis, expressed as a set of database clauses, that is complete and consistent with the given facts (Michalski 1983). We say that a hypothesis is *complete* iff it covers all positive facts; a hypothesis is *consistent* iff it does not cover any negative fact. A hypothesis *covers* a fact iff any of its clauses covers the fact. A clause $A \leftarrow L_0, \ldots, L_N$ covers a fact $A'$ iff there is a substitution $\Theta$ that unifies $A$ with $A'$, such that $(L_0, \ldots, L_N)\Theta$ true. Such a clause is called a *covering clause* (Shapiro 1982).

The learning procedure used in the system is based on the AQ learning algorithm (Michalski 1969) and proceeds as follows (Mozetič and Lavrač 1988). The *non-incremental* version of the algorithm starts with an empty inductive hypothesis. It selects a positive fact, generalizes it as much as possible (replaces all constants with distinct variables) and subsequently specializes it so that no negative fact is covered. The algorithm keeps several alternative covering clauses that maximize the number of positive facts covered and are as short as possible. Subject to the constraint that no negative fact is covered, it selects the best covering clause, adds it to the inductive hypothesis, and repeats the procedure until all positive facts are covered. There are three specialization operations used to uncover a negative fact: replacing a variable by a term, unifying two distinct variables, and adding a utility predicate in the condition of the clause.

An inductive hypothesis is not guaranteed to be true, but only complete and consistent with the facts seen so far. However, when new facts are encountered that contradict the hypothesis or are not covered by it, the hypothesis may be *incrementally* refined. First, all inconsistent clauses, i.e., clauses that cover some negative facts, are removed from the initial hypothesis. Next, covering clauses are induced that cover all positive facts not yet covered so that all negative facts remain uncovered. Finally, those covering clauses are added to the modified initial hypothesis. Note that the system does not discard any facts after the inductive hypothesis is found since they might be needed for further refinement (full memory incremental learning). Note also that inconsistent clauses are not specialized but rather removed from the initial hypothesis to avoid their over-specialization.

The time complexity of the learning task is proportional to the number of clauses the inductive hypothesis consists of. Therefore, in the case of a complex hypothesis, the incremental learning tends to be more efficient than the non-incremental learning. However, it also tends to produce a more complex hypothesis since it does not attempt to generalize consistent clauses from the initial hypothesis, but simply adds new clauses.

As an example, let us consider the task of completing the definition of the detailed model of the heart of the previous section. Initially, some instances of the detailed model behavior are provided by the user:

[atr_rhythm] $\implies$
    [P_wave = present] & [Rate = 60_100]         (1)

[atr_rhythm, av_block] $\implies$
    [P_wave = present] & [Rate = 60_100]   V    (2)
    [P_wave = present] & [Rate = zero_60]      (3)

The first example denotes the fact that the atrial rhythm causes the P wave to be present and the rate is between 60 and 100. The second example indicates a nondeterministic behavior of the model, since for a given arrhythmia two ECG descriptions are possible. An implicit assumption is made that for a given state (arrhythmia) all possible outputs (ECGs) are listed, and for that reason all other outputs are instances of impossible model behavior.

The user is expected to justify instances of the model behavior in terms of the components behavior. The justifications provide instances of the behavior for each component in the model. From these instances (positive or negative facts) the learner induces initial hypotheses, one for each component function. For example:

Some facts: **atria( atr_rhythm, 60_100 ), true**
             **atria( atr_rhythm, zero ), false**

Hypothesis: **atria( atr_rhythm, 60_100 ).**         (4)

Some facts: **av_node( normal, 60_100, 60_100 ), true**
             **av_node( av_block, 60_100, 60_100 ), true**
             **av_node( av_block, 60_100, zero_60 ), true**
             **av_node( av_block, 60_100, over_100 ), false**

Hypothesis: **av_node( normal, Rate, Rate ).**        (5)
           **av_node( av_block, _, Rate ) $\leftarrow$**      (6)
           **Rate in [zero_60, 60_100].**

This completes the initial learning stage.

# 5.4    Debugging a hypothesized model

The induced hypotheses are not guaranteed to be true, but are complete and consistent with the facts given so far. To verify them we can execute them and see if they behave the way we want them to. This is the usual program testing and debugging activity, applied here to a knowledge base instead of to a program. In our case, the knowledge base may be incomplete (a possible model behavior cannot be derived from it), or incorrect (an impossible behavior can be derived). The debugger that can locate and correct such faulty hypotheses in the knowledge base embodies and extends the techniques for debugging logic programs (Shapiro 1982).

To test the hypothesized model, the model interpreter is used for simulation on some new instance. For example:

[atr_tachy]  $\implies$  [P_wave = ?] & [Rate = ?]

In this example, the interpreter answers "no," meaning that it cannot derive any ECG for the given arrhythmia from the current model. The user concludes that the model does not behave as intended, more precisely, that the model is incomplete. The debugger is invoked, given the intended behavior of the model:

[atr_tachy]  $\implies$
  [P_wave = present] & [Rate = over_100]                    (7)

The debugger takes the current, hypothesized definition of the model, trying to derive the intended behavior from it. Since this fails, it inspects the finitely failed derivation tree (Lloyd 1984), reduced to a single path in this case:

heart(arr(atr_tachy, normal, quiet), ecg(present, over_100))
  \
  atria(atr_tachy, Impulse)
  |
  FAILURE

The first goal used in the derivation immediately fails since it cannot be unified with the head of the corresponding hypothesis (4). This indicates that the hypothesis is incomplete, i.e., it does not cover a positive fact denoting an instance of the possible behavior of the component. In such a case Shapiro's debugger (Shapiro 1982) would ask the user for all instances of the variable **Impulse** that make the goal true. In contrast, our debugger makes assumptions about the possible behavior of the component by itself. Only when the intended behavior of the model is achieved is the user asked for confirmation. In general, this task of making assumptions is difficult since more than one hypothesis may be incomplete. Even if only one hypothesis is incomplete, as in our case, a lot of futile guesses may be made. Here, the debugger takes into consideration the corresponding abstract model, thus reducing the search space. Namely, the behavior on the detailed level must be consistent with the behavior on the abstract level (Figure 5.6).

**Figure 5.6** Using the abstract level in proposing possible instances of a component behavior on the detailed level.

The debugger first tries with the assumption:

**atria( atr_tachy, 60_100 ), true**

which fails to produce the intended model behavior (7), and then succeeds with the following assumption:

**atria( atr_tachy, over_100 ), true**          (8)

Because of the requirement of consistency with the abstract level and hierarchies provided (Figure 5.5), the debugger does not even try the assumptions that are unsuccessful, for example:

**atria( atr_tachy, zero ), true**
**atria( atr_tachy, zero_60 ), true**

The assumption (8) that enables the derivation of the intended model behavior (7), is added as a positive exception (a positive fact) to the currect hypothesis (4).

The user proceeds with testing the model. The next example is slightly more complicated, where no advantage of the abstract level can be taken. The interpreter simulates the model on the following multiple arrhythmia, as chosen by the user:

[atr_tachy, av_block]  $\implies$  [P_wave = ?] & [Rate = ?]

The following behavior is derived:

[atr_tachy, av_block]  $\implies$
   [P_wave = present] & [Rate = zero_60]  ∨        (9)
   [P_wave = present] & [Rate = 60_100]        (10)

while the intended behavior is:

[atr_tachy, av_block]  $\implies$
   [P_wave = present] & [Rate = 60_100]  ∨        (10)
   [P_wave = present] & [Rate = over_100]        (11)

The derived and the intended model behavior are different in cases (9) and (11). An impossible behavior that was derived (9) indicates that the current model is incorrect, and therefore that at least one hypothesis is incorrect. The debugging task is to locate an incorrect hypothesis and provide a counterexample to it. The algorithm we implemented is based on the contradiction backtracing algorithm (Shapiro 1981, 1982). First, the debugger inspects the derivation that yields the impossible behavior in order to prevent it:

heart(arr(atr_tachy, av_block, quiet), ecg(present, zero_60))
    \
   atria(atr_tachy, over_100)
    |
   av_node(av_block, over_100, zero_60)
    |
   ventricles(quiet, zero)
    |
   sum(zero_60, zero, zero_60)
    |
   atr_ecg(over_100, present)
    |
   vent_ecg(zero_60, zero_60)
    |
   SUCCESS

At this point, Shapiro's algorithm would query the user for a subgoal, used in the derivation, that is false. In contrast, our debugger by itself makes assumptions about which subgoal might be false under the condition that all instances of the model behavior already known to be true are still derivable. In our case, there is only one assumption that prevents the above derivation, provided that (3,7) are still derivable:

$$\text{av\_node( av\_block, over\_100, zero\_60 ), false} \tag{12}$$

This assumption is added as an exception (a negative fact) to the current hypothesis (5,6).

Since a possible model behavior (11) cannot be derived from the current hypotheses, some hypotheses are still incomplete. The interpreter returns a finitely failed derivation tree, and the debugger tries to make at least one path in the tree successful:

**heart(arr(atr_tachy, av_block, quiet), ecg(present, over_100))**
|
**atria(atr_tachy, over_100)**

**av_node(av_block,over_100,zero_60)**
|
**FAILURE**

**av_node(av_block,over_100,60_100)**
|
**ventricles(quiet, zero)**
|
**sum(60_100,zero,60_100)**
|
**atr_ecg(over_100, present)**
|
**vent_ecg(60_100, over_100)**
|
**FAILURE**

The left branch of the tree fails due to the negative exception (12) added to the hypothesis (5,6). The right branch fails since the last goal cannot be satisfied. The debugger first tries with the immediately failed subgoal, making the assumption:

**vent_ecg( 60_100, over_100 ), true**

which would make the derivation possible. However, this is not acceptable since it also enables the derivation of an impossible model behavior with respect to (2,3), namely:

**[atr_rhythm, av_block]** $\Longrightarrow$
    **[P_wave = present] & [Rate = over_100]**

As it turns out, in this case only one hypothesis can be labeled as incomplete in order to prevent derivations of impossible model behaviors. After locating the incomplete hypothesis (5,6) the debugger also has to propose a positive exception that yields the intended model behavior:

**av_node( av_block, over_100, Rate=? ), true**

Since there is no abstract level to guide the search, the debugger has to nondeterministically try values from the variable domain, until the derivation succeeds:

**Rate = zero       FAILS**
**      zero_60    FAILS**
**      over_100   SUCCEEDS**

Finally, the assumption is added as a positive exception to the hypothesis (5,6):

**av_node( av_block, over_100, over_100 ), true**

All assumptions together, internally made by the debugger, guarantee that the derived behavior of the model is the same as the intended behavior. However, they may not be true. Therefore, at the end, the user is asked to confirm them. If they are not confirmed, the debugger backtracks and proposes another set of assumptions until the user is satisfied. Then the user decides either to simply accumulate the assumptions as positive and negative exceptions to the faulty hypotheses, or to actually modify the hypotheses in the incremental or the non-incremental way.

The incremental learning proceeds as follows. First, all inconsistent clauses, that is clauses that cover some negative facts, are removed from the initial hypothesis. In our example the clause (6) is removed since it covers a negative fact (12). Next, clauses that cover all positive facts not yet covered, or not covered any more, are induced. Finally, these covering clauses are added to the modified initial hypothesis (5) to form a new hypothesis:

**av_node( normal,    Rate1, Rate1 ).**
**av_node( av_block, Rate1, Rate1 ).**
**av_node( av_block, Rate1, Rate2 )  ←**
**    succ( Rate2, Rate1 ),**

**Rate2 in [zero_60, 60_100].**

The system does not discard any facts after the inductive hypothesis is found since they might be needed for further refinement (full memory incremental learning).

## 5.5 Interpreting a model

Once the user believes that a qualitative model behaves as intended, the model may be used for problem solving. In this section we concentrate on two ways in which a model can be used: simulation and diagnosis. A model has some internal qualitative state and is connected to the environment through information channels. A state of the model is defined by states of the individual components (e.g. normal or abnormal), and indicates the region within which some law of behavior is valid. The model accepts some input information, and, depending on the state, transforms it onto an output.

The simulation task is the following: given a state of the model and an input, derive the corresponding output. The diagnostic task is the opposite: given an input and an output from the model, find all possible states that may produce the given behavior of the model. Here we do not consider possible transitions in time between different qualitative states, also called "envisioning" (de Kleer and Brown 1983) or "qualitative simulation" (Kuipers 1985).

Both simulation and diagnosis are constraint satisfaction problems, or, in the logic programming terminology, problems of goal satisfaction. However, a qualitative model is primarily designed to be used in the "forward" direction, for simulation. When used in the "backward" direction, for diagnosis, the degree of nondeterminism in the model is usually higher. This causes more backtracking, thus increasing the time complexity of the diagnostic task.

We have designed and implemented three methods to improve the efficiency of the diagnostic task:

(1) Compilation and compression of the model into a base of operational diagnostic rules.

(2) Hierarchical diagnosis by representing and using the model on different levels of abstraction.

(3) Backward diagnosis by the use of a non-standard goal selection strategy (unlike the standard Prolog interpreters that implement the left-to-right selection).

The method (1) is described in Chapter 4 while methods (2) and (3) are in the following two sections.

## 5.5.1    Hierarchical diagnosis

Hierarchical diagnosis is based on the representation of a model on several levels of abstraction. The basic idea behind the method is to move the "greedy" search from a detailed to an abstract level of the model. The diagnosis at the abstract level is less precise, but easier because the model at this level is simpler. More detailed diagnoses are obtained through simulation at the detailed level. An illustration of the method is in Figure 5.7. While the method is general and domain independent (Mozetič, Bratko, and Urbančič 1987), in this chapter we are concerned with a particular diagnostic task of finding arrhythmias for a given electrocardiogram.

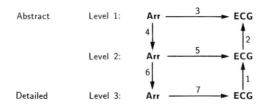

**Figure 5.7**  A scheme of hierarchical diagnosis. The diagnostic procedure consists of 7 steps in the order as indicated by labels.

Given a detailed ECG, the diagnostic algorithm climbs the hierarchies of values to find more abstract ECG (steps 1,2). The algorithm uses the model at the abstract level to find an arrhythmia that can actually produce the abstract ECG (step 3). If more detailed diagnosis is required, the algorithm uses hierarchies to further consider only arrhythmias that are below the abstract arrhythmia in the hierarchy (steps 4,6). Potential detailed arrhythmias are then verified by means of simulation if they actually produce the corresponding ECG (steps 5,7). If another diagnosis is required, the algorithm backtracks until there are no more possible arrhythmias.

Our model representation formalism allows for an abstract level to be incomplete with respect to the detailed level. In such a case the algorithm cannot take the advantage of hierarchies. In the degenerate case of total incompleteness, the method is in fact reduced to the naive "generate and test" strategy.

The diagnostic algorithm below is written in standard Prolog. For a given level of the model and output from the model the procedure **diagnose( Level, Out, In )** finds a corresponding input or state of the model (denoted by **In**). The problem is formally the same when, for a given output, either an input or an internal state is to be found. The procedure consists of two clauses. The first clause deals with the case when there are hierarchies, and the second clause deals with all instances of inputs or states that do not have abstract counterparts on the given level of abstraction:

```
diagnose( Level, Out, In )   :-
    Level > 1, Level0 is Level − 1,
    hierarchy( Out0, Out ),               % move level up
    diagnose( Level0, Out0, In0 ),
    hierarchy( In0, In ),                 % move level down
    simulate( Level, In, Out ).
diagnose( Level, Out, In )   :-
    no_abstract( Level, In ),             % there is no abstraction
    simulate( Level, In, Out ).
```

The following example illustrates the method. The model under consideration is our previous detailed model of the heart. The task is to find an arrhythmia, given the following ECG description:

**[P_wave = present] & [Rate = zero_60]**

Given the above detailed ECG:

**Detailed_ECG = ecg( present, zero_60 )**

the diagnostic algorithm climbs the hierarchies of values (Figure 5.5) to find more abstract ECG:

**Abstract_ECG = under_60**

The algorithm uses the model on the abstract level (section 5.2.3) to find an arrhythmia that actually produces this particular abstract ECG. The following arrhythmia is obtained by means of the generate and test method:

**Abstract_Arr = slow_rhythm**

To find more detailed diagnoses, the algorithm uses hierarchies to further consider only arrhythmias that are in the hierarchy under the abstract arrhythmia **slow_rhythm** (Figure 5.5) and satisfy given constraints over the states of the heart. Constraints specify which (multiple) arrhythmias are physiologically possible and medically interesting. Potentially possible detailed arrhythmias are then verified by means of simulation:

**Detailed_Arr =**
    **arr( atr_brady, normal, quiet )**      **SUCCEEDS**
    **arr( quiet, normal, vent_brady )**    **FAILS**

The following arrhythmias are not considered at all since they are not under the hierarchy of **slow_rhythm**:

**Detailed_Arr =**
    **arr( atr_rhythm, normal, quiet )**
    **arr( atr_tachy, normal, quiet )**
    **arr( quiet, normal, vent_rhythm )**
    **arr( quiet, normal, vent_tachy )**

However, the abstract level is incomplete, meaning that there are some detailed arrhythmias that do not have corresponding abstractions:

**no_abstract( 2, arr(_, av_block, _) ).**

They have to be explicitly verified if one wants all possible diagnoses for the given ECG:

**Detailed_Arr =**
    arr( atr_brady, av_block, quiet )    **SUCCEEDS**
    arr( atr_rhythm, av_block, quiet )   **SUCCEEDS**
    arr( atr_tachy, av_block, quiet )    **FAILS**

As compared to the naive diagnosis, in this example the search space was reduced by almost one half.

## 5.5.2   Backward diagnosis

As already mentioned, the standard Prolog interpreter uses left-to-right goal selection strategy. In the case of diagnosis, the output is given and the state of the model has to be found. The use of the components as constraints in the inverse direction better suits this problem. In the logic programming terminology, this is the right-to-left goal selection strategy.

To illustrate this method, let us consider the same example as in the previous section. Given is the structure of the model:

**heart( arr(Atr,AV,Vent), ecg(P_wave, Rate))** ←       (1)
    atria( Atr, ImpAtr ),
    av_node( AV, ImpAtr, ImpHis ),
    ventricles( Vent, ImpVent0 ),
    sum( ImpVent0, ImpHis, ImpVent ),
    atr_ecg( ImpAtr, P_wave ),
    vent_ecg( ImpVent, Rate ).

Further, we assume that correct and complete predicate definitions that specify functions of components were automatically constructed in previous stages:

**atria( quiet, zero ).**
**atria( atr_brady, zero_60 ).**
**atria( atr_rhythm, 60_100 ).**                          (2)
**atria( atr_tachy, over_100 ).**

**av_node( normal,   Rate1, Rate1 ).**                     (3)
**av_node( av_block, Rate1, Rate1 ).**                     (4)
**av_node( av_block, Rate1, Rate2 )** ←                    (5)

```
     succ( Rate2, Rate1 ),
     Rate2 in [zero_60, 60_100].
```

ventricles( quiet,         zero ).
ventricles( vent_brady,    zero_60 ).                    (6)
ventricles( vent_rhythm,   60_100 ).                     (7)
ventricles( vent_tachy,    over_100 ).

sum( zero, zero, zero ).
sum( zero, Rate, Rate )  ←  Rate ≠ zero.                 (8)
sum( Rate, zero, zero )  ←  Rate ≠ zero.                 (9)

atr_ecg( Rate, present )  ←  Rate ≠ zero.                (10)
atr_ecg( zero, absent   ).

vent_ecg( Rate, Rate ).                                  (11)

The diagnostic task is to find an arrythmia, given the same ECG description as in the previous section:

**ECG = ecg(present, zero_60)**

The interpreter is given the following goal

**heart( Arr, ecg(present, zero_60) )**

in order to find an arrhythmia that causes the given ECG. The interpreter unifies the goal with the head of the clause 1 and replaces the goal with the body of the clause 1. Since the right-to-left (in our example bottom-to-top) goal selection strategy is used, the last ("rightmost") subgoal of the clause 1 is selected next. The following is a trace of the first (unsuccessful) derivation:

```
vent_ecg( zero_60, zero_60 )
    |
atr_ecg( over_100, present )
    |
sum( zero, zero_60, zero_60 )
    |
ventricles( quiet, zero )
    |
av_node( av_block, over_100, zero_60 )
    |
FAILURE
```

The last subgoal cannot be satisfied since it cannot be unified with the heads of the clauses 3 and 4, and the condition in the body of the clause 5 cannot be satisfied either. However, the reason for the failure is actually in the clause 10, since for the second subgoal, namely **atr_ecg( Rate, present )**, the interpreter has to make a nondeterministic choice for the value of variable **Rate**, different from **zero**. The first choice above (**over_100**) leads to failure; therefore the interpreter backtracks to the last point of nondeterminism and tries the next possible choice:

> **sum( zero_60, zero, zero_60 )**
> |
> **ventricles( vent_brady, zero_60 )**
> |
> **av_node( av_block, over_100, zero )**
> |
> **FAILURE**

Again, failure occurs since just the clause 9 was selected instead of the clause 8. The system backtracks again and chooses the next possible value for **Rate** which now gets the value **60_100**. Now, the derivation is successful:

> **atr_ecg( 60_100, present )**
> |
> **sum( zero, zero_60, zero_60 )**
> |
> **ventricles( quiet, zero )**
> |
> **av_node( av_block, 60_100, zero_60 )**
> |
> **atria( atr_rhythm, 60_100 )**
> |
> **SUCCESS**

Since the initial goal was satisfied, the interpreter returns the substitution of the free variable **Arr** in the question:

> **Arr = arr(atr_rhythm, av_block, quiet)**

The other two possible diagnoses are obtained through backtracking in the same manner:

> **Arr = arr(atr_brady, normal, quiet)**
> **Arr = arr(atr_brady, av_block, quiet)**

## 5.6   Experiments and results

The hierarchical model representation and learning methods described in this chapter were used for the construction of a subset of the heart model for ECG diagnosis. The system embodies a model of the heart, represented on three levels of abstraction. Table 5.1 gives the complexity of the model at each level, with respect to the number of its constituent components, the number of possible states of the model (arrhythmias), and outputs from the model (ECG descriptions). The fourth column in the table indicates the number of arrhythmias that do not have a corresponding abstraction on the higher level; these are unique to the model on the detailed level.

| Level of abstr. | Components | States (Arr) | | Outputs (ECG) |
|---|---|---|---|---|
| | | All | Without abstr. | |
| 1 | 2 | 3 | 3 | 3 |
| 2 | 9 | 18 | 3 | 38 |
| 3 | 16 | 175 | 85 | 333 |

**Table 5.1**  Complexity of the heart model used in the experiments.

The system for semi-automatic construction of qualitative models was faced with the task of constructing a qualitative model of the heart on the third (most detailed) level of abstraction. The model relates all arrhythmias to their ECG descriptions through the underlying electrophysiology of the heart. We have designed three experiments to answer the following questions:

(1) How many cycles of debugging and incremental refinement are needed before the model is completely correct?

(2) Is there any advantage of having a qualitative model as opposed to surface rules in terms of predictive accuracy?

(3) What is the efficiency of different diagnostic methods?

For the first experiment, the system was given the structure of the electrical network in the heart (impulse generators, impulse conductors, impulse projection on the ECG, and connections between these components). Further, examples of all single disorders in the heart (25 arrhythmias), all the corresponding ECG descriptions (66 ECGs), and the behavior of the components for these cases were given. The hypothesized model was then tested on examples of all multiple disorders that may occur in the heart (150 arrhythmias with corresponding 267 ECGs) and its predictive accuracy was measured. In each model refinement cycle, the system was given a few additional examples of the intended model behavior until the model was completely correct, i.e., for all possible arrhythmias exactly all corresponding ECG descriptions were derivable. Figure 5.8 shows that 8 steps were needed for the refinement, where altogether 19 additional examples of arrhythmias and 37 corresponding ECGs were provided by the user. In the step 5* there was no debugging. At this point the user decided to discard an incrementally modified hypothesis since it was too complicated. The new hypothesis was then learned in the non-incremental way from all available examples.

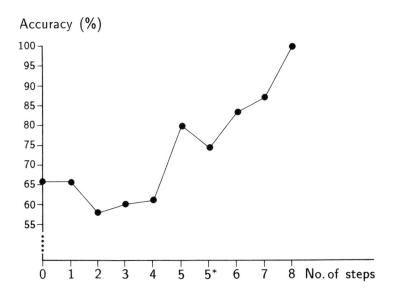

**Figure 5.8** Steps of debugging and incremental refinement of the model, and the corresponding predictive accuracy.

In the second experiment we automatically constructed a surface knowledge base from the same examples of input-output behavior as above. The resulting surface knowledge base consists of rules directly relating arrhythmias to ECG descriptions. We have measured the predictive accuracy of the surface rules twice; first, after the learning from the initial examples (25 arrhythmias with 66 ECGs), and second, after the last cycle of refining the model (additional 19 arrhythmias with 37 ECGs). The accuracy was measured on examples of 150 multiple arrhythmias with corresponding 267 ECGs. The results are shown in Table 5.2. Note that the system guarantees 100% accuracy if measured on the learning examples.

| Type of knowledge base | No. of learning examples (Arr-ECG) | |
|---|---|---|
| | 25-66 | 44-103 |
| Surface Arr-ECG rules | 48% | 77% |
| Deep model of the heart | 66% | 100% |

**Table 5.2** A comparison of the predictive accuracy of surface rules and the structured model of the heart. The predictive accuracy is measured as the percentage of correctly predicted ECG descriptions for each multiple arrhythmia.

These results show that the structured model of the heart reached higher predictive accuracy than surface rules, when they were both constructed from the same examples. This is not surprising, since the system for learning deep models accepts more information, namely, the model structure and initial examples of the components behavior.

In the third experiment we compared the efficiency of different diagnostic methods with the model on the third level of abstraction. We compared:

(1) naive generate and test method,

(2) hierarchical diagnosis with simulation (see section 5.5.1),

(3) one level backward diagnosis (see section 5.5.2),

(4) combined method that uses hierarchical diagnosis (when there are abstractions) and backward diagnosis (for arrhythmias that do not have corresponding abstraction).

A randomly selected subset of 12 ECG descriptions was used to measure the time that each method needed to find possible arrhythmias. Table 5.3 gives average times needed to find the first and the rest of possible arrhythmias (the second and the third column, respectively). The analysis of results revealed that times highly depend on whether the possible arrhythmia does have an abstraction or it does not. Therefore, four more columns are included in Table 5.3, two for each case. The first subcolumn in each case indicates the time needed to find the first arrhythmia, and the second subcolumn indicates the time that was spent until all possibilities were exhausted.

| Diagnostic method | Together (12 cases) | | Without abstr. (3 cases) | | With abstr. (9 cases) | |
|---|---|---|---|---|---|---|
| | First | Rest | First | Rest | First | Rest |
| Naive | 305 | 500 | 283 | 519 | 313 | 493 |
| Hierarchical | 108 | 408 | 335 | 125 | 32 | 502 |
| Backward | 50 | 34 | 160 | 40 | 14 | 32 |
| Combined | 68 | 92 | 172 | 44 | 33 | 108 |

**Table 5.3** Average times per diagnosis (in CPU seconds on VAX 11/750) for different diagnostic methods implemented in Prolog (two levels of interpretation).

The results show that the naive generate and test diagnosis can be considerably improved. Hierarchical diagnosis is much faster when it can take the advantage of abstractions (consider the 6th column, 32 seconds vs. 313 seconds). Even when the arrhythmia that is actually possible does not have the abstraction, the search space is reduced (4th and 5th column together, 460 seconds vs. 802 seconds) since all detailed arrhythmias that do have abstractions need not be considered. Backward diagnosis is the most efficient in this model, but mostly due to the relatively large number of detailed diagnoses without abstractions. When there are abstractions, hierarchical diagnosis with simulation is not much slower than backward diagnosis. Here it should be stressed that relatively large absolute times needed for diagnosis (a few minutes) are not inherent to the problem. They are a result of the inefficient model interpreter (itself written in C-Prolog interpreter) and were in subsequent experiments reduced by a factor of 100 when the model was compiled by Quintus Prolog compiler.

To conclude, in this chapter we outlined a system for the automated construction and refinement of qualitative models. The system is based on logic and is domain independent. Its power was demonstrated on the problem of constructing a model of the electrical activity of the heart. Results of experiments support the conclusion that the system can serve as a useful knowledge acquisition tool for the construction of deep knowledge bases in difficult domains.

# References

Arity (1986) *The Arity/Prolog programming language.* Concord, MA: Arity Corporation.

Becker, J. (1985) Inductive learning of decision rules with exceptions. MSc Thesis, University of Illinois at Urbana-Champaign, Department of Computer Science.

Bratko, I. (1986) *Prolog programming for artificial intelligence.* Addison-Wesley.

Bratko, I. and Kononenko, I. (1987) Learning diagnostic rules from incomplete and noisy data. In: Phelps, B. (ed.) *Interactions in AI and statistics.* London: Gower Technical Press.

Bratko, I. and Lavrač, N. (eds.) (1987) *Progress in machine learning.* Wilmslow: Sigma Press.

Bratko, I., Lavrač, N., Mozetič, I., Zrimec, T., Horvat, M. and Rode, P. (1982) The development of an expert system for intensive medical treatment. *Proc. Technical Conference on Theory and Practice of Knowledge-based Systems,* London.

Bratko, I., Mozetič, I. and Lavrač, N. (1986) Automatic synthesis and compression of cardiological knowledge. In: Michie, D. and Bratko, I. (eds.) *Expert systems—Automating knowledge acquisition.* Handbook and video, Addison-Wesley. Also in: Hayes, J., Michie, D. and Richards, J. (eds.) *Machine intelligence 11,* pp. 435–454. 1988. Oxford: Oxford University Press.

Brazdil, P. and Clark, P. (1988) Learning from imperfect data. *Proc. Int. Workshop on Machine Learning, Meta Reasoning and Logics,* Sesimbra, Portugal.

Cestnik, B., Kononenko, I. and Bratko, I. (1987) ASSISTANT 86: A knowledge elicitation tool for sophisticated users. In: Bratko, I. and Lavrač, N. (eds.) *Progress in machine learning.* Wilmslow: Sigma Press.

Clocksin, W. F. and Mellish, C. S. (1981) *Programming in Prolog.* Springer-Verlag.

de Kleer, J. and Brown, J. S. (1983) The origin, form and logic of qualitative physical laws. *Proc. Eighth Int. Joint Conference on Artificial Intelligence*, Karlsruhe, West Germany: Morgan Kaufmann.

de Kleer, J. and Brown, J. S. (1984) A qualitative physics based on confluences. *Artificial Intelligence 24* (1-3), pp. 7–83.

Forbus, K. D. (1984) Qualitative process theory. *Artificial Intelligence 24* (1-3), pp. 85–168.

Goldman, M. J. (1976) *Principles of clinical electrocardiography.* Los Altos: Lange Medical Publications.

Grad, A. and Čerček, B. (1984) Evaluation of the applicability of the KARDIO-E expert system. ISSEK Workshop 84, Bled, Yugoslavia.

Hong, J., Mozetič, I. and Michalski, R. S. (1986) AQ15: Incremental learning of attribute-based descriptions from examples, the method and user's guide. Report ISG 86-5, UIUCDCS-F-86-949, University of Illinois at Urbana-Champaign, Department of Computer Science.

Hunter, J., Gotts, N. and Hamlet, I. (1988) Qualitative spatial and temporal reasoning in cardiac electrophysiology. *Proc. Second Workshop on Qualitative Physics*, Paris.

Kodratoff, Y. (1988) *Introduction to Machine Learning.* London: Pitman.

Kuipers, B. (1985) The limits of qualitative simulation. *Proc. Ninth Int. Joint Conference on Artificial Intelligence*, Los Angeles: Morgan Kaufmann.

Kuipers, B. (1986) Qualitative simulation. *Artificial Intelligence 29*, pp. 289–338.

Kuipers, B. (1987) Qualitative simulation as causal explanation. *IEEE Trans. Systems, Man and Cybernetics SMC-17*, pp. 432–444.

Kuipers, B. and Kassirer, J. P. (1985) Qualitative simulation in medical physiology: A progress report. Memorandum MIT/LCS/TM-280, Massachusetts Institute of Technology, Laboratory for Computer Science.

Lavrač, N., Bratko, I., Mozetič, I., Čerček, B., Horvat, M. and Grad, A. (1985) KARDIO-E: An expert system for electrocardiographic diagnosis of cardiac arrhythmias. *Expert Systems 2* (1), pp. 46–49. Also in: *Proc. First Int. Expert Systems Conference*, London.

Lee, W. W., Chiu, C. and Kuipers, B. J. (1987) Developments towards constraining qualitative simulation. Technical report AI TR87-44, University of Texas at Austin, AI Laboratory.

Lloyd, J. W. (1984) *Foundations of logic programming.* Springer-Verlag.

Lloyd, J. W. and Topor, R. W. (1984) Making Prolog more expressive. *Journal of Logic Programming 1* (3), pp. 225–240.

Lloyd, J. W. and Topor, R. W. (1985) A basis for deductive database systems. *Journal of Logic Programming 2* (2), pp. 93–109.

Lloyd, J. W. and Topor, R. W. (1986) A basis for deductive database systems II. *Journal of Logic Programming 3* (1), pp. 55–67.

Michalski, R. S. (1969) On the quasi-minimal solution of the general covering problem. *Proc. Fifth Int. Symposium on Information Processing (FCIP 69)*, Vol. A3 (Switching Circuits) pp. 125–128, Bled, Yugoslavia.

Michalski, R. S. (1983) A theory and methodology of inductive learning. In: Michalski, R. S., Carbonell, J. G. and Mitchell, T. M. (eds.) *Machine learning: An artificial intelligence approach.* Palo Alto: Tioga Publishing Company.

Michalski, R. S., Carbonell, J. G. and Mitchell, T. M. (eds.) (1983) *Machine learning: An artificial intelligence approach.* Palo Alto: Tioga Publishing Company.

Michalski, R. S., Carbonell, J. G. and Mitchell, T. M. (eds.) (1986) *Machine learning: An artificial intelligence approach, Volume II.* Los Altos: Morgan Kaufmann.

Michalski, R. S. and Larson, J. (1975) AQVAL/1 (AQ7) User's guide and program description. Report No. 731, University of Illinois at Urbana-Champaign, Department of Computer Science.

Michalski, R. S. and Chilausky, R. L. (1980) Learning by being told and learning from examples: An experimental comparison of the two methods for knowledge acquisition in the context of developing an expert system for soybean disease diagnosis. *Int. Journal for Policy Analysis and Information Systems 4* (2), pp. 125–161.

Michalski, R. S., Mozetič, I., Hong, J. and Lavrač, N. (1986a) The AQ15 inductive learning system: An overview and experiments. Report ISG 86-20, UIUCDCS-R-8601260, University of Illinois at Urbana-Champaign, Department of Computer Science.

Michalski, R. S., Mozetič, I., Hong, J. and Lavrač, N. (1986b) The multi-purpose incremental learning system AQ15 and its testing application to three medical domains. *Proc. National Conference on Artificial Intelligence*, AAAI-86, Philadelphia, PA: Morgan Kaufmann.

Michie, D. (1986a) The superarticulacy phenomenon in the context of software manufacture. In: Michie, D. and Bratko, I. (eds.) *Expert systems—Automating knowledge acquisition.* Handbook and video, Addison-Wesley.

Michie, D. (1986b) Machine learning and knowledge acquisition. In: Michie, D. and Bratko, I. (eds.) *Expert systems—Automating knowledge acquisition.* Handbook and video, Addison-Wesley. Also published as New developments in expert systems. In: Quinlan, J. R. (ed.) Applications of expert systems, 1987. Addison-Wesley.

Mitchell, T. M., Carbonell, J. G. and Michalski, R. S. (eds.) (1986) *Machine learning: A guide to current research.* Boston: Kluwer Academic Publishers.

Mozetič, I. (1984) Qualitative model of the heart (in Slovene). Ljubljana: MSc Thesis, E. Kardelj University, Faculty of Electrical Engineering, Department of Computer Science and Informatics, Ljubljana, Yugoslavia.

Mozetič, I. (1985a) Compression of the ECG knowledge-base using the AQ inductive learning algorithms. Report ISG 85-13, UIUCDCS-F-85-943, University of Illinois at Urbana-Champaign, Department of Computer Science.

Mozetič, I. (1985b) NEWGEM: Program for learning from examples, technical documentation and user's guide. Report, University of Illinois at Urbana-Champaign, Department of Computer Science. Also: Report IJS-DP-4390, Jozef Stefan Institute, Ljubljana.

Mozetič, I. (1986) Knowledge extraction through learning from examples. In: Mitchell, T. M., Carbonell, J. G. and Michalski, R. S. (eds.) *Machine learning: A guide to current research.* Boston: Kluwer Academic Publishers.

Mozetič, I. (1987a) Learning of qualitative models. In: Bratko, I. and Lavrač, N. (eds.) *Progress in machine learning.* Wilmslow: Sigma Press.

Mozetič, I. (1987b) The role of abstractions in learning qualitative models. *Proc. Fourth Int. Workshop on Machine Learning,* Irvine, CA: Morgan Kaufmann.

Mozetič, I. (1988) Learning of qualitative models (in Slovene). PhD Thesis, E. Kardelj University, Faculty of Electrical Engineering, Department of Computer Science and Informatics, Ljubljana, Yugoslavia.

Mozetič, I., Bratko, I. and Lavrač, N. (1983) An experiment in automatic synthesis of expert knowledge through qualitative modelling. *Proc. Logic Programming Workshop 83,* Albufeira, Portugal.

Mozetič, I., Bratko, I. and Lavrač, N. (1984) The derivation of medical knowledge from a qualitative model of the heart. ISSEK Workshop 84, Bled, Yugoslavia.

Mozetič, I., Bratko, I. and Urbančič, T. (1987) Varying level of abstraction in qualitative modelling. Machine Intelligence Workshop 12, Tallin. Also in: Hayes, J., Michie, D. and Tyugu, E. (eds.) *Machine intelligence 12.* Oxford University Press (in press).

Mozetič, I. and Lavrač, N. (1988) Incremental learning from examples in a logic-based formalism. *Proc. Int. Workshop on Machine Learning, Meta Reasoning and Logics*, Sesimbra, Portugal.

Nicolosi, E. and Leaning, M. S. (1988) Qualitative simulation of compartmental models. *Proc. IFAC Conf. Modelling and Control in Biomedical Systems*, Venice, Italy.

Pearce, D. A. (1988) The induction of fault diagnosis systems from qualitative models. *Proc. National Conference on Artificial Intelligence*, AAAI-88, Saint Paul, MN: Morgan Kaufmann.

Pereira, L. M., Pereira, F. and Warren, D. H. D. (1978) The DECsystems 10 Prolog user's guide. University of Edinburgh, Artificial Intelligence Department.

Phibbs, B. (1973) *The cardiac arrhythmias.* St. Louis: The C. V. Mosby Co.

Quinlan, J. R. (1983) Learning efficient classification procedures and their application to chess end games. In: Michalski, R. S., Carbonell, J. G. and Mitchell, T. M. (eds.) *Machine learning: An artificial intelligence approach.* Palo Alto: Tioga Publishing Company.

Quinlan, J. R. (1986) Induction of decision trees. *Machine Learning 1* (1), pp. 81–106.

Quinlan, J. R., Compton, P., Horn, K. A. and Lazarus, L. (1986) Inductive knowledge acquisition: A case study. *Proc. Second Australian Conference on the Applications of Expert Systems*, pp. 183–204. Sydney: New South Wales Institute of Technology.

Reinke, R. E. (1984) Knowledge-acquisition and refinement tools for the ADVISE META-EXPERT system. MSc Thesis, Report ISG 84-4, UIUCDCS-F-84-921, University of Illinois at Urbana-Champaign, Department of Computer Science.

Reinke, R. E. and Michalski, R. S. (1988) Incremental learning of concept descriptions: A method and experimental results.
In: Hayes, J., Michie, D. and Richards, J. (eds.) *Machine intelligence 11*, pp. 263–288. Oxford: Oxford University Press.

Sammut, C. and Banerji, R. B. (1986) Learning concepts by asking questions. In: Michalski, R. S., Carbonell, J. G. and Mitchell, T. M. (eds.) *Machine learning: An artificial intelligence approach, Volume II*. Los Altos: Morgan Kaufmann.

Schamroth, L. (1980) *The disorders of cardiac rhythm*. Blackwell Scientific Publications.

Shapiro, E. Y. (1981) Inductive inference of theories from facts. Research Report 192, New Haven, CT: Yale University.

Shapiro, E. Y. (1982) *Algorithmic program debugging*. Cambridge, MA: The MIT Press.

Shibahara, T. (1985) On using causal knowledge to recognize vital signals: Knowledge-based interpretation of arrhythmias. *Proc. Ninth Int. Joint Conference on Artificial Intelligence*, Los Angeles: Morgan Kaufmann.

Steels, L. (1985) Second generation expert systems. *Future Generation Computer Systems 1* (4), pp. 213–221.

Struss, P. (1988) Global filters for qualitative behaviors. *Proc. National Conference on Artificial Intelligence*, AAAI-88, Saint Paul, MN: Morgan Kaufmann.

WHO (ISFC Task Force) (1978) Definition of terms related to cardiac rhythm. *American Heart Journal 95* (6), pp. 796–806. St. Louis: The C. V. Mosby Company.

WHO (ISFC Task Force) (1979) Classification of cardiac arrhythmias and conduction disturbances. *American Heart Journal 98* (2), pp. 263–267. St. Louis: The C. V. Mosby Company.

# Appendix A

# Part of Surface Arrhythmia-ECG Base

This appendix contains part of the original arrhythmia-ECG knowledge base, generated by the model of the heart. There are all simple arrhythmias, occuring either alone or in combination (usually with sinus rhythm). At the end, there are also examples of more complicated multiple arrhythmias (combinations of four, five, six and seven simple arrhythmias).

[sinus_rhythm] ⟹
    [rhythm_QRS = regular] &
    [dominant_P = normal] &
    [rate_of_P = between_60_100] &
    [relation_P_QRS = after_P_always_QRS] &
    [dominant_PR = normal] &
    [dominant_QRS = normal] &
    [rate_of_QRS = between_60_100]

[sinus_arrhythmia] ⟹
    [rhythm_QRS = irregular] &
    [dominant_P = normal] &
    [rate_of_P = between_60_100] &
    [relation_P_QRS = after_P_always_QRS] &
    [dominant_PR = normal] &
    [dominant_QRS = normal] &
    [rate_of_QRS = between_60_100]
    V
    [rhythm_QRS = irregular] &
    [dominant_P = normal] &

        [rate_of_P = under_60] &
        [relation_P_QRS = after_P_always_QRS] &
        [dominant_PR = normal] &
        [dominant_QRS = normal] &
        [rate_of_QRS = under_60]

[sinus_bradycardia]  ⟹
        [rhythm_QRS = regular] &
        [dominant_P = normal] &
        [rate_of_P = under_60] &
        [relation_P_QRS = after_P_always_QRS] &
        [dominant_PR = normal] &
        [dominant_QRS = normal] &
        [rate_of_QRS = under_60]

[sinus_tachycardia]  ⟹
        [rhythm_QRS = regular] &
        [dominant_P = normal] &
        [rate_of_P = between_100_250] &
        [relation_P_QRS = after_P_always_QRS] &
        [dominant_PR = normal] &
        [dominant_QRS = normal] &
        [rate_of_QRS = between_100_250]

[sa_node_disorders]  ⟹
        [rhythm_QRS = irregular] &
        [dominant_P = normal] &
        [rate_of_P = between_60_100] &
        [relation_P_QRS = after_P_always_QRS] &
        [dominant_PR = normal] &
        [dominant_QRS = normal] &
        [rate_of_QRS = between_60_100]
        ∨
        [rhythm_QRS = irregular] &
        [dominant_P = normal] &
        [rate_of_P = under_60] &
        [relation_P_QRS = after_P_always_QRS] &
        [dominant_PR = normal] &
        [dominant_QRS = normal] &
        [rate_of_QRS = under_60]

[wandering_pacemaker]  $\implies$
  [rhythm_QRS = irregular] &
  [dominant_P = changing] &
  [rate_of_P = between_60_100] &
  [relation_P_QRS = after_P_always_QRS] &
  [dominant_PR = normal ∨ changing] &
  [dominant_QRS = normal] &
  [rate_of_QRS = between_60_100]

[atrial_tachycardia]  $\implies$
  [rhythm_QRS = regular] &
  [dominant_P = abnormal] &
  [rate_of_P = between_100_250] &
  [relation_P_QRS = after_P_always_QRS] &
  [dominant_PR = normal ∨ shortened ∨ prolonged] &
  [dominant_QRS = normal] &
  [rate_of_QRS = between_100_250]

[multi_atrial_tachycardia]  $\implies$
  [rhythm_QRS = irregular] &
  [dominant_P = changing] &
  [rate_of_P = between_100_250] &
  [relation_P_QRS = after_P_always_QRS] &
  [dominant_PR = normal ∨ changing] &
  [dominant_QRS = normal] &
  [rate_of_QRS = between_100_250]

[atrial_flutter]  $\implies$
  [rhythm_QRS = irregular ∨ regular] &
  [dominant_P = abnormal] &
  [rate_of_P = between_250_350] &
  [relation_P_QRS = after_P_some_QRS_miss] &
  [dominant_PR = meaningless] &
  [dominant_QRS = normal] &
  [rate_of_QRS = under_60 ∨ between_60_100 ∨
                between_100_250]

[atrial_fibrillation]  $\implies$
  [rhythm_QRS = irregular] &
  [dominant_P = abnormal] &

[rate_of_P = over_350] &
[relation_P_QRS = meaningless ∨ independent_P_QRS ∨
                   after_P_some_QRS_miss] &
[dominant_PR = meaningless] &
[dominant_QRS = normal] &
[rate_of_QRS = under_60 ∨ between_60_100 ∨
                between_100_250]
∨
[rhythm_QRS = irregular] &
[dominant_P = absent] &
[rate_of_P = zero] &
[relation_P_QRS = meaningless] &
[dominant_PR = meaningless] &
[dominant_QRS = normal] &
[rate_of_QRS = under_60 ∨ between_60_100 ∨
                between_100_250]

[junctional_rhythm]  ⟹
[rhythm_QRS = regular] &
[dominant_P = abnormal] &
[rate_of_P = under_60] &
[relation_P_QRS = after_P_always_QRS] &
[dominant_PR = shortened ∨ after_QRS_is_P] &
[dominant_QRS = normal] &
[rate_of_QRS = under_60]
∨
[rhythm_QRS = regular] &
[dominant_P = absent] &
[rate_of_P = zero] &
[relation_P_QRS = meaningless] &
[dominant_PR = meaningless] &
[dominant_QRS = normal] &
[rate_of_QRS = under_60]

[accelerated_junctional_rhythm]  ⟹
[rhythm_QRS = regular] &
[dominant_P = abnormal] &
[rate_of_P = between_60_100] &
[relation_P_QRS = after_P_always_QRS] &

   [dominant_PR = shortened ∨ after_QRS_is_P] &
   [dominant_QRS = normal] &
   [rate_of_QRS = between_60_100]
   ∨
   [rhythm_QRS = regular] &
   [dominant_P = absent] &
   [rate_of_P = zero] &
   [relation_P_QRS = meaningless] &
   [dominant_PR = meaningless] &
   [dominant_QRS = normal] &
   [rate_of_QRS = between_60_100]

[junctional_tachycardia] ⟹
   [rhythm_QRS = regular] &
   [dominant_P = abnormal] &
   [rate_of_P = between_100_250] &
   [relation_P_QRS = after_P_always_QRS] &
   [dominant_PR = shortened ∨ after_QRS_is_P] &
   [dominant_QRS = normal] &
   [rate_of_QRS = between_100_250]
   ∨
   [rhythm_QRS = regular] &
   [dominant_P = absent] &
   [rate_of_P = zero] &
   [relation_P_QRS = meaningless] &
   [dominant_PR = meaningless] &
   [dominant_QRS = normal] &
   [rate_of_QRS = between_100_250]

[ventricular_rhythm] ⟹
   [rhythm_QRS = regular] &
   [dominant_P = absent] &
   [rate_of_P = zero] &
   [relation_P_QRS = meaningless] &
   [dominant_PR = meaningless] &
   [dominant_QRS = wide_RBBB ∨ wide_LBBB ∨
                      wide_non_specific] &
   [rate_of_QRS = under_60]
   ∨

        [rhythm_QRS = regular] &
        [dominant_P = abnormal] &
        [rate_of_P = under_60] &
        [relation_P_QRS = after_P_always_QRS] &
        [dominant_PR = after_QRS_is_P] &
        [dominant_QRS = wide_RBBB ∨ wide_LBBB ∨
                            wide_non_specific] &
        [rate_of_QRS = under_60]

[accelerated_ventricular_rhythm]  ⟹
        [rhythm_QRS = regular] &
        [dominant_P = absent] &
        [rate_of_P = zero] &
        [relation_P_QRS = meaningless] &
        [dominant_PR = meaningless] &
        [dominant_QRS = wide_RBBB ∨ wide_LBBB ∨
                            wide_non_specific] &
        [rate_of_QRS = between_60_100]
        ∨
        [rhythm_QRS = regular] &
        [dominant_P = abnormal] &
        [rate_of_P = between_60_100] &
        [relation_P_QRS = after_P_always_QRS] &
        [dominant_PR = after_QRS_is_P] &
        [dominant_QRS = wide_RBBB ∨ wide_LBBB ∨
                            wide_non_specific] &
        [rate_of_QRS = between_60_100]

[ventricular_tachycardia]  ⟹
        [rhythm_QRS = regular] &
        [dominant_P = absent] &
        [rate_of_P = zero] &
        [relation_P_QRS = meaningless] &
        [dominant_PR = meaningless] &
        [dominant_QRS = wide_RBBB ∨ wide_LBBB ∨
                            wide_non_specific] &
        [rate_of_QRS = between_100_250]
        ∨
        [rhythm_QRS = regular] &

  [dominant_P = -abnormal] &
  [rate_of_P = between_100_250] &
  [relation_P_QRS = after_P_always_QRS] &
  [dominant_PR = after_QRS_is_P] &
  [dominant_QRS = wide_RBBB ∨ wide_LBBB ∨
                      wide_non_specific] &
  [rate_of_QRS = between_100_250]

[ventricular_flutter] ⟹
  [rhythm_QRS = regular] &
  [dominant_P = absent] &
  [rate_of_P = zero] &
  [relation_P_QRS = meaningless] &
  [dominant_PR = meaningless] &
  [dominant_QRS = wide_RBBB ∨ wide_LBBB ∨
                      wide_non_specific] &
  [rate_of_QRS = between_250_350]

[ventricular_fibrillation] ⟹
  [rhythm_QRS = irregular] &
  [dominant_P = absent] &
  [rate_of_P = zero] &
  [relation_P_QRS = meaningless] &
  [dominant_PR = meaningless] &
  [dominant_QRS = absent] &
  [rate_of_QRS = over_350]

[sinus_rhythm,
 atrial_ectopic_beats] ⟹
  [rhythm_QRS = regular] &
  [dominant_P = normal] &
  [rate_of_P = between_60_100] &
  [relation_P_QRS = after_P_always_QRS] &
  [dominant_PR = normal] &
  [dominant_QRS = normal] &
  [rate_of_QRS = between_60_100] &
  [ectopic_P(1) = abnormal] &
  [ectopic_PR(1) = normal ∨ shortened ∨ prolonged] &
  [ectopic_QRS(1) = normal]

[sinus_rhythm,
  av_block_1]  ⟹
    [rhythm_QRS = regular] &
    [dominant_P = normal] &
    [rate_of_P = between_60_100] &
    [relation_P_QRS = after_P_always_QRS] &
    [dominant_PR = prolonged] &
    [dominant_QRS = normal] &
    [rate_of_QRS = between_60_100]

[sinus_rhythm,
  wenckebach]  ⟹
    [rhythm_QRS = irregular] &
    [dominant_P = normal] &
    [rate_of_P = between_60_100] &
    [relation_P_QRS = after_P_some_QRS_miss] &
    [dominant_PR = prolonged] &
    [dominant_QRS = normal] &
    [rate_of_QRS = between_60_100 ∨ under_60]

[sinus_rhythm,
  mobitz_2]  ⟹
    [rhythm_QRS = regular] &
    [dominant_P = normal] &
    [rate_of_P = between_60_100] &
    [relation_P_QRS = after_P_some_QRS_miss] &
    [dominant_PR = normal] &
    [dominant_QRS = normal] &
    [rate_of_QRS = between_60_100 ∨ under_60]

[sinus_rhythm,
  wpw_syndrome]  ⟹
    [rhythm_QRS = regular] &
    [dominant_P = normal] &
    [rate_of_P = between_60_100] &
    [relation_P_QRS = after_P_always_QRS] &
    [dominant_PR = shortened] &
    [dominant_QRS = delta_LBBB ∨ delta_RBBB] &
    [rate_of_QRS = between_60_100]

[sinus_rhythm,
 lgl_syndrome]  ⟹
   [rhythm_QRS = regular] &
   [dominant_P = normal] &
   [rate_of_P = between_60_100] &
   [relation_P_QRS = after_P_always_QRS] &
   [dominant_PR = shortened] &
   [dominant_QRS = normal] &
   [rate_of_QRS = between_60_100]

[sinus_rhythm,
 junctional_ectopic_beats]  ⟹
   [rhythm_QRS = regular] &
   [dominant_P = normal] &
   [rate_of_P = between_60_100] &
   [relation_P_QRS = after_P_always_QRS] &
   [dominant_PR = normal] &
   [dominant_QRS = normal] &
   [rate_of_QRS = between_60_100] &
   [ectopic_P(1) = abnormal] &
   [ectopic_PR(1) = shortened ∨ after_QRS_is_P] &
   [ectopic_QRS(1) = normal]
   ∨
   [rhythm_QRS = regular] &
   [dominant_P = normal] &
   [rate_of_P = between_60_100] &
   [relation_P_QRS = after_P_always_QRS] &
   [dominant_PR = normal] &
   [dominant_QRS = normal] &
   [rate_of_QRS = between_60_100] &
   [ectopic_P(1) = absent] &
   [ectopic_PR(1) = meaningless] &
   [ectopic_QRS(1) = normal]

[sinus_rhythm,
 left_bundle_branch_block]  ⟹
   [rhythm_QRS = regular] &
   [dominant_P = normal] &
   [rate_of_P = between_60_100] &
   [relation_P_QRS = after_P_always_QRS] &

[dominant_PR = normal] &
[dominant_QRS = wide_LBBB] &
[rate_of_QRS = between_60_100]

[sinus_rhythm,
 right_bundle_branch_block]  $\implies$
   [rhythm_QRS = regular] &
   [dominant_P = normal] &
   [rate_of_P = between_60_100] &
   [relation_P_QRS = after_P_always_QRS] &
   [dominant_PR = normal] &
   [dominant_QRS = wide_RBBB] &
   [rate_of_QRS = between_60_100]

[sinus_rhythm,
 ventricular_ectopic_beats]  $\implies$
   [rhythm_QRS = regular] &
   [dominant_P = normal] &
   [rate_of_P = between_60_100] &
   [relation_P_QRS = after_P_always_QRS] &
   [dominant_PR = normal] &
   [dominant_QRS = normal] &
   [rate_of_QRS = between_60_100] &
   [ectopic_P(1) = absent] &
   [ectopic_PR(1) = meaningless] &
   [ectopic_QRS(1) = wide_RBBB $\vee$ wide_LBBB $\vee$
                        wide_non_specific]
   $\vee$
   [rhythm_QRS = regular] &
   [dominant_P = normal] &
   [rate_of_P = between_60_100] &
   [relation_P_QRS = after_P_always_QRS] &
   [dominant_PR = normal] &
   [dominant_QRS = normal] &
   [rate_of_QRS = between_60_100] &
   [ectopic_P(1) = abnormal] &
   [ectopic_PR(1) = after_QRS_is_P] &
   [ectopic_QRS(1) = wide_RBBB $\vee$ wide_LBBB $\vee$
                        wide_non_specific]

[sinus_rhythm,
  multi_ventricular_ectopic_beats] ⟹
    [rhythm_QRS = regular] &
    [dominant_P = normal] &
    [rate_of_P = between_60_100] &
    [relation_P_QRS = after_P_always_QRS] &
    [dominant_PR = normal] &
    [dominant_QRS = normal] &
    [rate_of_QRS = between_60_100] &
    [ectopic_P(1) = absent] &
    [ectopic_PR(1) = meaningless] &
    [ectopic_QRS(1) = wide_RBBB ∨ wide_LBBB ∨
                    wide_non_specific] &
    [ectopic_P(2) = absent] &
    [ectopic_PR(2) = meaningless] &
    [ectopic_QRS(2) = wide_RBBB ∨ wide_LBBB ∨
                    wide_non_specific]
    ∨
    [rhythm_QRS = regular] &
    [dominant_P = normal] &
    [rate_of_P = between_60_100] &
    [relation_P_QRS = after_P_always_QRS] &
    [dominant_PR = normal] &
    [dominant_QRS = normal] &
    [rate_of_QRS = between_60_100] &
    [ectopic_P(1) = absent] &
    [ectopic_PR(1) = meaningless] &
    [ectopic_QRS(1) = wide_RBBB ∨ wide_LBBB ∨
                    wide_non_specific] &
    [ectopic_P(2) = abnormal] &
    [ectopic_PR(2) = after_QRS_is_P] &
    [ectopic_QRS(2) = wide_RBBB ∨ wide_LBBB ∨
                    wide_non_specific]
    ∨
    [rhythm_QRS = regular] &
    [dominant_P = normal] &
    [rate_of_P = between_60_100] &
    [relation_P_QRS = after_P_always_QRS] &

[dominant_PR = normal] &
[dominant_QRS = normal] &
[rate_of_QRS = between_60_100] &
[ectopic_P(1) = abnormal] &
[ectopic_PR(1) = after_QRS_is_P] &
[ectopic_QRS(1) = wide_RBBB ∨ wide_LBBB ∨
                         wide_non_specific] &
[ectopic_P(2) = absent] &
[ectopic_PR(2) = meaningless] &
[ectopic_QRS(2) = wide_RBBB ∨ wide_LBBB ∨
                         wide_non_specific]
∨
[rhythm_QRS = regular] &
[dominant_P = normal] &
[rate_of_P = between_60_100] &
[relation_P_QRS = after_P_always_QRS] &
[dominant_PR = normal] &
[dominant_QRS = normal] &
[rate_of_QRS = between_60_100] &
[ectopic_P(1) = abnormal] &
[ectopic_PR(1) = after_QRS_is_P] &
[ectopic_QRS(1) = wide_RBBB ∨ wide_LBBB ∨
                         wide_non_specific] &
[ectopic_P(2) = abnormal] &
[ectopic_PR(2) = after_QRS_is_P] &
[ectopic_QRS(2) = wide_RBBB ∨ wide_LBBB ∨
                         wide_non_specific]

[sinus_rhythm,
 av_block_3,
 accelerated_junctional_rhythm]  ⟹
   [rhythm_QRS = regular] &
   [dominant_P = normal] &
   [rate_of_P = between_60_100] &
   [relation_P_QRS = independent_P_QRS] &
   [dominant_PR = meaningless] &
   [dominant_QRS = normal] &
   [rate_of_QRS = between_60_100]

[sinus_rhythm,
 av_block_3,
 ventricular_rhythm]  $\implies$
   [rhythm_QRS = regular] &
   [dominant_P = normal] &
   [rate_of_P = between_60_100] &
   [relation_P_QRS = independent_P_QRS] &
   [dominant_PR = meaningless] &
   [dominant_QRS = wide_RBBB ∨ wide_LBBB ∨
                      wide_non_specific] &
   [rate_of_QRS = under_60]

[atrial_tachycardia,
 wenckebach,
 right_bundle_branch_block,
 ventricular_ectopic_beats]  $\implies$
   [rhythm_QRS = irregular] &
   [dominant_P = abnormal] &
   [rate_of_P = between_100_250] &
   [relation_P_QRS = after_P_some_QRS_miss] &
   [dominant_PR = prolonged] &
   [dominant_QRS = wide_RBBB] &
   [rate_of_QRS = between_100_250 ∨ between_60_100] &
   [ectopic_P(1) = absent] &
   [ectopic_PR(1) = meaningless] &
   [ectopic_QRS(1) = wide_RBBB ∨ wide_LBBB ∨
                      wide_non_specific]
   ∨
   [rhythm_QRS = irregular] &
   [dominant_P = abnormal] &
   [rate_of_P = between_100_250] &
   [relation_P_QRS = after_P_some_QRS_miss] &
   [dominant_PR = prolonged] &
   [dominant_QRS = wide_RBBB] &
   [rate_of_QRS = between_100_250 ∨ between_60_100] &
   [ectopic_P(1) = abnormal] &

```
    [ectopic_PR(1) = after_QRS_is_P] &
    [ectopic_QRS(1) = wide_RBBB ∨ wide_LBBB ∨
                            wide_non_specific]
[sinus_bradycardia,
 wpw_syndrome,
 junctional_ectopic_beats,
 left_bundle_branch_block]  ⟹
    [rhythm_QRS = regular] &
    [dominant_P = normal] &
    [rate_of_P = under_60] &
    [relation_P_QRS = after_P_always_QRS] &
    [dominant_PR = shortened] &
    [dominant_QRS = delta_LBBB ∨ delta_RBBB] &
    [rate_of_QRS = under_60] &
    [ectopic_P(1) = abnormal] &
    [ectopic_PR(1) = shortened ∨ after_QRS_is_P] &
    [ectopic_QRS(1) = wide_LBBB]
    ∨
    [rhythm_QRS = regular] &
    [dominant_P = normal] &
    [rate_of_P = under_60] &
    [relation_P_QRS = after_P_always_QRS] &
    [dominant_PR = shortened] &
    [dominant_QRS = delta_LBBB ∨ delta_RBBB] &
    [rate_of_QRS = under_60] &
    [ectopic_P(1) = absent] &
    [ectopic_PR(1) = meaningless] &
    [ectopic_QRS(1) = wide_LBBB]
[multi_atrial_tachycardia,
 av_block_3,
 junctional_rhythm,
 left_bundle_branch_block,
 ventricular_ectopic_beats]  ⟹
    [rhythm_QRS = regular] &
    [dominant_P = changing] &
    [rate_of_P = between_100_250] &
    [relation_P_QRS = independent_P_QRS] &
```

```
   [dominant_PR = meaningless] &
   [dominant_QRS = wide_LBBB] &
   [rate_of_QRS = under_60] &
   [ectopic_P(1) = absent] &
   [ectopic_PR(1) = meaningless] &
   [ectopic_QRS(1) = wide_RBBB ∨ wide_LBBB ∨
                          wide_non_specific]
[sinus_tachycardia,
 atrial_ectopic_beats,
 mobitz_2,
 junctional_ectopic_beats,
 ventricular_ectopic_beats]  ⟹
   [rhythm_QRS = regular] &
   [dominant_P = normal] &
   [rate_of_P = between_100_250] &
   [relation_P_QRS = after_P_some_QRS_miss] &
   [dominant_PR = normal] &
   [dominant_QRS = normal] &
   [rate_of_QRS = between_100_250 ∨ between_60_100] &
   [ectopic_P(1) = absent] &
   [ectopic_PR(1) = meaningless] &
   [ectopic_QRS(1) = wide_RBBB ∨ wide_LBBB ∨
                          wide_non_specific] &
   [ectopic_P(2) = abnormal] &
   [ectopic_PR(2) = shortened ∨ after_QRS_is_P] &
   [ectopic_QRS(2) = normal] &
   [ectopic_P(3) = abnormal] &
   [ectopic_PR(3) = normal] &
   [ectopic_QRS(3) = normal]
   ∨
   [rhythm_QRS = regular] &
   [dominant_P = normal] &
   [rate_of_P = between_100_250] &
   [relation_P_QRS = after_P_some_QRS_miss] &
   [dominant_PR = normal] &
   [dominant_QRS = normal] &
   [rate_of_QRS = between_100_250 ∨ between_60_100] &
   [ectopic_P(1) = absent] &
```

[ectopic_PR(1) = meaningless] &
[ectopic_QRS(1) = wide_RBBB ∨ wide_LBBB ∨
                       wide_non_specific] &
[ectopic_P(2) = absent] &
[ectopic_PR(2) = meaningless] &
[ectopic_QRS(2) = normal] &
[ectopic_P(3) = abnormal] &
[ectopic_PR(3) = normal] &
[ectopic_QRS(3) = normal]
∨
[rhythm_QRS = regular] &
[dominant_P = normal] &
[rate_of_P = between_100_250] &
[relation_P_QRS = after_P_some_QRS_miss] &
[dominant_PR = normal] &
[dominant_QRS = normal] &
[rate_of_QRS = between_100_250 ∨ between_60_100] &
[ectopic_P(1) = abnormal] &
[ectopic_PR(1) = after_QRS_is_P] &
[ectopic_QRS(1) = wide_RBBB ∨ wide_LBBB ∨
                       wide_non_specific] &
[ectopic_P(2) = abnormal] &
[ectopic_PR(2) = shortened ∨ after_QRS_is_P] &
[ectopic_QRS(2) = normal] &
[ectopic_P(3) = abnormal] &
[ectopic_PR(3) = normal] &
[ectopic_QRS(3) = normal]
∨
[rhythm_QRS = regular] &
[dominant_P = normal] &
[rate_of_P = between_100_250] &
[relation_P_QRS = after_P_some_QRS_miss] &
[dominant_PR = normal] &
[dominant_QRS = normal] &
[rate_of_QRS = between_100_250 ∨ between_60_100] &
[ectopic_P(1) = abnormal] &
[ectopic_PR(1) = after_QRS_is_P] &

   [ectopic_QRS(1) = wide_RBBB ∨ wide_LBBB ∨
                       wide_non_specific] &
   [ectopic_P(2) = absent] &
   [ectopic_PR(2) = meaningless] &
   [ectopic_QRS(2) = normal] &
   [ectopic_P(3) = abnormal] &
   [ectopic_PR(3) = normal] &
   [ectopic_QRS(3) = normal]
[sinus_arrhythmia,
 atrial_ectopic_beats,
 av_block_3,
 junctional_ectopic_beats,
 accelerated_ventricular_rhythm,
 ventricular_ectopic_beats]  ⟹
   [rhythm_QRS = regular] &
   [dominant_P = normal] &
   [rate_of_P = between_60_100] &
   [relation_P_QRS = independent_P_QRS] &
   [dominant_PR = meaningless] &
   [dominant_QRS = wide_RBBB ∨ wide_LBBB ∨
                       wide_non_specific] &
   [rate_of_QRS = between_60_100] &
   [ectopic_P(1) = absent] &
   [ectopic_PR(1) = meaningless] &
   [ectopic_QRS(1) = wide_RBBB ∨ wide_LBBB ∨
                       wide_non_specific] &
   [ectopic_P(2) = absent] &
   [ectopic_PR(2) = meaningless] &
   [ectopic_QRS(2) = normal] &
   [ectopic_P(3) = abnormal] &
   [ectopic_PR(3) = meaningless] &
   [ectopic_QRS(3) = absent]
   ∨
   [rhythm_QRS = regular] &
   [dominant_P = normal] &
   [rate_of_P = under_60] &
   [relation_P_QRS = independent_P_QRS] &
   [dominant_PR = meaningless] &

[dominant_QRS = wide_RBBB ∨ wide_LBBB ∨
                        wide_non_specific] &
[rate_of_QRS = between_60_100] &
[ectopic_P(1) = absent] &
[ectopic_PR(1) = meaningless] &
[ectopic_QRS(1) = wide_RBBB ∨ wide_LBBB ∨
                        wide_non_specific] &
[ectopic_P(2) = absent] &
[ectopic_PR(2) = meaningless] &
[ectopic_QRS(2) = normal] &
[ectopic_P(3) = abnormal] &
[ectopic_PR(3) = meaningless] &
[ectopic_QRS(3) = absent]

[atrial_tachycardia,
 av_block_3,
 junctional_ectopic_beats,
 right_bundle_branch_block,
 ventricular_rhythm,
 multi_ventricular_ectopic_beats]   ⟹
   [rhythm_QRS = regular] &
   [dominant_P = abnormal] &
   [rate_of_P = between_100_250] &
   [relation_P_QRS = independent_P_QRS] &
   [dominant_PR = meaningless] &
   [dominant_QRS = wide_RBBB ∨ wide_LBBB ∨
                        wide_non_specific] &
   [rate_of_QRS = under_60] &
   [ectopic_P(1) = absent] &
   [ectopic_PR(1) = meaningless] &
   [ectopic_QRS(1) = wide_RBBB ∨ wide_LBBB ∨
                        wide_non_specific] &
   [ectopic_P(2) = absent] &
   [ectopic_PR(2) = meaningless] &
   [ectopic_QRS(2) = wide_RBBB ∨ wide_LBBB ∨
                        wide_non_specific] &
   [ectopic_P(3) = absent] &
   [ectopic_PR(3) = meaningless] &
   [ectopic_QRS(3) = wide_RBBB]

[sa_node_disorders,
 atrial_ectopic_beats,
 av_block_3,
 junctional_ectopic_beats,
 right_bundle_branch_block,
 ventricular_tachycardia,
 ventricular_ectopic_beats]  ⟹
   [rhythm_QRS = regular] &
   [dominant_P = normal] &
   [rate_of_P = between_60_100] &
   [relation_P_QRS = independent_P_QRS] &
   [dominant_PR = meaningless] &
   [dominant_QRS = wide_RBBB ∨ wide_LBBB ∨
                        wide_non_specific] &
   [rate_of_QRS = between_100_250] &
   [ectopic_P(1) = absent] &
   [ectopic_PR(1) = meaningless] &
   [ectopic_QRS(1) = wide_RBBB ∨ wide_LBBB ∨
                        wide_non_specific] &
   [ectopic_P(2) = absent] &
   [ectopic_PR(2) = meaningless] &
   [ectopic_QRS(2) = wide_RBBB] &
   [ectopic_P(3) = abnormal] &
   [ectopic_PR(3) = meaningless] &
   [ectopic_QRS(3) = absent]
   ∨
   [rhythm_QRS = regular] &
   [dominant_P = normal] &
   [rate_of_P = under_60] &
   [relation_P_QRS = independent_P_QRS] &
   [dominant_PR = meaningless] &
   [dominant_QRS = wide_RBBB ∨ wide_LBBB ∨
                        wide_non_specific] &
   [rate_of_QRS = between_100_250] &
   [ectopic_P(1) = absent] &
   [ectopic_PR(1) = meaningless] &
   [ectopic_QRS(1) = wide_RBBB ∨ wide_LBBB ∨
                        wide_non_specific] &

[ectopic_P(2) = absent] &
[ectopic_PR(2) = meaningless] &
[ectopic_QRS(2) = wide_RBBB] &
[ectopic_P(3) = abnormal] &
[ectopic_PR(3) = meaningless] &
[ectopic_QRS(3) = absent]

[sinus_tachycardia,
 atrial_ectopic_beats,
 av_block_3,
 junctional_ectopic_beats,
 left_bundle_branch_block,
 ventricular_rhythm,
 ventricular_ectopic_beats]  $\Longrightarrow$
   [rhythm_QRS = regular] &
   [dominant_P = normal] &
   [rate_of_P = between_100_250] &
   [relation_P_QRS = independent_P_QRS] &
   [dominant_PR = meaningless] &
   [dominant_QRS = wide_RBBB ∨ wide_LBBB ∨
                         wide_non_specific] &
   [rate_of_QRS = under_60] &
   [ectopic_P(1) = absent] &
   [ectopic_PR(1) = meaningless] &
   [ectopic_QRS(1) = wide_RBBB ∨ wide_LBBB ∨
                         wide_non_specific] &
   [ectopic_P(2) = absent] &
   [ectopic_PR(2) = meaningless] &
   [ectopic_QRS(2) = wide_LBBB] &
   [ectopic_P(3) = abnormal] &
   [ectopic_PR(3) = meaningless] &
   [ectopic_QRS(3) = absent]

# Appendix B

# Compressed Diagnostic Rules

This appendix contains the compressed diagnostic rules and the diagnostic algorithm. Diagnostic rules consist of a complete set of descriptions of individual ECG features in terms of the states of the heart. Diagnostic rules were obtained by the NEWGEM program through compression of the reduced arrhythmia-ECG base (943 arrhythmias with 5240 ECG descriptions).

NEWGEM has a set of user defined parameters that influence the form of derived concept descriptions. Here we explain their meaning and their possible values.

| Parameter | Value | Meaning |
|---|---|---|
| • mode | • intersecting covers (ic) | • Rules may intersect over parts of the space where there are no learning events. |
| | • disjoint covers (dc) | • Rules do not intersect at all. |
| | • variable-valued logic (vl) | • Rules are order dependant; rule for class N assumes that rules for classes 1 through N-1 are not satisfied. |
| • ambig | • negative (neg) | • Ambiguous examples are always taken as negative and are not covered by any rule. |
| | • positive (pos) | • Ambiguous examples are taken as positive and are covered by more than one rule. |

| | | |
|---|---|---|
| | • empty (empty) | • Ambiguous examples are ignored and may or may not be covered by some rule. |
| • trim | • general (gen) | • Rules are as general as possible having min. number of selectors and max. number of values. |
| | • minimal (mini) | • Rules are as simple as possible having min. number of selectors and min. number of values. |
| | • specific (spec) | • Rules are as specific as possible having max. number of selectors and min. number of values. |
| • wts | • no weights (no) | • No weights. |
| | • complexes (cpx) | • Two weights are associated with each complex: the total number of covered positive examples and number of examples covered by this and no other complex. |
| | • all | • Besides weights of complexes there are also two weights of selectors: total number of positive examples covered by a selector and number of negative examples covered by a selector (independently of other selectors). |
| • maxstar | • N | • Parameter controls the number of alternative solutions to be kept during a complex formation: its value must be an integer between 1 and 100. |

| • criteria | • maxnew | • Maximize the number of newly covered positive examples, i.e. examples not covered by previous complexes. |
| | • maxtot | • Maximize the total number of covered positive examples. |
| | • newvsneg | • Maximize the ratio between newly covered positive examples and all covered negative examples. |
| | • totvsneg | • Maximize the ration between total number of covered positive examples and all covered negative examples. |
| | • mincost | • Minimize the total cost of variables used. |
| | • minsel | • Minimize the number of selectors. |
| | • maxsel | • Maximize the number of selectors. |
| | • minref | • Minimize the number of references in selectors. |

In the experiment the following values of NEWGEM parameters were selected:

- mode = ic
- ambig = pos
- trim = mini
- wts = cpx
- maxstar = 10
- criteria = maxnew, minsel, minref

Here are definitions of domains of attributes that define heart disorders:

```
domain( sa_node, [quiet, sr, sb, st, sa, sad]).
domain( atr_focus, [quiet, wp, at, mat, afl, af, aeb]).
domain( av_conduct, [normal, avb1, wen, mob2, avb3, wpw, lgl]).
domain( av_junction , [quiet, jr, ajr, jt, jeb]).
domain( bundle_branches, [normal, lbbb, rbbb]).
domain( reg_vent_focus, [quiet, vr, avr, vt, vfl, vf]).
domain( ect_vent_focus, [quiet, veb]).
```

The following are definitions of domains of attributes that define ECG descriptions:

```
domain(    rhythm_QRS, [regular,
                          irregular]).
domain(    dominant_P, [normal,
                          abnormal,
                          changing,
                          absent]).
domain(     rate_of_P, [zero,                  % ordered domain
                          under_60,
                          between_60_100,
                          between_100_250,
                          between_250_350,
                          over_350]).
domain(relation_P_QRS, [meaningless,
                          after_P_always_QRS,
                          after_P_some_QRS_miss,
                          independent_P_QRS]).
domain(   dominant_PR, [meaningless,
                          normal,
                          prolonged,
                          shortened,
                          changing,
                          after_QRS_is_P]).
domain( dominant_QRS, [normal,
                          wide_LBBB,
                          wide_RBBB,
                          wide_non_specific,
                          delta_LBBB,
                          delta_RBBB,
```

```
                            absent]]).
    domain(    rate_of_QRS, [zero,                    % ordered domain
                            under_60,
                            between_60_100,
                            between_100_250,
                            between_250_350,
                            over_350]]).
    domain(      ectopic_P, [none,
                            abnormal,
                            absent]]).
    domain(     ectopic_PR, [none,
                            meaningless,
                            normal,
                            prolonged,
                            shortened,
                            after_QRS_is_P]]).
    domain(    ectopic_QRS, [none,
                            normal,
                            wide_LBBB,
                            wide_RBBB,
                            wide_non_specific,
                            delta_LBBB,
                            delta_RBBB,
                            absent]]).
```

The following is a complete set of compressed diagnostic rules.

```
[rhythm_QRS = regular]  ⇒
   [sa_node = sr ∨ sb ∨ st ∨ quiet] &
   [atr_focus = at ∨ afl ∨ aeb ∨ quiet] &
   [av_conduct = avb1 ∨ mob2 ∨ avb3 ∨
                    wpw ∨ lgl ∨ normal] &
   [reg_vent_focus = vr ∨ avr ∨ vt ∨ vfl ∨ quiet] (2194:1645)
 ∨ [av_conduct = avb3] (1413:864)

[rhythm_QRS = irregular]  ⇒
   [sa_node = sa ∨ sad ∨ quiet] &
   [atr_focus = wp ∨ mat ∨ af ∨ aeb ∨ quiet] &
   [av_junction = jeb ∨ quiet] &
   [reg_vent_focus = vf ∨ quiet] (1867:1549)
```

∨ [atr_focus = afl] &
  [av_conduct = normal] (90:90)
∨ [av_conduct = wen] (543:225)


[dominant_P = normal]  ⇒
  [sa_node = sr ∨ sb ∨ st ∨ sa ∨ sad] (2532:2532)

[dominant_P = abnormal]  ⇒
  [sa_node = quiet] &
  [atr_focus = at ∨ afl ∨ af ∨ aeb ∨ quiet] &
  [reg_vent_focus = vr ∨ avr ∨ vt ∨ quiet] (1457:1457)

[dominant_P = changing]  ⇒
  [atr_focus = wp ∨ mat] (742:742)

[dominant_P = absent]  ⇒
  [sa_node = quiet] &
  [atr_focus = af ∨ aeb ∨ quiet] (509:509)


[rate_of_P = zero]  ⇒
  [sa_node = quiet] &
  [atr_focus = af ∨ aeb ∨ quiet] (509:509)

[rate_of_P = under_60]  ⇒
  [sa_node = sb ∨ sa ∨ sad] (972:972)
∨ [sa_node = quiet] &
  [atr_focus = aeb ∨ quiet] &
  [av_junction = jr ∨ jeb ∨ quiet] &
  [reg_vent_focus = vr ∨ quiet] (135:135)

[rate_of_P = between_60_100]  ⇒
  [sa_node = sr ∨ sa ∨ sad ∨ quiet] &
  [atr_focus = wp ∨ aeb ∨ quiet] &
  [av_junction = ajr ∨ jeb ∨ quiet] &
  [reg_vent_focus = avr ∨ quiet] (1376:1226)
∨ [sa_node = sr ∨ sa ∨ sad ∨ quiet] &
  [atr_focus = wp ∨ aeb ∨ quiet] &
  [av_conduct = avb3] (450:300)

[rate_of_P = between_100_250]  ⇒
   [sa_node = st ∨ quiet] &
   [atr_focus = at ∨ mat ∨ aeb ∨ quiet] &
   [av_junction = jt ∨ jeb ∨ quiet] &
   [reg_vent_focus = vt ∨ quiet] (1087:982)
 ∨ [sa_node = st ∨ quiet] &
   [atr_focus = at ∨ mat ∨ aeb ∨ quiet] &
   [av_conduct = avb3] (315:210)

[rate_of_P = between_250_350]  ⇒
   [atr_focus = afl] (281:281)

[rate_of_P = over_350]  ⇒
   [atr_focus = af] (370:370)

[relation_P_QRS = meaningless]  ⇒
   [sa_node = quiet] &
   [atr_focus = af ∨ aeb ∨ quiet] &
   [av_conduct = wpw ∨ normal] (501:501)
 ∨ [atr_focus = afl] &
   [av_conduct = wpw] (2:2)

[relation_P_QRS = after_P_always_QRS]  ⇒
   [atr_focus = wp ∨ at ∨ mat ∨ aeb ∨ quiet] &
   [av_conduct = avb1 ∨ wpw ∨ lgl ∨ normal] &
   [reg_vent_focus = vr ∨ avr ∨ vt ∨ quiet] (1878:1878)

[relation_P_QRS = after_P_some_QRS_miss]  ⇒
   [av_conduct = wen ∨ mob2] (1086:1086)
 ∨ [atr_focus = afl ∨ af] &
   [av_conduct = normal] (270:270)

[relation_P_QRS = independent_P_QRS]  ⇒
   [av_conduct = avb3] (1413:1413)
 ∨ [atr_focus = af] &
   [av_conduct = normal] (90:90)

[dominant_PR = meaningless]  ⇒
   [av_conduct = avb3] (1413:1116)
 ∨ [sa_node = quiet] &
   [atr_focus = afl ∨ af ∨ aeb ∨ quiet] (1160:863)

[dominant_PR = normal]  ⇒
  [atr_focus = wp ∨ at ∨ mat ∨ aeb ∨ quiet] &
  [av_conduct = mob2 ∨ normal] &
  [av_junction = jeb ∨ quiet] &
  [reg_vent_focus = quiet] (906:906)

[dominant_PR = prolonged]  ⇒
  [av_conduct = avb1 ∨ wen] (864:864)
 ∨ [atr_focus = at] &
  [av_conduct = normal] (30:30)

[dominant_PR = shortened]  ⇒
  [atr_focus = wp ∨ at ∨ mat ∨ aeb ∨ quiet] &
  [av_conduct = wpw ∨ lgl] (669:669)
 ∨ [sa_node = quiet] &
  [atr_focus = at ∨ aeb ∨ quiet] &
  [av_conduct = normal] &
  [reg_vent_focus = quiet] (120:120)

[dominant_PR = changing]  ⇒
  [atr_focus = wp ∨ mat] &
  [av_conduct = normal] (60:60)

[dominant_PR = after_QRS_is_P]  ⇒
  [sa_node = quiet] &
  [atr_focus = aeb ∨ quiet] &
  [reg_vent_focus = vr ∨ avr ∨ vt ∨ quiet] (315:315)

[dominant_QRS = normal]  ⇒
  [av_conduct = avb1 ∨ wen ∨ mob2 ∨
               avb3 ∨ lgl ∨ normal] &
  [bundle_branches = normal] &
  [reg_vent_focus = quiet] (1184:1184)

[dominant_QRS = wide_LBBB] ⇒
  [av_conduct = avb1 ∨ wen ∨ mob2 ∨
                avb3 ∨ lgl ∨ normal] &
  [bundle_branches = lbbb] (1259:1184)
 ∨ [reg_vent_focus = vr ∨ avr ∨ vt ∨ vfl] (445:370)

[dominant_QRS = wide_RBBB] ⇒
  [av_conduct = avb1 ∨ wen ∨ mob2 ∨
                avb3 ∨ lgl ∨ normal] &
  [bundle_branches = rbbb] (1259:1184)
 ∨ [reg_vent_focus = vr ∨ avr ∨ vt ∨ vfl] (445:370)

[dominant_QRS = wide_non_specific] ⇒
  [reg_vent_focus = vr ∨ avr ∨ vt ∨ vfl] (445:445)

[dominant_QRS = delta_LBBB] ⇒
  [atr_focus = wp ∨ at ∨ mat ∨ afl ∨ aeb ∨ quiet] &
  [av_conduct = wpw] (175:175)

[dominant_QRS = delta_RBBB] ⇒
  [atr_focus = wp ∨ at ∨ mat ∨ afl ∨ aeb ∨ quiet] &
  [av_conduct = wpw] (175:175)

[dominant_QRS = absent] ⇒
  [atr_focus = af] &
  [av_conduct = wpw] (2:2)
 ∨ [reg_vent_focus = vf] (1:1)

[rate_of_QRS = zero] ⇒ false (0:0)

[rate_of_QRS = under_60] ⇒
  [sa_node = sb ∨ sa ∨ sad ∨ quiet] &
  [atr_focus = afl ∨ af ∨ aeb ∨ quiet] &
  [av_conduct = avb1 ∨ wen ∨ mob2 ∨
                avb3 ∨ lgl ∨ normal] &
  [av_junction = jr ∨ jeb ∨ quiet] &
  [reg_vent_focus = vr ∨ quiet] (1359:1065)
 ∨ [sa_node = sr ∨ quiet] &
  [atr_focus = wp ∨ aeb ∨ quiet] &
  [av_conduct = wen ∨ mob2 ∨ avb3] &
  [av_junction = jr ∨ jeb ∨ quiet] &

[reg_vent_focus = vr ∨ quiet] (198:126)
∨ [sa_node = sb ∨ sa ∨ sad] &
[av_conduct = wpw] (108:108)
∨ [av_conduct = avb3] &
[av_junction = jr ∨ jeb ∨ quiet] &
[reg_vent_focus = vr ∨ quiet] (471:105)

[rate_of_QRS = between_60_100]  ⇒
[sa_node = sr ∨ sa ∨ sad ∨ quiet] &
[atr_focus = wp ∨ afl ∨ af ∨ aeb ∨ quiet] &
[av_conduct = avb1 ∨ wen ∨ mob2 ∨
                      avb3 ∨ lgl ∨ normal] &
[av_junction = ajr ∨ jeb ∨ quiet] &
[reg_vent_focus = avr ∨ quiet] (1440:1053)
∨ [sa_node = st ∨ quiet] &
[av_conduct = wen ∨ mob2 ∨ avb3] &
[av_junction = ajr ∨ jeb ∨ quiet] &
[reg_vent_focus = avr ∨ quiet] (483:186)
∨ [sa_node = sr ∨ sa ∨ sad ∨ quiet] &
[atr_focus = wp ∨ aeb ∨ quiet] &
[av_conduct = wpw] (140:140)
∨ [av_conduct = avb3] &
[av_junction = ajr ∨ jeb ∨ quiet] &
[reg_vent_focus = avr ∨ quiet] (471:39)

[rate_of_QRS = between_100_250]  ⇒
[sa_node = st ∨ quiet] &
[atr_focus = at ∨ mat ∨ afl ∨ af ∨ aeb ∨ quiet] &
[av_conduct = avb1 ∨ wen ∨ mob2 ∨
                      avb3 ∨ lgl ∨ normal] &
[av_junction = jt ∨ jeb ∨ quiet] &
[reg_vent_focus = vt ∨ quiet] (1185:981)
∨ [sa_node = st ∨ quiet] &
[atr_focus = at ∨ mat ∨ aeb ∨ quiet] &
[av_conduct = wpw] (100:100)
∨ [av_conduct = avb3] &
[av_junction = jt ∨ jeb ∨ quiet] &
[reg_vent_focus = vt ∨ quiet] (471:267)

[rate_of_QRS = between_250_350] ⇒
  [reg_vent_focus = vfl] (3:3)
∨ [atr_focus = afl] &
  [av_conduct = wpw] (2:2)

[rate_of_QRS = over_350] ⇒
  [atr_focus = af] &
  [av_conduct = wpw] (2:2)
∨ [reg_vent_focus = vf] (1:1)

[ectopic_P = none] ⇒
  [atr_focus = wp ∨ at ∨ mat ∨ afl ∨ af ∨ quiet] &
  [av_junction = jr ∨ ajr ∨ jt ∨ quiet] &
  [ect_vent_focus = quiet] (565:565)

[ectopic_P = abnormal] ⇒
  [av_conduct = avb1 ∨ wen ∨ mob2 ∨
               wpw ∨ lgl ∨ normal] &
  [ect_vent_focus = veb] (969:969)
∨ [av_conduct = avb1 ∨ wen ∨ mob2 ∨
               wpw ∨ lgl ∨ normal] &
  [av_junction = jeb] (744:744)
∨ [atr_focus = aeb] (568:568)

[ectopic_P = absent] ⇒
  [ect_vent_focus = veb] (1671:1671)
∨ [av_junction = jeb] (723:723)

[ectopic_PR = none] ⇒
  [atr_focus = wp ∨ at ∨ mat ∨ afl ∨ af ∨ quiet] &
  [av_junction = jr ∨ ajr ∨ jt ∨ quiet] &
  [ect_vent_focus = quiet] (565:565)

[ectopic_PR = meaningless] ⇒
  [ect_vent_focus = veb] (1671:1671)
∨ [av_junction = jeb] (723:723)
∨ [atr_focus = aeb] &
  [av_conduct = avb3] (126:126)

[ectopic_PR = normal] ⇒
  [atr_focus = aeb] &
  [av_conduct = mob2 ∨ normal] (135:135)

[ectopic_PR = prolonged]  ⇒
  [atr_focus = aeb] &
  [av_conduct = avb1 ∨ wen ∨ normal] (156:156)

[ectopic_PR = shortened]  ⇒
  [av_conduct = avb1 ∨ wen ∨ mob2 ∨
                wpw ∨ lgl ∨ normal] &
  [av_junction = jeb] (372:372)
 ∨ [atr_focus = aeb] &
  [av_conduct = wpw ∨ lgl ∨ normal] (151:151)

[ectopic_PR = after_QRS_is_P]  ⇒
  [av_conduct = avb1 ∨ wen ∨ mob2 ∨
                wpw ∨ lgl ∨ normal] &
  [ect_vent_focus = veb] (969:969)
 ∨ [av_conduct = avb1 ∨ wen ∨ mob2 ∨
                wpw ∨ lgl ∨ normal] &
  [av_junction = jeb] (372:372)


[ectopic_QRS = none]  ⇒
  [atr_focus = wp ∨ at ∨ mat ∨ afl ∨ af ∨ quiet] &
  [av_junction = jr ∨ ajr ∨ jt ∨ quiet] &
  [ect_vent_focus = quiet] (565:565)

[ectopic_QRS = normal]  ⇒
  [av_junction = jeb] &
  [bundle_branches = normal] (489:489)
 ∨ [atr_focus = aeb] &
  [av_conduct = avb1 ∨ wen ∨ mob2 ∨ lgl ∨ normal] &
  [bundle_branches = normal] (138:138)

[ectopic_QRS = wide_LBBB]  ⇒
  [ect_vent_focus = veb] (880:880)
 ∨ [av_junction = jeb] &
  [bundle_branches = lbbb] (489:489)
 ∨ [atr_focus = aeb] &
  [av_conduct = avb1 ∨ wen ∨ mob2 ∨ lgl ∨ normal] &
  [bundle_branches = lbbb] (138:138)

[ectopic_QRS = wide_RBBB] ⇒
  [ect_vent_focus = veb] (880:880)
 V [av_junction = jeb] &
  [bundle_branches = rbbb] (489:489)
 V [atr_focus = aeb] &
  [av_conduct = avb1 V wen V mob2 V lgl V normal] &
  [bundle_branches = rbbb] (138:138)

[ectopic_QRS = wide_non_specific] ⇒
  [ect_vent_focus = veb] (880:880)

[ectopic_QRS = delta_LBBB] ⇒
  [atr_focus = aeb] &
  [av_conduct = wpw] (14:14)

[ectopic_QRS = delta_RBBB] ⇒
  [atr_focus = aeb] &
  [av_conduct = wpw] (14:14)

[ectopic_QRS = absent] ⇒
  [atr_focus = aeb] &
  [av_conduct = avb3] (126:126)

The following is a part of the Prolog program that implements a diagnostic algorithm on the basis of compressed diagnostic rules. The algorithm also incorporates rules for the reconstruction of the original arrhythmia-ECG base, with several ectopic beats occuring simultaneously.

```
%   An ECG description is represented as a list of lists, where
%   the first list contains dominant attributes and next lists
%   contain triples of ectopic attributes:

sample_ECG( [ [ rhythm_QRS : [regular],
                dominant_P : [normal],
                rate_of_P : [between_60_100],
                relation_P_QRS : [after_P_always_QRS],
                dominant_PR : [normal],
                dominant_QRS : [normal],
                rate_of_QRS : [between_60_100]  ],
```

```
                    [ ectopic_P : [abnormal],
                      ectopic_PR : [normal, shortened, prolonged],
                      ectopic_QRS : [normal]  ],
                    [ ectopic_P : [absent],
                      ectopic_PR : [meaningless],
                      ectopic_QRS : [wide_LBBB]  ]  ] ).
```

%   Compressed diagnostic rules are represented as Prolog
%   unit clauses of the following form:

```
rule( rhythm_QRS, regular, [mini], [
    [ sa_node : [sr, sb, st, quiet],
      atr_focus : [at, afl, aeb, quiet],
      av_cond : [avb1, mob2, avb3, wpw, lgl, normal],
      reg_vent : [vr, avr, vt, vfl, quiet] ] :2194:1645,
    [ av_cond : [avb3] ] :1413:864 ] ).

rule( rhythm_QRS, irregular, [mini], [
    [ sa_node : [sa, sad, quiet],
      atr_focus : [wp, mat, af, aeb, quiet],
      junction : [jeb, quiet],
      reg_vent : [vf, quiet] ] :1867:1549,
    [ atr_focus : [afl],
      av_cond : [normal] ] :90:90,
    [ av_cond : [wen] ] :543:225 ] ).
```

%   For an ECG description finds list Diag of all possible
%   combined arrhythmias.

```
ecg_diag( [Regular], Diag ) :-
    ecg_cond( Regular, [[]], Disj ),
    setof( Arrs, cond_no_ectop( Disj, Arrs ), Diag ).
ecg_diag( [Regular | Ectopic], Diag ) :-
    ecg_cond( Regular, [[]], Disj0 ),
    ect_diag( Ectopic, Disj0, Diag_list ),
    setof( Arrs, find_arrs( Diag_list, [], Arrs ), Diag ).

    ect_diag( [], _, [] ).
    ect_diag( [Ect | Ectopic], Disj0, [Diag | Diag_list] ) :-
        ecg_cond( Ect, Disj0, Disj ),
        setof( Arrs, cond_one_ectop( Disj, Arrs ), Diag ),
        ect_diag( Ectopic, Disj0, Diag_list ).
```

```
% For a given list of ECG attributes calculates condition
% EDiag (using induced diagnostic rules) that must be satisfied
% by any possible diagnosis.

ecg_cond( [], Disj, Disj ).
ecg_cond( [Feature | ECG], Disj0, Disj ) :-
    ecg_cond( ECG, Disj0, Disj1 ),
    apply_rule( Feature, Disj2 ),
    mult_disj( Disj2, Disj1, Disj3 ),
    refine( Disj3, Disj ).

    apply_rule( _ : [], [] ).
    apply_rule( Attr : [Val | Values], Disj ) :-
        rule( Attr, Val, _, Disj0 ),
        conc( Disj0, Disj1, Disj ),
        apply_rule( Attr : Values, Disj1 ).

    refine( [], [] ).
    refine( [Conj0 | Disj0], [Conj | Disj] ) :-
        general( Conj0, Disj0, Conj, Disj1 ),
        refine( Disj1, Disj ).

        general( Conj, [], Conj, [] ).
        general( Conj0, [Conj1 | Disj0], Conj, Disj ) :-
            subsume( Conj1, Conj0 ), !,
            general( Conj1, Disj0, Conj, Disj ).
        general( Conj0, [Conj1 | Disj0], Conj, Disj ) :-
            subsume( Conj0, Conj1 ), !,
            general( Conj0, Disj0, Conj, Disj ).
        general( Conj0, [Conj1 | Disj0], Conj, [Conj1 | Disj] ) :-
            general( Conj0, Disj0, Conj, Disj ).

            subsume( [], _ ).
            subsume( [Group : Arrs0 | Conj0], Conj1 ) :-
                mem( Group : Arrs1, Conj1, Conj2 ),
                subset( Arrs1, Arrs0 ),
                subsume( Conj0, Conj2 ).

    mult_disj( [], _, [] ).
    mult_disj( [Conj:_:_ | Disj1], Disj0, Disj ) :-
        mult_disj_conj( Disj0, Conj, Disj, Tail ),
        mult_disj( Disj1, Disj0, Tail ).
```

```
mult_disj_conj( [], _, Tail, Tail ).
mult_disj_conj( [Conj0 | Disj0], Conj1, [Conj | Disj], Tail ) :-
    merge_conj( Conj1, Conj0, Conj ), !,
    mult_disj_conj( Disj0, Conj1, Disj, Tail ).
mult_disj_conj( [_ | Disj0], Conj1, Disj, Tail ) :-
    mult_disj_conj( Disj0, Conj1, Disj, Tail ).


merge_conj( [], Conj, Conj ).
merge_conj( [Atom1 | Conj1], Conj0, Conj ) :-
    merge_conj_atom( Conj0, Atom1, Conj00, Conj, Tail ), !,
    merge_conj( Conj1, Conj00, Tail ).


merge_conj_atom( [], Group:Arrs, [], [Group:Arrs | Tail], Tail ).
merge_conj_atom( [Group:Arrs0 | Conj0], Group:Arrs1, Conj0,
                 [Group:Arrs | Tail], Tail ) :- !,
    intersect( Arrs0, Arrs1, Arrs ), Arrs = [_|_].
merge_conj_atom( [Atom0 | Conj0], Atom1,
                 [Atom0 | Conj00], Conj, Tail ) :-
    merge_conj_atom( Conj0, Atom1, Conj00, Conj, Tail ).



%   Finds multiple arrhythmias without any ectopic arrhythmia
%   or with exactly one ectopic arrhythmia.

cond_no_ectop( Disj, Arrs ) :-
    cond_diag( Disj, Arrs ),
    ectop_arr( Ectop ),
    no_ectop( Arrs, Ectop ).

cond_one_ectop( Disj, Arrs ) :-
    cond_diag( Disj, Arrs ),
    ectop_arr( Ectop ),
    one_ectop( Arrs, Ectop ).

ectop_arr( [aeb, jeb, veb, mveb] ).
```

```
one_ectop( [Arr | Arrs], Ectop ) :-
    mem( Arr, Ectop ), !,
    no_ectop( Arrs, Ectop ).
one_ectop( [_ | Arrs], Ectop ) :-
    one_ectop( Arrs, Ectop ).

no_ectop( [], _ ).
no_ectop( [Arr | Arrs], Ectop ) :-
    not mem( Arr, Ectop ),
    no_ectop( Arrs, Ectop ).
```

% Finds combined arrhythmia Diag satisfying condition Disj
% and legality constraints.

```
cond_diag( Disj, Arrs ) :-
    groups( Groups ),
    mem( Conj, Disj ),
    augment_sel( Groups, Conj, Arrs ),
    trans_constr( Arrs ).

    augment_sel( [], _, [] ).
    augment_sel( [Group:_ | Groups], Conj, Arrs ) :-
        mem( Group:Arrs0, Conj ), !,
        mem( Arr, Arrs0 ),
        sel_arr( Arr, Arrs, Tail ),
        augment_sel( Groups, Conj, Tail ).
    augment_sel( [Group:Arrs0 | Groups], Conj, Arrs ) :-
        mem( Arr, Arrs0 ),
        sel_arr( Arr, Arrs, Tail ),
        augment_sel( Groups, Conj, Tail ).

        sel_arr( none, Arrs, Arrs ) :- !.
        sel_arr( Arr, [Arr | Arrs], Arrs ).
```

% Combine multiple arrhythmias with one constituent ectopic
% arrhythmia into several ectopic arrhythmias. Takes into
% consideration legality constraints.

```
find_arrs( [], Diag, Arrs ) :-
    comb_diag( Diag, Arrs ), !,
    trans_constr( Arrs ).
```

```
find_arrs( [Diag0 | Diag_list], Diag1, Arrs ) :-
    mem( Arrs0, Diag0 ),
    find_arrs( Diag_list, [Arrs0 | Diag1], Arrs ).

    comb_diag( [Arrs], Arrs ) :- !.
    comb_diag( [Arrs0 | Diag], Arrs ) :-
        comb_diag( Diag, Arrs1 ),
        comb_arrs( Arrs0, Arrs1, Arrs ).

        comb_arrs( Arrs0, Arrs1, Arrs ) :-
            ectop_arr( Ectop ),
            differ( Arrs0, Ectop, Reg0 ),
            differ( Arrs1, Ectop, Reg1 ),
            union( Reg0, Reg1, Reg ),
            intersect( Ectop, Arrs0, Ect0 ),
            intersect( Ectop, Arrs1, Ect1 ),
            union_ect( Ect0, Ect1, Ect ),
            conc( Reg, Ect, Arrs ).

            union_ect( [], Ect, Ect ).
            union_ect( [Arr | Ect0], Ect1, _ ) :-
                (Arr = aeb ; Arr = jeb ),
                mem( Arr, Ect1 ), !,
                fail.
            union_ect( [veb | Ect0], Ect1, [mveb | Ect] ) :-
                (mem( veb, Ect1, Ect2 ) ;
                 mem( mveb, Ect1, Ect2 )), !,
                union_ect( Ect0, Ect2, Ect ).
            union_ect( [Arr | Ect0], Ect1, [Arr | Ect] ) :-
                union_ect( Ect0, Ect1, Ect ).
```

%   Transforms and checks for legality constraints.

```
trans_constr( Arr_comb ) :-
    abnormal_heart( Arr_comb, Heart0 ),
    rest_heart( Heart1 ),
    complete_state( Heart1, Heart0, Heart2 ),
    legality_constraints( Heart2, notrace ).
```

# Appendix C

# Compressed Prediction Rules

This appendix contains the compressed prediction rules, i.e. the complete set of descriptions of selected heart disorders obtained through compression by the NEWGEM algorithm. Compression was performed on the reduced arrhythmia-ECG base (943 arrhythmias with 5240 ECG descriptions).

In the sequel we present the complete set of compressed prediction rules, defining descriptions of selected arrhythmias. Each complex has associated a pair of numbers **(Total:Unique)**. **Total** denotes the number of positive examples covered by the complex, and **Unique** denotes the number of examples covered by this and no other complex in the rule. Binary functor "`..`" is used in values of attributes **rate_of_P** and **rate_of_QRS**, that both have ordered domains. $\mathbf{v}_0..\mathbf{v}_n$ denotes the internal disjunction of the set of values $\mathbf{v}_0 \vee \mathbf{v}_1 \vee \ldots \vee \mathbf{v}_n$.

[sa_node = quiet] ⇒
    [dominant_P = abnormal ∨ changing ∨ absent] (2708:2708)

[sa_node = sr] ⇒                                  % sinus rhythm
    [rhythm_QRS = regular] &
    [dominant_P = normal] &
    [rate_of_P = between_60_100] (324:324)
  ∨ [dominant_P = normal] &
    [rate_of_P = between_60_100] &
    [relation_P_QRS = after_P_some_QRS_miss] &
    [dominant_PR = prolonged] (66:66)

[sa_node = sb]  ⇒                                    % sinus bradycardia
  [rhythm_QRS = regular] &
  [dominant_P = normal] &
  [rate_of_P = under_60] (291:291)
 V [rate_of_P = under_60] &
  [relation_P_QRS = after_P_some_QRS_miss] &
  [dominant_PR = prolonged] (33:33)

[sa_node = st]  ⇒                                    % sinus tachycardia
  [dominant_P = normal] &
  [rate_of_P = between_100_250] (390:390)

[sa_node = sa]  ⇒                                    % sinus arrrhythmia
  [rhythm_QRS = irregular] &
  [dominant_P = normal] &
  [rate_of_P = under_60..between_60_100] (480:480)
 V [dominant_P = normal] &
  [rate_of_P = under_60..between_60_100] &
  [relation_P_QRS = independent_P_QRS] (234:234)

[sa_node = sad]  ⇒                                   % SA node disorders
  [rhythm_QRS = irregular] &
  [dominant_P = normal] &
  [rate_of_P = under_60..between_60_100] (480:480)
 V [dominant_P = normal] &
  [rate_of_P = under_60..between_60_100] &
  [relation_P_QRS = independent_P_QRS] (234:234)

[atr_focus = quiet]  ⇒
  [dominant_P = normal] &
  [ectopic_PR(1) = meaningless V shortened V
           after_QRS_is_P V none] &
  [ectopic_QRS(1) = normal V wide_LBBB V wide_RBBB V
           wide_non_specific V none] (2207:2132)
 V [rhythm_QRS = regular] &
  [relation_P_QRS = meaningless V after_P_always_QRS] &
  [dominant_PR = meaningless V shortened V after_QRS_is_P] &
  [dominant_QRS = normal V wide_LBBB V wide_RBBB V
           wide_non_specific] &
  [ectopic_PR(1) = meaningless V after_QRS_is_P V none] &

[ectopic_QRS(1) = wide_LBBB ∨ wide_RBBB ∨
                        wide_non_specific ∨ none] (465:138)
∨ [rhythm_QRS = regular] &
  [relation_P_QRS = meaningless ∨ after_P_always_QRS] &
  [dominant_PR = meaningless ∨ after_QRS_is_P] &
  [dominant_QRS = wide_LBBB ∨ wide_RBBB ∨
                        wide_non_specific] &
  [ectopic_PR(1) = meaningless ∨ shortened ∨
                        after_QRS_is_P] (342:90)
∨ [rate_of_P = zero] &
  [relation_P_QRS = meaningless] &
  [dominant_QRS = absent] &
  [ectopic_PR(1) = none] (1:1)

[atr_focus = wp]  ⇒                        % wandering pacemaker
  [dominant_P = changing] &
  [rate_of_P = between_60_100] (371:371)

[atr_focus = at]  ⇒                        % atrial tachycardia
  [dominant_P = abnormal] &
  [rate_of_P = between_100_250] &
  [dominant_PR = meaningless ∨ normal ∨
                        prolonged ∨ shortened] &
  [ectopic_PR(1) = meaningless ∨ shortened ∨
                        after_QRS_is_P ∨ none] (401:401)

[atr_focus = mat]  ⇒                % multifocal atrial tachycardia
  [dominant_P = changing] &
  [rate_of_P = between_100_250] (371:371)

[atr_focus = afl]  ⇒                        % atrial flutter
  [rate_of_P = between_250_350] (281:281)

[atr_focus = af]  ⇒                        % atrial fibrillation
  [rate_of_P = over_350] (370:279)
∨ [rhythm_QRS = irregular] &
  [relation_P_QRS = meaningless] (182:91)
∨ [dominant_P = absent] &
  [relation_P_QRS = independent_P_QRS] (99:99)

[atr_focus = aeb]  ⇒                              % atrial ectopic beats
  [ectopic_P(1) = abnormal] &
  [ectopic_PR(1) = meaningless ∨ normal ∨ prolonged] (417:417)
∨ [rhythm_QRS = regular] &
  [dominant_P = normal ∨ abnormal ∨ absent] &
  [rate_of_P = zero..between_60_100] &
  [relation_P_QRS = meaningless ∨ after_P_always_QRS] &
  [dominant_PR = meaningless ∨ normal ∨ shortened ∨
                      after_QRS_is_P] &
  [dominant_QRS = normal ∨ wide_LBBB ∨ wide_RBBB ∨
                      wide_non_specific] &
  [ectopic_PR(1) = shortened] (78:36)
∨ [ectopic_QRS(1) = delta_LBBB ∨ delta_RBBB] (28:28)
∨ [rhythm_QRS = regular] &
  [dominant_PR = shortened ∨ after_QRS_is_P] &
  [dominant_QRS = normal ∨ wide_LBBB ∨ wide_RBBB ∨
                      wide_non_specific] &
  [ectopic_PR(1) = shortened] (54:15)
∨ [dominant_P = normal] &
  [relation_P_QRS = after_P_always_QRS] &
  [dominant_PR = normal ∨ shortened] &
  [dominant_QRS = normal ∨ wide_LBBB ∨ wide_RBBB] &
  [ectopic_PR(1) = shortened] (42:27)

[av_conduct = normal]  ⇒
  [relation_P_QRS = meaningless ∨ after_P_always_QRS] &
  [dominant_PR = meaningless ∨ normal ∨ changing ∨
                      after_QRS_is_P] &
  [dominant_QRS = normal ∨ wide_LBBB ∨ wide_RBBB ∨
                      wide_non_specific] (1236:828)
∨ [dominant_P = abnormal ∨ absent] &
  [rate_of_P = zero ∨ between_100_250] &
  [relation_P_QRS = meaningless ∨ after_P_always_QRS] &
  [dominant_PR = meaningless ∨ prolonged] (439:31)
∨ [dominant_P = abnormal] &
  [relation_P_QRS = after_P_always_QRS ∨
                      after_P_some_QRS_miss] &
  [dominant_PR = meaningless ∨ shortened] &

[dominant_QRS = normal ∨ wide_LBBB ∨
                                wide_RBBB] (390:390)
 ∨ [rhythm_QRS = irregular] &
   [relation_P_QRS = independent_P_QRS] (90:90)

[av_conduct = avb1]   ⇒                    % AV block of 1st degree
   [relation_P_QRS = after_P_always_QRS] &
   [dominant_PR = prolonged] (321:321)

[av_conduct = wen]   ⇒             % AV block of Wenckebach type
   [relation_P_QRS = after_P_some_QRS_miss] &
   [dominant_PR = prolonged] (543:543)

[av_conduct = mob2]   ⇒            % AV block of Mobitz II type
   [relation_P_QRS = after_P_some_QRS_miss] &
   [dominant_PR = normal] (543:543)

[av_conduct = avb3]    ⇒             % AV block of 3rd degree
   [rhythm_QRS = regular] &
   [relation_P_QRS = independent_P_QRS] (1413:1413)

[av_conduct = wpw]   ⇒                        % WPW syndrome
   [dominant_QRS = delta_LBBB ∨ delta_RBBB ∨
                                absent] (352:352)

[av_conduct = lgl]   ⇒                         % LGL syndrome
   [dominant_P = normal ∨ changing] &
   [dominant_PR = shortened] &
   [dominant_QRS = normal ∨ wide_LBBB ∨
                                wide_RBBB] (291:228)
 ∨ [rate_of_P = between_100_250] &
   [dominant_PR = shortened] &
   [dominant_QRS = normal ∨ wide_LBBB ∨ wide_RBBB] &
   [ectopic_PR(1) = meaningless ∨ shortened ∨
                    after_QRS_is_P ∨ none] (93:30)

[av_junction = quiet]   ⇒
   [dominant_P = normal ∨ abnormal ∨ changing] &
   [relation_P_QRS = meaningless ∨ after_P_always_QRS ∨
                    after_P_some_QRS_miss] &
   [dominant_PR = meaningless ∨ normal ∨
                    prolonged ∨ changing] &

[ectopic_PR(1) = meaningless ∨ normal ∨ prolonged ∨
                    after_QRS_is_P ∨ none] &
[ectopic_QRS(1) = wide_LBBB ∨ wide_RBBB ∨
                    wide_non_specific ∨ none] (1538:401)
∨ [dominant_P = normal ∨ changing] &
[dominant_PR = shortened] &
[ectopic_PR(1) = meaningless ∨ after_QRS_is_P ∨ none] &
[ectopic_QRS(1) = wide_LBBB ∨ wide_RBBB ∨
                    wide_non_specific ∨ none] (315:70)
∨ [rhythm_QRS = irregular] &
[ectopic_PR(1) = meaningless ∨ after_QRS_is_P ∨ none] &
[ectopic_QRS(1) = wide_LBBB ∨ wide_RBBB ∨
                    wide_non_specific ∨ none] (1389:128)
∨ [rhythm_QRS = regular] &
[relation_P_QRS = meaningless ∨ after_P_always_QRS ∨
                    independent_P_QRS] &
[dominant_PR = meaningless ∨ after_QRS_is_P] &
[dominant_QRS = wide_LBBB ∨ wide_RBBB ∨
                    wide_non_specific] &
[ectopic_QRS(1) = wide_LBBB ∨ wide_RBBB ∨
                    wide_non_specific ∨ absent ∨ none] (768:768)
∨ [dominant_PR = shortened] &
[rate_of_QRS = between_100_250] &
[ectopic_PR(1) = meaningless ∨ after_QRS_is_P ∨ none] &
[ectopic_QRS(1) = wide_LBBB ∨ wide_RBBB ∨
                    wide_non_specific ∨ none] (126:56)
∨ [dominant_P = normal] &
[ectopic_PR(1) = normal ∨ prolonged] (129:43)
∨ [dominant_P = normal] &
[relation_P_QRS = after_P_always_QRS] &
[dominant_PR = normal ∨ shortened] &
[dominant_QRS = normal ∨ wide_LBBB ∨ wide_RBBB] &
[ectopic_PR(1) = shortened] (42:42)
∨ [dominant_QRS = wide_LBBB ∨ wide_RBBB ∨
                    wide_non_specific] &
[ectopic_PR(1) = normal ∨ prolonged ∨ shortened] &
[ectopic_QRS(1) = normal] (54:54)
∨ [ectopic_QRS(1) = delta_LBBB ∨ delta_RBBB] (28:28)

[av_junction = jr]  ⇒                                    % junctional rhythm
    [rhythm_QRS = regular] &
    [relation_P_QRS = independent_P_QRS] &
    [dominant_QRS = normal ∨ wide_LBBB ∨ wide_RBBB] &
    [rate_of_QRS = under_60] &
    [ectopic_QRS(1) = wide_LBBB ∨ wide_RBBB ∨
                    wide_non_specific ∨ absent ∨ none] (177:169)
  ∨ [rhythm_QRS = regular] &
    [dominant_P = abnormal ∨ absent] &
    [relation_P_QRS = meaningless ∨ after_P_always_QRS] &
    [dominant_QRS = normal ∨ wide_LBBB ∨ wide_RBBB] &
    [rate_of_QRS = under_60] &
    [ectopic_PR(1) = meaningless ∨ after_QRS_is_P ∨ none] &
    [ectopic_QRS(1) = wide_LBBB ∨ wide_RBBB ∨
                    wide_non_specific ∨ none] (63:20)
  ∨ [rhythm_QRS = regular] &
    [rate_of_P = zero..under_60] &
    [dominant_PR = meaningless ∨ after_QRS_is_P] &
    [dominant_QRS = wide_LBBB] &
    [rate_of_QRS = under_60] &
    [ectopic_QRS(1) = wide_LBBB] (14:6)
  ∨ [rhythm_QRS = regular] &
    [dominant_P = abnormal ∨ absent] &
    [relation_P_QRS = meaningless ∨ after_P_always_QRS] &
    [dominant_QRS = wide_RBBB] &
    [rate_of_QRS = under_60] &
    [ectopic_QRS(1) = wide_RBBB] (15:6)
  ∨ [rhythm_QRS = regular] &
    [dominant_P = abnormal ∨ absent] &
    [rate_of_P = zero..under_60] &
    [dominant_QRS = normal] &
    [rate_of_QRS = under_60] (34:6)
  ∨ [dominant_P = abnormal] &
    [dominant_PR = shortened] &
    [rate_of_QRS = under_60] (30:3)

[av_junction = ajr]  ⇒                          % accelerated junctional rhythm
    [dominant_P = normal ∨ changing ∨ absent] &
    [relation_P_QRS = independent_P_QRS] &

[dominant_QRS = normal ∨ wide_LBBB ∨ wide_RBBB] &
[rate_of_QRS = between_60_100] &
[ectopic_QRS(1) = wide_LBBB ∨ wide_RBBB ∨
                    wide_non_specific ∨ absent ∨ none] (141:129)
∨ [rhythm_QRS = regular] &
[dominant_P = abnormal ∨ absent] &
[relation_P_QRS = meaningless ∨ after_P_always_QRS ∨
                    independent_P_QRS] &
[dominant_QRS = normal ∨ wide_LBBB ∨ wide_RBBB] &
[rate_of_QRS = between_60_100] &
[ectopic_PR(1) = meaningless ∨ after_QRS_is_P ∨ none] &
[ectopic_QRS(1) = wide_LBBB ∨ wide_RBBB ∨
                    wide_non_specific ∨ none] (111:56)
∨ [rhythm_QRS = regular] &
[relation_P_QRS = meaningless ∨ after_P_always_QRS] &
[dominant_PR = meaningless ∨ after_QRS_is_P] &
[dominant_QRS = wide_RBBB] &
[rate_of_QRS = between_60_100] &
[ectopic_QRS(1) = wide_RBBB] (10:6)
∨ [rhythm_QRS = regular] &
[relation_P_QRS = meaningless ∨ after_P_always_QRS] &
[dominant_PR = meaningless ∨ after_QRS_is_P] &
[dominant_QRS = wide_LBBB] &
[rate_of_QRS = between_60_100] &
[ectopic_QRS(1) = wide_LBBB] (10:6)
∨ [rhythm_QRS = regular] &
[dominant_P = abnormal ∨ absent] &
[rate_of_P = zero ∨ between_60_100] &
[dominant_QRS = normal] &
[rate_of_QRS = between_60_100] (34:6)
∨ [dominant_P = abnormal] &
[rate_of_P = between_60_100] &
[dominant_PR = shortened] (30:6)

[av_junction = jt] ⇒                    % junctional tachycardia
    [rate_of_P = under_60..between_100_250] &
    [dominant_PR = meaningless] &
    [dominant_QRS = normal ∨ wide_LBBB ∨ wide_RBBB] &
    [rate_of_QRS = between_100_250] &

```
    [ectopic_QRS(1) = wide_LBBB ∨ wide_RBBB ∨
                            wide_non_specific ∨ absent ∨ none] (141:118)
 ∨ [rhythm_QRS = regular] &
   [dominant_P = abnormal ∨ absent] &
   [relation_P_QRS = meaningless ∨ after_P_always_QRS ∨
                            independent_P_QRS] &
   [dominant_PR = meaningless ∨ shortened ∨ after_QRS_is_P] &
   [dominant_QRS = normal ∨ wide_LBBB ∨ wide_RBBB] &
   [rate_of_QRS = between_100_250] &
   [ectopic_PR(1) = meaningless ∨ after_QRS_is_P ∨ none] &
   [ectopic_QRS(1) = wide_LBBB ∨ wide_RBBB ∨
                            wide_non_specific ∨ none] (111:72)
 ∨ [rhythm_QRS = regular] &
   [relation_P_QRS = meaningless ∨ after_P_always_QRS] &
   [dominant_PR = meaningless ∨ after_QRS_is_P] &
   [dominant_QRS = wide_LBBB] &
   [rate_of_QRS = between_100_250] &
   [ectopic_QRS(1) = wide_LBBB] (10:6)
 ∨ [rhythm_QRS = regular] &
   [rate_of_P = zero ∨ between_100_250] &
   [dominant_PR = meaningless ∨ after_QRS_is_P] &
   [dominant_QRS = wide_RBBB] &
   [rate_of_QRS = between_100_250] &
   [ectopic_QRS(1) = wide_RBBB] (14:6)
 ∨ [rhythm_QRS = regular] &
   [rate_of_P = zero ∨ between_100_250] &
   [dominant_PR = meaningless ∨ after_QRS_is_P] &
   [dominant_QRS = normal] &
   [rate_of_QRS = between_100_250] (37:6)
 ∨ [dominant_P = abnormal] &
   [dominant_PR = shortened] &
   [dominant_QRS = normal ∨ wide_LBBB ∨ wide_RBBB] &
   [rate_of_QRS = between_100_250] &
   [ectopic_PR(1) = normal ∨ prolonged ∨ shortened] (9:9)

[av_junction = jeb]   ⇒                    % junctional ectopic beats
   [rhythm_QRS = regular] &
   [relation_P_QRS = meaningless ∨ after_P_always_QRS ∨
                            independent_P_QRS] &
```

[dominant_PR = meaningless ∨ after_QRS_is_P] &
[dominant_QRS = wide_LBBB ∨ wide_RBBB ∨
                wide_non_specific] &
[ectopic_PR(1) = meaningless ∨ shortened ∨
                after_QRS_is_P] &
[ectopic_QRS(1) = normal ∨ wide_LBBB ∨
                wide_RBBB] (513:254)
∨ [dominant_P = normal ∨ changing ∨ absent] &
[dominant_QRS = wide_RBBB ∨ delta_LBBB ∨
                delta_RBBB] &
[ectopic_PR(1) = meaningless ∨ shortened ∨
                after_QRS_is_P] &
[ectopic_QRS(1) = normal ∨ wide_RBBB] (372:183)
∨ [dominant_P = normal ∨ changing ∨ absent] &
[dominant_QRS = wide_LBBB ∨ delta_LBBB ∨
                delta_RBBB] &
[ectopic_PR(1) = meaningless ∨ shortened ∨
                after_QRS_is_P] &
[ectopic_QRS(1) = wide_LBBB] (279:183)
∨ [ectopic_PR(1) = meaningless ∨ after_QRS_is_P] &
[ectopic_QRS(1) = normal] (365:172)
∨ [dominant_P = normal ∨ changing] &
[ectopic_PR(1) = shortened] &
[ectopic_QRS(1) = normal] (77:9)
∨ [rate_of_P = between_100_250..over_350] &
[dominant_QRS = wide_RBBB ∨ delta_LBBB ∨
                delta_RBBB] &
[ectopic_PR(1) = meaningless ∨ shortened ∨
                after_QRS_is_P] &
[ectopic_QRS(1) = normal ∨ wide_RBBB] (189:78)
∨ [rate_of_P = between_100_250..over_350] &
[dominant_QRS = wide_LBBB ∨ delta_LBBB ∨
                delta_RBBB] &
[ectopic_PR(1) = meaningless ∨ shortened ∨
                after_QRS_is_P] &
[ectopic_QRS(1) = wide_LBBB] (153:78)
∨ [rhythm_QRS = irregular] &
[ectopic_PR(1) = shortened] &

[ectopic_QRS(1) = normal] (74:12)
∨ [rate_of_P = between_100_250..between_250_350] &
[dominant_PR = meaningless ∨ normal ∨ prolonged ∨
                        shortened] &
[ectopic_PR(1) = shortened] &
[ectopic_QRS(1) = normal] (35:10)


[bundle_branches = normal]  ⇒
   [dominant_QRS = normal ∨ wide_non_specific ∨
                        delta_LBBB ∨ delta_RBBB ∨ absent] &
   [ectopic_PR(1) = meaningless ∨ after_QRS_is_P ∨
                        none] (1470:766)
∨ [rhythm_QRS = regular] &
   [relation_P_QRS = meaningless ∨ after_P_always_QRS ∨
                        independent_P_QRS] &
   [dominant_PR = meaningless ∨ after_QRS_is_P] &
   [ectopic_PR(1) = meaningless ∨ after_QRS_is_P ∨
                        none] (1034:440)
∨ [ectopic_QRS(1) = normal ∨ delta_LBBB ∨
                        delta_RBBB] (655:290)

[bundle_branches = lbbb]  ⇒              % left bundle branch block
   [dominant_QRS = wide_LBBB] &
   [rate_of_QRS = under_60..between_100_250] &
   [ectopic_QRS(1) = wide_LBBB ∨ wide_non_specific ∨
                        absent ∨ none] (1030:1030)
∨ [dominant_QRS = wide_LBBB] &
   [ectopic_PR(1) = meaningless ∨ after_QRS_is_P] &
   [ectopic_QRS(1) = wide_RBBB] (229:229)
∨ [dominant_QRS = delta_LBBB ∨ delta_RBBB] &
   [ectopic_QRS(1) = wide_LBBB] (60:60)
∨ [rhythm_QRS = regular] &
   [relation_P_QRS = meaningless ∨ after_P_always_QRS ∨
                        independent_P_QRS] &
   [dominant_PR = meaningless ∨ after_QRS_is_P] &
   [dominant_QRS = wide_RBBB ∨ wide_non_specific] &
   [ectopic_QRS(1) = wide_LBBB] (150:150)

[bundle_branches = rbbb]   ⇒                  % right bundle branch block
   [dominant_QRS = wide_RBBB] &
   [rate_of_QRS = under_60..between_100_250] &
   [ectopic_QRS(1) = wide_RBBB ∨ wide_non_specific ∨
                      absent ∨ none] (1030:1030)
 ∨ [dominant_QRS = wide_RBBB] &
   [ectopic_PR(1) = meaningless ∨ after_QRS_is_P] &
   [ectopic_QRS(1) = wide_LBBB] (229:229)
 ∨ [dominant_QRS = delta_LBBB ∨ delta_RBBB] &
   [ectopic_QRS(1) = wide_RBBB] (60:60)
 ∨ [rhythm_QRS = regular] &
   [relation_P_QRS = meaningless ∨ after_P_always_QRS ∨
                      independent_P_QRS] &
   [dominant_PR = meaningless ∨ after_QRS_is_P] &
   [dominant_QRS = wide_LBBB ∨ wide_non_specific] &
   [ectopic_QRS(1) = wide_RBBB] (150:150)

[reg_vent_focus = quiet]   ⇒
   [dominant_QRS = normal ∨ wide_LBBB ∨ wide_RBBB ∨
                      delta_LBBB ∨ delta_RBBB] &
   [rate_of_QRS = under_60..between_100_250] &
   [ectopic_PR(1) = meaningless ∨ after_QRS_is_P ∨ none] &
   [ectopic_QRS(1) = wide_LBBB ∨ wide_RBBB ∨
                   wide_non_specific ∨ absent ∨ none] (3090:1226)
 ∨ [dominant_QRS = normal ∨ delta_LBBB ∨ delta_RBBB ∨
                    absent] (1536:474)
 ∨ [dominant_QRS = wide_RBBB] &
   [ectopic_QRS(1) = wide_RBBB] (571:170)
 ∨ [dominant_QRS = wide_LBBB] &
   [ectopic_QRS(1) = wide_LBBB] (571:170)

[reg_vent_focus = vr]   ⇒                      % ventricular rhythm
   [rhythm_QRS = regular] &
   [relation_P_QRS = meaningless ∨ after_P_always_QRS ∨
                    independent_P_QRS] &
   [dominant_PR = meaningless ∨ after_QRS_is_P] &
   [dominant_QRS = wide_LBBB ∨ wide_RBBB ∨
                   wide_non_specific] & .
   [rate_of_QRS = under_60] (444:444)

[reg_vent_focus = avr] ⇒                   % accelerated ventricular rhythm
   [rhythm_QRS = regular] &
   [relation_P_QRS = meaningless ∨ after_P_always_QRS ∨
                   independent_P_QRS] &
   [dominant_PR = meaningless ∨ after_QRS_is_P] &
   [dominant_QRS = wide_LBBB ∨ wide_RBBB ∨
                   wide_non_specific] &
   [rate_of_QRS = between_60_100] (444:444)

[reg_vent_focus = vt] ⇒                   % ventricular tachycardia
   [rhythm_QRS = regular] &
   [relation_P_QRS = meaningless ∨ after_P_always_QRS ∨
                   independent_P_QRS] &
   [dominant_PR = meaningless ∨ after_QRS_is_P] &
   [dominant_QRS = wide_LBBB ∨ wide_RBBB ∨
                   wide_non_specific] &
   [rate_of_QRS = between_100_250] (444:444)

[reg_vent_focus = vfl] ⇒                   % ventricular flutter
   [dominant_QRS = wide_LBBB ∨ wide_RBBB ∨
                   wide_non_specific] &
   [rate_of_QRS = between_250_350] (3:3)

[reg_vent_focus = vf] ⇒                   % ventricular fibrilation
   [dominant_P = absent] &
   [dominant_QRS = absent] (1:1)

[ect_vent_focus = quiet] ⇒
   [ectopic_P(1) = abnormal ∨ none] &
   [ectopic_PR(1) = meaningless ∨ normal ∨ prolonged ∨
                 shortened ∨ none] (1505:731)
 ∨ [ectopic_QRS(1) = normal] (627:365)
 ∨ [rhythm_QRS = regular] &
   [relation_P_QRS = meaningless ∨ after_P_always_QRS ∨
                   independent_P_QRS] &
   [dominant_PR = meaningless ∨ after_QRS_is_P] &
   [dominant_QRS = wide_LBBB ∨ wide_RBBB ∨
                   wide_non_specific] &
   [ectopic_QRS(1) = wide_LBBB ∨ wide_RBBB] (486:212)
 ∨ [dominant_PR = meaningless ∨ normal ∨
                 prolonged ∨ changing] &

[dominant_QRS = wide_LBBB] &
[ectopic_QRS(1) = wide_LBBB] (341:28)
∨ [dominant_P = normal ∨ changing ∨ absent] &
[dominant_QRS = wide_RBBB ∨ delta_LBBB ∨
               delta_RBBB] &
[ectopic_QRS(1) = wide_RBBB] (354:122)
∨ [dominant_P = normal ∨ changing] &
[dominant_QRS = wide_LBBB ∨ delta_LBBB ∨
               delta_RBBB] &
[ectopic_QRS(1) = wide_LBBB] (315:42)
∨ [rate_of_P = between_100_250..over_350] &
[dominant_QRS = wide_RBBB ∨ delta_LBBB ∨
               delta_RBBB] &      .
[ectopic_QRS(1) = wide_RBBB] (171:52)
∨ [dominant_QRS = wide_LBBB ∨ delta_LBBB ∨
               delta_RBBB] &
[rate_of_QRS = between_100_250] &
[ectopic_QRS(1) = wide_LBBB] (131:8)


[ect_vent_focus = veb]  ⇒                    % ventricular ectopic beats
   [ectopic_PR(1) = meaningless ∨ after_QRS_is_P] &
   [ectopic_QRS(1) = wide_LBBB ∨ wide_RBBB ∨
                     wide_non_specific]  (2640:2640)


Exception rules have to be added to compressed prediction rules in order to preserve the equivalence with the reduced arrhythmia-ECG surface knowledge base. The following are four examples of exception rules.

[af]  ⇒  not
   [rhythm_QRS = irregular] &
   [dominant_P = absent] &
   [rate_of_P = zero] &
   [relation_P_QRS = meaningless] &
   [dominant_PR = meaningless] &
   [dominant_QRS = absent] &
   [rate_of_QRS = over_350]

[jr, veb]  ⇒  not
    [rhythm_QRS = regular] &
    [dominant_P = absent] &
    [rate_of_P = zero] &
    [relation_P_QRS = meaningless] &
    [dominant_PR = meaningless] &
    [dominant_QRS = wide_RBBB ∨ wide_LBBB] &
    [rate_of_QRS = under_60] &
    [ectopic_P(1) = absent] &
    [ectopic_PR(1) = meaningless] &
    [ectopic_QRS(1) = wide_LBBB ∨ wide_non_specific ∨
                        wide_RBBB]

    ∨

    [rhythm_QRS = regular] &
    [dominant_P = absent] &
    [rate_of_P = zero] &
    [relation_P_QRS = meaningless] &
    [dominant_PR = meaningless] &
    [dominant_QRS = wide_RBBB ∨ wide_LBBB] &
    [rate_of_QRS = under_60] &
    [ectopic_P(1) = abnormal] &
    [ectopic_PR(1) = after_QRS_is_P] &
    [ectopic_QRS(1) = wide_LBBB ∨ wide_non_specific ∨
                        wide_RBBB]

    ∨

    [rhythm_QRS = regular] &
    [dominant_P = abnormal] &
    [rate_of_P = under_60] &
    [relation_P_QRS = after_P_always_QRS] &
    [dominant_PR = after_QRS_is_P] &
    [dominant_QRS = wide_RBBB ∨ wide_LBBB] &
    [rate_of_QRS = under_60] &
    [ectopic_P(1) = absent] &
    [ectopic_PR(1) = meaningless] &
    [ectopic_QRS(1) = wide_LBBB ∨ wide_non_specific ∨
                        wide_RBBB]

    ∨

    [rhythm_QRS = regular] &

```
        [dominant_P = abnormal] &
        [rate_of_P = under_60] &
        [relation_P_QRS = after_P_always_QRS] &
        [dominant_PR = after_QRS_is_P] &
        [dominant_QRS = wide_RBBB ∨ wide_LBBB] &
        [rate_of_QRS = under_60] &
        [ectopic_P(1) = abnormal] &
        [ectopic_PR(1) = after_QRS_is_P] &
        [ectopic_QRS(1) = wide_LBBB ∨ wide_non_specific ∨
                            wide_RBBB]

[at, wpw, jeb]   ⇒   not
        [rhythm_QRS = regular] &
        [dominant_P = abnormal] &
        [rate_of_P = between_100_250] &
        [relation_P_QRS = after_P_always_QRS] &
        [dominant_PR = shortened] &
        [dominant_QRS = delta_RBBB ∨ delta_LBBB] &
        [rate_of_QRS = between_100_250] &
        [ectopic_P(1) = absent] &
        [ectopic_PR(1) = meaningless] &
        [ectopic_QRS(1) = wide_LBBB ∨ wide_RBBB]
        ∨
        [rhythm_QRS = regular] &
        [dominant_P = abnormal] &
        [rate_of_P = between_100_250] &
        [relation_P_QRS = after_P_always_QRS] &
        [dominant_PR = shortened] &
        [dominant_QRS = delta_RBBB ∨ delta_LBBB] &
        [rate_of_QRS = between_100_250] &
        [ectopic_P(1) = abnormal] &
        [ectopic_PR(1) = after_QRS_is_P] &
        [ectopic_QRS(1) = wide_LBBB ∨ wide_RBBB]

[st, avb3, jeb, rbbb, avr]   ⇒   not
        [rhythm_QRS = regular] &
        [dominant_P = normal] &
        [rate_of_P = between_100_250] &
        [relation_P_QRS = independent_P_QRS] &
```

[dominant_PR = meaningless] &
[dominant_QRS = wide_RBBB] &
[rate_of_QRS = between_60_100] &
[ectopic_P(1) = absent] &
[ectopic_PR(1) = meaningless] &
[ectopic_QRS(1) = wide_LBBB]

The complete set of exception rules consists of 255 combined arrhytmias (out of 943) with altogether 1,029 ECG descriptions. For complete equivalence with the original arrhythmia-ECG base, exception rules have to be added for the list of combined arrhythmias below. For space reasons we do not give complete exeption rules.

[af]
[af,avb3,jr]
[af,avb3,jr,lbbb,veb]
[af,avb3,jr,rbbb,veb]
[af,avb3,jr,veb]
[af,avb3,jeb,avr]
[af,avb3,jeb,lbbb,avr]
[af,avb3,jeb,lbbb,vr]
[af,avb3,jeb,lbbb,vt]
[af,avb3,jeb,rbbb,avr]
[af,avb3,jeb,rbbb,vr]
[af,avb3,jeb,rbbb,vt]
[af,avb3,jeb,vr]
[af,avb3,jeb,vt]
[af,avb3,ajr]
[af,avb3,ajr,lbbb,veb]
[af,avb3,ajr,rbbb,veb]
[af,avb3,ajr,veb]
[af,avb3,jt]
[af,avb3,jt,lbbb,veb]
[af,avb3,jt,rbbb,veb]
[af,avb3,jt,veb]
[afl,avb3,jr]
[afl,avb3,jr,lbbb,veb]
[afl,avb3,jr,rbbb,veb]

[afl,avb3,jr,veb]
[afl,avb3,jeb,avr]
[afl,avb3,jeb,lbbb,avr]
[afl,avb3,jeb,lbbb,vr]
[afl,avb3,jeb,lbbb,vt]
[afl,avb3,jeb,rbbb,avr]
[afl,avb3,jeb,rbbb,vr]
[afl,avb3,jeb,rbbb,vt]
[afl,avb3,jeb,vr]
[afl,avb3,jeb,vt]
[afl,avb3,ajr]
[afl,avb3,ajr,lbbb,veb]
[afl,avb3,ajr,rbbb,veb]
[afl,avb3,ajr,veb]
[afl,avb3,jt]
[afl,avb3,jt,lbbb,veb]
[afl,avb3,jt,rbbb,veb]
[afl,avb3,jt,veb]
[at,avb3,jr]
[at,avb3,jr,lbbb,veb]
[at,avb3,jr,rbbb,veb]
[at,avb3,jr,veb]
[at,avb3,jeb,avr]
[at,avb3,jeb,lbbb,avr]
[at,avb3,jeb,lbbb,vr]

[at,avb3,jeb,lbbb,vt]
[at,avb3,jeb,rbbb,avr]
[at,avb3,jeb,rbbb,vr]
[at,avb3,jeb,rbbb,vt]
[at,avb3,jeb,vr]
[at,avb3,jeb,vt]
[at,avb3,ajr]
[at,avb3,ajr,lbbb,veb]
[at,avb3,ajr,rbbb,veb]
[at,avb3,ajr,veb]
[at,avb3,jt]
[at,avb3,jt,lbbb,veb]
[at,avb3,jt,rbbb,veb]
[at,avb3,jt,veb]
[at,wpw,jeb]
[jr]
[jr,lbbb,veb]
[jr,rbbb,veb]
[jr,veb]
[jeb,avr]
[jeb,lbbb,avr]
[jeb,lbbb,vr]
[jeb,lbbb,vt]
[jeb,rbbb,avr]
[jeb,rbbb,vr]
[jeb,rbbb,vt]
[jeb,vr]
[jeb,vt]
[ajr]
[ajr,lbbb,veb]
[ajr,rbbb,veb]
[ajr,veb]
[jt]
[jt,lbbb,veb]
[jt,rbbb,veb]
[jt,veb]
[mat,avb3,jr]
[mat,avb3,jr,lbbb,veb]

[mat,avb3,jr,rbbb,veb]
[mat,avb3,jr,veb]
[mat,avb3,jeb,avr]
[mat,avb3,jeb,lbbb,avr]
[mat,avb3,jeb,lbbb,vr]
[mat,avb3,jeb,lbbb,vt]
[mat,avb3,jeb,rbbb,avr]
[mat,avb3,jeb,rbbb,vr]
[mat,avb3,jeb,rbbb,vt]
[mat,avb3,jeb,vr]
[mat,avb3,jeb,vt]
[mat,avb3,ajr]
[mat,avb3,ajr,lbbb,veb]
[mat,avb3,ajr,rbbb,veb]
[mat,avb3,ajr,veb]
[mat,avb3,jt]
[mat,avb3,jt,lbbb,veb]
[mat,avb3,jt,rbbb,veb]
[mat,avb3,jt,veb]
[mat,wpw,jeb]
[sa,aeb,avb3,jr]
[sa,aeb,avb3,ajr]
[sa,aeb,avb3,jt]
[sa,avb3,jr]
[sa,avb3,jr,lbbb,veb]
[sa,avb3,jr,rbbb,veb]
[sa,avb3,jr,veb]
[sa,avb3,jeb,avr]
[sa,avb3,jeb,lbbb,avr]
[sa,avb3,jeb,lbbb,vr]
[sa,avb3,jeb,lbbb,vt]
[sa,avb3,jeb,rbbb,avr]
[sa,avb3,jeb,rbbb,vr]
[sa,avb3,jeb,rbbb,vt]
[sa,avb3,jeb,vr]
[sa,avb3,jeb,vt]
[sa,avb3,ajr]
[sa,avb3,ajr,lbbb,veb]

[sa,avb3,ajr,rbbb,veb]
[sa,avb3,ajr,veb]
[sa,avb3,jt]
[sa,avb3,jt,lbbb,veb]
[sa,avb3,jt,rbbb,veb]
[sa,avb3,jt,veb]
[sa,wpw,jeb]
[sad,aeb,avb3,jr]
[sad,aeb,avb3,ajr]
[sad,aeb,avb3,jt]
[sad,avb3,jr]
[sad,avb3,jr,lbbb,veb]
[sad,avb3,jr,rbbb,veb]
[sad,avb3,jr,veb]
[sad,avb3,jeb,avr]
[sad,avb3,jeb,lbbb,avr]
[sad,avb3,jeb,lbbb,vr]
[sad,avb3,jeb,lbbb,vt]
[sad,avb3,jeb,rbbb,avr]
[sad,avb3,jeb,rbbb,vr]
[sad,avb3,jeb,rbbb,vt]
[sad,avb3,jeb,vr]
[sad,avb3,jeb,vt]
[sad,avb3,ajr]
[sad,avb3,ajr,lbbb,veb]
[sad,avb3,ajr,rbbb,veb]
[sad,avb3,ajr,veb]
[sad,avb3,jt]
[sad,avb3,jt,lbbb,veb]
[sad,avb3,jt,rbbb,veb]
[sad,avb3,jt,veb]
[sad,wpw,jeb]
[sb,aeb,avb3,jr]
[sb,aeb,avb3,ajr]
[sb,aeb,avb3,jt]
[sb,avb3,jr]
[sb,avb3,jr,lbbb,veb]
[sb,avb3,jr,rbbb,veb]

[sb,avb3,jr,veb]
[sb,avb3,jeb,avr]
[sb,avb3,jeb,lbbb,avr]
[sb,avb3,jeb,lbbb,vr]
[sb,avb3,jeb,lbbb,vt]
[sb,avb3,jeb,rbbb,avr]
[sb,avb3,jeb,rbbb,vr]
[sb,avb3,jeb,rbbb,vt]
[sb,avb3,jeb,vr]
[sb,avb3,jeb,vt]
[sb,avb3,ajr]
[sb,avb3,ajr,lbbb,veb]
[sb,avb3,ajr,rbbb,veb]
[sb,avb3,ajr,veb]
[sb,avb3,jt]
[sb,avb3,jt,lbbb,veb]
[sb,avb3,jt,rbbb,veb]
[sb,avb3,jt,veb]
[sb,wpw,jeb]
[sr,aeb,avb3,jr]
[sr,aeb,avb3,ajr]
[sr,aeb,avb3,jt]
[sr,avb3,jr]
[sr,avb3,jr,lbbb,veb]
[sr,avb3,jr,rbbb,veb]
[sr,avb3,jr,veb]
[sr,avb3,jeb,avr]
[sr,avb3,jeb,lbbb,avr]
[sr,avb3,jeb,lbbb,vr]
[sr,avb3,jeb,lbbb,vt]
[sr,avb3,jeb,rbbb,avr]
[sr,avb3,jeb,rbbb,vr]
[sr,avb3,jeb,rbbb,vt]
[sr,avb3,jeb,vr]
[sr,avb3,jeb,vt]
[sr,avb3,ajr]
[sr,avb3,ajr,lbbb,veb]
[sr,avb3,ajr,rbbb,veb]

[sr,avb3,ajr,veb]
[sr,avb3,jt]
[sr,avb3,jt,lbbb,veb]
[sr,avb3,jt,rbbb,veb]
[sr,avb3,jt,veb]
[sr,wpw,jeb]
[st,aeb,avb3,jr]
[st,aeb,avb3,ajr]
[st,aeb,avb3,jt]
[st,avb3,jr]
[st,avb3,jr,lbbb,veb]
[st,avb3,jr,rbbb,veb]
[st,avb3,jr,veb]
[st,avb3,jeb,avr]
[st,avb3,jeb,lbbb,avr]
[st,avb3,jeb,lbbb,vr]
[st,avb3,jeb,lbbb,vt]
[st,avb3,jeb,rbbb,avr]
[st,avb3,jeb,rbbb,vr]
[st,avb3,jeb,rbbb,vt]
[st,avb3,jeb,vr]
[st,avb3,jeb,vt]
[st,avb3,ajr]
[st,avb3,ajr,lbbb,veb]
[st,avb3,ajr,rbbb,veb]
[st,avb3,ajr,veb]
[st,avb3,jt]

[st,avb3,jt,lbbb,veb]
[st,avb3,jt,rbbb,veb]
[st,avb3,jt,veb]
[st,wpw,jeb]
[wp,avb3,jr]
[wp,avb3,jr,lbbb,veb]
[wp,avb3,jr,rbbb,veb]
[wp,avb3,jr,veb]
[wp,avb3,jeb,avr]
[wp,avb3,jeb,lbbb,avr]
[wp,avb3,jeb,lbbb,vr]
[wp,avb3,jeb,lbbb,vt]
[wp,avb3,jeb,rbbb,avr]
[wp,avb3,jeb,rbbb,vr]
[wp,avb3,jeb,rbbb,vt]
[wp,avb3,jeb,vr]
[wp,avb3,jeb,vt]
[wp,avb3,ajr]
[wp,avb3,ajr,lbbb,veb]
[wp,avb3,ajr,rbbb,veb]
[wp,avb3,ajr,veb]
[wp,avb3,jt]
[wp,avb3,jt,lbbb,veb]
[wp,avb3,jt,rbbb,veb]
[wp,avb3,jt,veb]
[wp,wpw,jeb]

# Index

AQ, 17, 39, 131, 163, 172.
AQ15, 131, 134.
arrhythmia,
    cardiac, 23, 55.
    combined, 24, 68, 139, 142,
        145.
    dictionary of, 26.
    multiple, 23, 199.
    simple, 23, 60–61, 68, 73, 118,
        140, 199.
arrhythmia-ECG base, 137.
    reduced, 137, 219, 237.
Assistant Professional, 17.
atria, 22, 54.
atrial rhythm, 73.
atrio-ventricular (AV) node, 54.
AV conduction, 74.
AV node, 54.
av-conduct, 32.
backward chaining, 109.
backward diagnosis, 180, 183,
    188, 189.
beat,
    dominant, 57.
    ectopic, 57, 76, 137.
    permanent, 137.
breadth-first search, 36, 100.
bundle branches, 54, 74.
Bundle of His, 54.
C-Prolog, 189.

causal relation, 28.
class, 128, 130, 132, 143.
closed world assumption, 114,
    165.
commonsense knowledge, 10.
complete, 129, 172.
complex, 131.
compression, 12, 127.
compresssion procedure, 39.
concept, 128.
concept description, (see also
    cover; inductive hypothe-
    sis), 131.
    complete, 129.
    consistent, 129.
conduction pathway, 27, 71.
confluence, 48.
consistent, 129, 172.
constraints, 76.
constructive induction, 135.
cover, (see also concept descrip-
    tion; inductive hypothesis),
    132.
covering clause, 172.
data-driven learning, 163.
database clause, 164.
debugger, 162, 174.
decision tree, 17.
deductive database, 164.
depth-first search, 35, 98.

diagnosis, 179.
diagnostic method, 188.
diagnostic rule, 40, 42, 138, 150, 219.
diagnostic task, 179, 184.
dominant beat, 57.
ECG, 22, 54.
ECG description, 29.
ECG feature, 23, 24, 46–47, 127.
  selected, 144, 151.
ECG generator, 27.
ectopic beat, 57, 76, 137.
electrocardiogram (ECG), 22, 54.
example, 128, 130.
  negative, 129, 143.
  positive, 129, 143.
EXCELL, 39.
expert system, 1.
  first generation, 2.
  second generation, 44.
fact, 164, 167, 171, 173.
first order predicate calculus, 96.
function of a component, 167, 171.
GEM, 39.
global rule, 79, 96.
heart, 21.
  model of, 25.
  state of, 28, 69.
heart component, 68.
  state of, 140.
heart disorder, 22–23.
  selected, 143, 150.
  single, 186.
  multiple, 187.

hierarchical diagnosis, 180, 188–189.
ID3, 163.
impulse conduction, 85, 87, 89.
impulse conduction pathway, 68.
impulse generation, 81.
impulse generator, 27, 68, 71.
impulse summator, 27.
incomplete, 174, 177–178, 182.
incorrect, 174.
incremental, 172.
incremental learning, 134, 172, 178.
individual view, 51.
inductive hypothesis, (*see also* concept description; cover), 171–172.
inductive learning, 12, 44.
internal disjunctions, 131.
interpreter, 162, 174, 184.
junction, 54.
junctional rhythm, 74.
KARDIO, 1.
knowledge acquisition cycle, 13.
knowledge,
  causal, 10.
  deep, 1–2, 42.
  operational, 2.
  shallow, 1.
  surface, 1, 3, 12, 42.
  transformation of, 11.
learner, 162.
learning
  data-driven, 163.
  machine, 127.
learning from examples, 128.
learning task, 171.

legality constraints, 26, 28.
level of abstraction, 164, 167,
    180.
local rule, 26.
logic programming, 44.
machine learning, 127.
MARVIN, 163.
maxstar, 133–134.
MIS, 163.
model,
    compilation of, 36–37.
    deep, 3, 12.
    hierarchical, 44.
    qualitative, 2, 5.
    quantitative, 2–3.
    structure of, 48, 162, 166,
        169.
model-driven, 163.
multiple arrhythmias, 199.
multiple heart disorders, 187.
naive physics, 10.
naive physiology, 10.
NEWGEM, 19, 39, 131, 134,
    219.
noise, 129.
non-incremental learning, 172,
    187.
nondeterminism, 8.
nonrecursive, 164.
nonrecursive types, 165.
P wave, 29, 55.
pacemaker, 54.
permanent beat, 137.
PR interval, 30, 55.
prediction rule, 40–42, 138, 150,
    237.
process, 48, 51.

producing ECG description, 90,
    93.
Prolog, 7, 44, 119.
QPT, 48.
QRS complex, 30, 47, 55.
qualitative modeling, 44, 47.
Qualitative Process Theory
    (QTP), 48.
qualitative simulation, 95.
quantity space, 7, 51.
question,
    control type, 10.
    diagnostic type, 8, 35.
    prediction type, 8, 35.
rate, 71.
representation,
    extensional, 12.
    intensional, 12.
rhythm, 71.
rule,
    diagnostic, 40, 42, 138, 150,
        219.
    general, 134.
    global, 26, 28, 79, 96.
    local, 26, 28.
    minimal, 134, 151.
    prediction, 40–42, 138, 150.
    specific, 134, 151.
SA node, 54.
search,
    breadth-first, 36, 100.
    depth-first, 35, 98.
seed, 132.
selected ECG feature, 144, 151.
selected heart disorder, 143,
    150.
selector, 131.

simple cardiac arrhythmia, 23,
    60–61, 68, 73, 118, 140,
    199.
simulation, 179.
simulation task, 179.
single heart disorders, 186.
sino-atrial (SA) node, 54.
sinus rhythm, 30, 73.
soundness, 113.
ST segment, 55.
star, 132.
state of the heart, 28, 69.
structure of the model, 48, 162,
    166, 169.

summation, 68.
surface knowledge, 1, 3, 12, 42,
    188.
TDIDT, 17.
T wave, 55.
Top-Down Induction of Decision
    Trees (TDIDT), 17.
type, 169.
typed, 165.
utility predicate, 167, 171.
ventricle, 22, 54.
ventricular rhythm, 75.
ventricular tachycardia, 30.
VL1, 131.

*The MIT Press, with Peter Denning, general consulting editor, and Brian Randall, European consulting editor, publishes computer science books in the following series:*

**ACM Doctoral Dissertation Award and Distinguished Dissertation Series**

**Artificial Intelligence**, Patrick Henry Winston and J. Michael Brady founding editors; J. Michael Brady, Daniel G. Bobrow, and Randall Davis, current editors

**Charles Babbage Institute Reprint Series for the History of Computing,** Martin Campbell-Kelly, editor

**Computer Systems**, Herb Schwetman, editor

**Exploring with Logo**, E. Paul Goldenberg, editor

**Foundations of Computing**, Michael Garey and Albert Meyer, editors

**History of Computing**, I. Bernard Cohen and William Aspray, editors

**Information Systems**, Michael Lesk, editor

**Logic Programming**, Ehud Shapiro, editor; Fernando Pereira, Koichi Furukawa, and D. H. D. Warren, associate editors

**The MIT Electrical Engineering and Computer Science Series**

**Research Monographs in Parallel and Distributed Processing,** Christopher Jesshope and David Klappholz, editors

**Scientific Computation**, Dennis Gannon, editor

**Technical Communication**, Edward Barrett, editor